Farnsworth's Classical English Rhetoric

Farnsworth's

CLASSICAL

 DAVID R. GODINE · *Publisher* · *Boston*

ENGLISH RHETORIC

by WARD FARNSWORTH

For Annie and Sam

First published in 2011 by
David R. Godine · *Publisher*
Post Office Box 450
Jaffrey, New Hampshire 03452
www.godine.com

LIBRARY OF CONGRESS
CATALOGING-IN-PUBLICATION DATA

Farnsworth, Ward, 1967–
Farnsworth's classical English rhetoric / by Ward Farnsworth.
p.   cm.
ISBN 978-1-56792-385-8
1. English language—Rhetoric. I. Title. II. Title: Classical English rhetoric.
PE1408.F285 2009
808'.042—dc22
2009022385

FIRST EDITION 2011
Printed in the United States of America

CONTENTS

PREFACE

EVERYONE SPEAKS and writes in patterns. Usually the patterns arise from unconscious custom; they are models we internalize from the speech around us without thinking much about it. But it also is possible to study the patterns deliberately and to learn more about how to use the ones that make the words they arrange more emphatic or memorable or otherwise effective. The most famous such patterns, known as *rhetorical figures*, were first identified and studied in ancient Greece and Rome. Most of them amount to departures from simple and literal statement, such as repeating words, putting words into an unexpected order, leaving out words that might have been expected, asking questions and then answering them, and so forth. Figures of these kinds amount to practical ways of working with large aesthetic principles – repetition and variety, suspense and relief, concealment and surprise, the creation of expectations and then the satisfaction or frustration of them – all as they apply to the composition of a simple sentence or paragraph. This book is meant as a help to those who wish to be on better terms with such techniques. It aims to show in detail what can be done with major rhetorical figures and the best of what has been done with them in English, to present the occasions for their use in systematic fashion, and to offer explanatory comments in moderation.

Rhetoric is a vast, old, and honorable discipline. It may be defined most broadly and simply as the use of language to persuade or otherwise affect an audience. The decline of rhetoric in our times is thus a much broader phenomenon than any mere decline in familiarity with figures of speech, but figures nevertheless are a good place to begin a study of the subject because they tend to be easy to explain, instructive to examine, and frequently useful. It certainly is possible to write well without rhetorical figures, but most of the best writers and speakers – the ones whose work has stood up the longest – have made important use of them, and figures tend to show up often in utterances that are long remembered. The point is not that figures are useful for writing things that one hopes will last, for writing anything in that hope is almost always a mistake. The point, rather, is that durability is one measure of the excellence of a style and the value of the techniques that it employs. It helps us think about quality in ways more interesting than asking what panders best to the fashions of the moment.

Rhetorical figures also show up often, of course, in a lot of bad speech and writing. When used in contemporary political speeches and read from tele-prompters, figures often sound tinny – like clichés, or strained efforts to make dull claims sound snappy. This is partly because today's politician tends to be a creature of very modest literacy and wit who spoils what he touches, but there are more specific reasons as well. First, figures sound splendid when used to say things worth saying. They can show a worthy sentiment to great advantage. But they merely are grating when used to inflate the sound of words that are trite or trivial in substance, a regrettably common use of figures that has helped give a bad name to rhetoric in general. Secondly, an otherwise promising use of a figure often goes wrong because the speaker overdoes it. Too much ornament in any art tends to leave a worse impression than too little. Skilled and experienced students of rhetoric sometimes are able to use a high density of figures to strong effect (we will see examples soon enough), but for most people most of the time an attractive use of these patterns requires moderation and restraint. Thirdly, rhetorical figures only become powerful when they sound spontaneous and are integrated smoothly into the rest of the way a speaker talks. Most of them come to notice in the first place because people use them unwittingly when they speak from passion and with a dash of inspiration. (My young children, when wrathful, are masters of hypophora.) Thus a mediocre speech or piece of writing often announces itself by the forced use of a rhetorical figure too freshly learned or deliberately employed.

But then how does one study techniques that succeed only when they seem unstudied? The answer lies in examples. Rhetorical figures start to sound natural once one has spent so much time with them that they come to mind without effort, and finally serve as shapes into which words assemble themselves by instinct when the situation calls for it. Examples also can do more than exposition to teach lessons about the beauty of a device, about its technical details, and about the occasions for its use – for a sense of the occasion is as important as anything in the mastery of rhetorical figures. Some of them are suited to the expression of certain sorts of ideas or feelings, but sound strange otherwise; some fit well into certain kinds of writing and speech, but have little or no place in others; some things that can be done with figures are rarely useful at all, yet are indispensable once or twice in a lifetime. (One wants to be ready.) Examples, if they are to teach all these things, must be not only apt but extensive. Seeing just a few examples invites direct imitation of them, which tends to be clumsy. Immersion in many examples allows them to do their work by way of a subtler process of influence, with a gentler and happier effect on the resulting style.

As a practical matter this approach to the study of figures means spending a great deal of time in the company of writers who know the devices intimately and have good taste. This book performs the necessary introductions. It contains more than a thousand illustrations drawn from British, Irish, and American oratory and literature. The right first question about any pattern for the arrangement of words, and the question asked in each chapter of this book, is what use masters of the language have made of it: how Lincoln put it to work, or Churchill, or Burke, or the American founding fathers; or Dickens and Melville, or Shaw and Chesterton, or the Irish orators Henry Grattan and Richard Lalor Sheil – but the reader will see. The masters of the rhetorical figure in English include many storied writers and talkers, but also others less well known. Making your own first acquaintance with them is part of the fun of studying their craft.

Most of the examples here are from English prose rather than verse. They start around 1600, the age of Shakespeare and the King James Bible, and end around 1950. The largest share are from the nineteenth century and the latter part of the eighteenth. This selection reflects one of the chief purposes of the book, which is to help recover a rhetorical tradition in English that is less familiar because it is outside of living memory and is fast becoming more distant as a cultural and stylistic matter. (Thus the word *classical* in the title.) The better authors and statesmen of those earlier periods studied rhetoric more closely than it tends to be studied today, and the English of their times was more hospitable to its charms. We may not want to talk now quite as people did in earlier times; in some respects we are indeed forbidden to talk that way by our culture. But the ablest of the older writers still make the best teachers of rhetoric.

Last, a few notes on what this book does not do. It does not come close to discussing every known rhetorical figure. It just covers the eighteen or so that, in my judgment, are of most practical value. Metaphor and simile are omitted here, too, not because they are unimportant but because they are too important; they are large enough topics to require separate treatment of their own. The book also avoids anything translated into English from other languages, with the exception of the King James Bible and passing mention of some famous French examples. The details that give a rhetorical figure its entire sound tend not to come through in translation, and in any event the use of rhetorical figures in English is extensive enough to support treatment by itself and important enough to need it. For this reason, too, the book pays relatively slight attention to classical origins of the devices it considers. In each case I do give the name for the device derived from Ancient Greek (or, occasionally, from Latin); those labels, however strange they may sound at first, end up being highly convenient if you spend much time with this subject. But the chapter titles also identify the devices with English words that are more likely to be clear, and in some chapters I also offer, near the start, a familiar example or two of the use of the figure in relatively recent times. More generally the book spends little time on details of taxonomy. There are hundreds of names for all the rhetorical figures that have ever been identified, and arguments about which names apply to which figures, and then more distinctions to draw between figures of speech and figures of thought, between schemes and tropes, and on and on. I do not disparage those distinctions, but this book is not about them. The reader unhappy with the book's insouciance on these points, or who just would like to pursue taxonomy in more detail, has plenty of recourse, some examples of which will be mentioned in the bibliographical notes.

I have various acknowledgements to make. I wish to thank my rhetoric students and research assistants at the Boston University law school who read and commented on parts of the manuscript, helped find examples for it, or both: Graham Foster, Susan Frauenhoffer, Salem Fussell, Sarah McCabe, Wells Miller, Nadia Oussayef, Joanna Rauh, Kevin Teng, Brian Vito, and Dustin Guzior. Daniel Norland was especially helpful early in the life of the project. Emily Tucker was especially helpful with suggestions toward the end of it. I am grateful as well to Marlowe Bergendoff, Brian Brooks, Daniel Cantor, Janet Farnsworth, Ted Frank, David R. Godine, Lisa Hills, Kelly Klaus, Christopher Kylin, Gary Lawson, Adam Long, Christopher Roberts, James Sanders, David Seipp, Ted Skillman, Jack Taylor, and John Thornton for their helpful comments and encouragement; and thanks in particular to Andrew Kull, a especially reliable supplier of each of those good things. Carl W. Scarbrough lent his consummate skill to the design of the book. Jon Barlow and the late Patrick Flaherty were friends to the subject matter and to my enthusiasm for it.

Boston, April 2010

Farnsworth's Classical English Rhetoric

Simple Repetition of Words and Phrases:
EPIZEUXIS, EPIMONE, *etc.*

Repetition is one of the most important general ideas in rhetoric, and later chapters consider a wide range of ways in which it can be used: repetition of words and phrases at the beginning or end of successive sentences or clauses, or repetition of sentence structure, of conjunctions, and so forth. But the most basic use of the principle, and our subject here, is the simple repetition of words *per se* for the sake of emphasis, drama, or beauty. The best-known line from Conrad's *Heart of Darkness* – *The horror! The horror!* – is an example of one scheme from this family: EPIMONE (e-*pi*-mo-nee), or the repetition of phrases. The same device also figures prominently in the most celebrated speech in French history, Charles de Gaulle's *Appeal of 18 June*. France had just fallen to the Nazis, and de Gaulle was speaking to the people of his country by radio from London:

> Car la France n'est pas seule! Elle n'est pas seule!
> Elle n'est pas seule!

(*For France is not alone! She is not alone! She is not alone!*) The speech is generally credited as the formal start of the French Resistance.

Repetition can create memorable effects in still simpler forms. Consider a pair of utterances made within two years of each other in the middle of the twentieth century. One is a famous line from the movie *Casablanca*: *Of all the gin joints in all the towns in all the world, she walks into mine*. Another is an enduring moment from a speech of Winston Churchill's praising the pilots who had fended off German air strikes during the Battle of Britain: *Never in the field of human conflict was so much owed by so many to so few*. Both of these quotations are remembered well today, and both of them owe much of their fame to the same rhetorical device: the use of the same word repeatedly, with other words between each repetition – a figure known as CONDUPLICATIO (con-du-pli-*cat*-ee-oh), or, especially when there are just a few other words between the repeated ones, DIACOPE (di-*ac*-o-pee).

Let us turn to a more systematic look at the uses of repeated words.

1. *Epizeuxis*. Our first device, EPIZEUXIS (e-pi-*zeux*-is), is the repetition of words consecutively. The simple and classic form repeats a word thrice: a verbal pounding of the table.

Othello, 2, 3	Reputation, reputation, reputation! Oh, I have lost my reputation! I have lost the immortal part of myself, and what remains is bestial. My reputation, Iago, my reputation!
Thoreau, *Walden* (1854)	Simplicity, simplicity, simplicity! I say, let your affairs be as two or three, and not a hundred or a thousand; instead of a million count half a dozen, and keep your accounts on your thumb-nail.
Grattan, speech in the Irish Parliament (1787)	Like the Draconian laws, this bill had blood! blood! – felony! felony! felony! in every period and in every sentence.
de Quincey, *Confessions of an English Opium Eater* (1821)	[U]pon all that has been hitherto written on the subject of opium, whether by travellers in Turkey (who may plead their privilege of lying as an old immemorial right), or by professors of medicine, writing *ex cathedra*, I have but one emphatic criticism to pronounce – Lies! lies! lies!

A common variation on the triplet starts with two repetitions of a word but delays the last one for a moment. The couplet at the start typically comes off as a cry or gasp or call to battle; the singlet then arrives with more thought attached, and explains the feeling behind the couplet, or elaborates on it, or makes it more articulate.

O Romeo, Romeo! wherefore art thou Romeo?	*Romeo and Juliet*, 2, 2
A horse! a horse! my kingdom for a horse!	*Richard III*, 5, 4
The heart! the heart! 'tis God's anointed; let me pursue the heart!	Melville, *Pierre* (1852)

The common prose applications put more space between the couplet at the start and the repetition that comes later.

[T]o these evils, monstrous as they are, you owe it to your national character, to truth, to justice, to every consideration, political, social, religious, moral, at once to provide the cure. What shall it be? Public opinion! Public opinion! We have been hearing of it this long time – this many a day we have been hearing of public opinion.	Sheil, speech in the House of Commons (1843)
Ill! Ill! I am bearded and bullied by a shop-boy, and she beseeches him to pity me and remember I am ill!	Dickens, *Nicholas Nickleby* (1839)
Owners, owners? Thou art always prating to me, Starbuck, about those miserly owners, as if the owners were my conscience.	Melville, *Moby-Dick* (1851)
We were told – told emphatically and abundantly – that the method of their going would be a masterpiece of tactical skill. Tactics! Tactics! Ladies and gentlemen, the country is tired of their tactics.	Campbell-Bannerman, speech at London (1905)

The reverse order is less common but also effective: one, then two, in which case the pattern is not quite one of exclamation followed by explanation; it more commonly is a statement about a thing, then an extra blast of emphasis as if the speaker can't contain himself:

Damn her, lewd minx! O damn her, damn her!	*Othello*, 3, 3

Dickens, *Nicholas Nickleby*
(1839)

Mr. Nickleby against all the world. There's nobody like him. A giant among pigmies, a giant, a giant!

Melville, *Moby-Dick* (1851)

Death and devils! men, it is Moby Dick ye have seen – Moby Dick – Moby Dick!

Strictly speaking these last examples are cases of *epimone* (the repetition of phrases), not just epizeuxis (repetition of individual words); epimone is considered in more detail below. Here as elsewhere in the book, minor liberties sometimes are taken with the placement of examples for the sake of showing them where they will be most instructive.

2. *Conduplicatio generally.* As mentioned in the introduction to this chapter, conduplicatio likewise involves repetition of the same word, but this time with each instance separated by other words. Some examples with repeated nouns:

Grattan, speech in the Irish
Parliament (1793)

No lawyer can say so; because no lawyer could say so without forfeiting his character as a lawyer.

Dickens, *Great Expectations*
(1861)

Before I had been standing at the window five minutes, they somehow conveyed to me that they were all toadies and humbugs, but that each of them pretended not to know that the others were toadies and humbugs: because the admission that he or she did know it, would have made him or her out to be a toady and humbug.

Coming back to the same word makes it a theme of the utterance and leaves it strongly in the listener's ear. Some examples with repeated modifiers:

Paine, *The American Crisis*
(1783)

A bad cause will ever be supported by bad means and bad men. . . .

Melville, *Mardi* (1849)

Verily, her ways were as the ways of the inscrutable penguins in building their inscrutable nests, which baffle all science, and make a fool of a sage.

Too often the American that himself makes his fortune, builds him a great metropolitan house, in
the most metropolitan street of the most metropolitan town.

Melville, *Pierre* (1852)

Eighteen of Mr. Tangle's learned friends, each
armed with a little summary of eighteen hundred
sheets, bob up like eighteen hammers in a piano-
forte, make eighteen bows, and drop into their
eighteen places of obscurity.

Dickens, *Bleak House* (1853)

Cases of conduplicatio can be combined, as in this fine
case where several nouns and modifiers (*empire*, *revenue*,
army, *worst*) are repeated to create a tightly wound effect:

I allow, indeed, that the Empire of Germany raises
her revenue and her troops by quotas and contin-
gents; but the revenue of the Empire and the army
of the Empire is the worst revenue and the worst
army in the world.

Burke, Speech on Conciliation with the Colonies
(1775)

3. *Conduplicatio for enlargement.* A distinctive type of
conduplicatio, worth treating separately, occurs when the
speaker repeats a word for the sake of elaborating on it in
some way.

a. *To strengthen a statement.* The repetition of a word with
more emphatic language around it often comes as a little
surprise, and when it is just for the sake of being more
pejorative it can produce a bit of amusement.

Mr. Urquiza had the misfortune (equally common
in the old world and the new) of being a knave;
and also a showy specious knave.

de Quincey, *The Spanish Nun*
(1847)

Omar Khayyam's wine-bibbing is bad, not because
it is wine-bibbing. It is bad, and very bad, because
it is medical wine-bibbing.

Chesterton, *Heretics* (1905)

Butchers we are, that is true. But butchers, also, and
butchers of the bloodiest badge have been all

Melville, *Moby-Dick* (1851)

Martial Commanders whom the world invariably delights to honor.

b. *To expand a statement or further define it.*

Burke, *Reflections on the Revolution in France* (1791)

This pulpit style, revived after so long a discontinuance, had to me the air of novelty, and of a novelty not wholly without danger.

Shelley, *Frankenstein* (1818)

You can blast my other passions, but revenge remains – revenge, henceforth dearer than light or food!

Conduplicatio of this kind may be extended beyond just the one repetition; the word can be repeated again to permit enlargement upon it in different directions.

Webster, speech in the Senate (1834)

Sir, I pronounce the author of such sentiments to be guilty of attempting a detestable fraud on the community; a double fraud; a fraud which is to cheat men out of their property, and out of the earnings of their labor, by first cheating them out of their understandings.

Lincoln, debate with Stephen Douglas at Peoria (1854)

I think, and shall try to show, that it is wrong – wrong in its direct effect, letting slavery into Kansas and Nebraska, and wrong in its prospective principle, allowing it to spread to every other part of the wide world where men can be found inclined to take it.

c. *To add explanation.*

Trollope, *The Prime Minister* (1876)

And the odious letters in the writing became very long; – odious because he had to confess in them over and over again that his daughter, the very apple of his eye, had been the wife of a scoundrel.

Burke, *Reflections on the Revolution in France* (1791)

The public interests, because about them they have no real solicitude, they abandon wholly to chance; I say to chance, because their schemes have nothing in experience to prove their tendency beneficial.

d. *The double use of conduplicatio.* A classic pattern in the use of this scheme involves two initial claims, each of which is then repeated with elaboration or reasons for it.

> Sir, he was a scoundrel, and a coward: a scoundrel, for charging a blunderbuss against religion and morality; a coward, because he had not resolution to fire it off himself, but left half a crown to a beggarly Scotchman, to draw the trigger after his death!

Johnson, in Boswell's *Life* (1791)

> We are dregs and scum, sir: the dregs very filthy, the scum very superior.

Shaw, *Man and Superman* (1903)

> I need not excuse myself to your lordship, nor, I think, to any honest man, for the zeal I have shown in this cause; for it is an honest zeal, and in a good cause.

Burke, *A Vindication of Natural Society* (1756)

e. *Churchillian uses of conduplicatio.* Churchill made frequent and good use of conduplicatio.

> If the Government and people of the USA have a word to speak for the salvation of the world, now is the time and now is the last time when words will be of any use.

Churchill, speech at London (1938)

The repetition of *time* emphasizes it, and the fresh language afterwards is emphasized as well because it is the excuse for saying the word a second time.

> Now all the difficulty about the tribunal has been removed, and removed by the simple process of complete surrender on our part of the whole case.

Churchill, speech in the House of Commons (1938)

The device adds rhetorical power because each initial clause sounds complete in itself; then comes a bit of repetition and elaboration, slightly against expectations – and then perhaps still another round of the same, as here:

> [I]n the east, take Constantinople; take it by ships if you can; take it by soldiers if you must; take it by whichever plan, military or naval, commends itself

Churchill, speech in the House of Commons (1915)

to your military experts, but take it, and take it soon, and take it while time remains.

Since *take it* is a phrase rather than a single word, this also can be considered a case of epimone – to which we now turn.

4. *Epimone*. We now examine the repetition of entire phrases.

a. *Doublets*.

Goldsmith, *She Stoops to Conquer* (1773)

I tell you, sir, I'm serious! and now that my passions are roused, I say this house is mine, sir; this house is mine, and I command you to leave it directly.

Pitt, speech in the House of Lords (1777)

[T]o send forth the infidel savage – against whom? against your Protestant brethren; to lay waste their country, to desolate their dwellings, and extirpate their race and name with these horrible hell-hounds of savage war – *hell-hounds, I say, of savage war!*

Webster, speech in the Senate (1833)

The cause, then, Sir, the cause! Let the world know the cause which has thus induced one State of the Union to bid defiance to the power of the whole, and openly to talk of secession.

b. *Triplets*. The longer the phrase, the less consecutive repetition it will stand; so the triplets in a case of epimone tend to be shorter.

Romeo and Juliet, 4, 5

Most lamentable day, most woful day,
That ever, ever, I did yet behold!
O day! O day! O day! O hateful day!

Dickens, *David Copperfield* (1850)

"He was a beggar, perhaps." Mr. Dick shook his head, as utterly renouncing the suggestion; and having replied a great many times, and with great confidence, "No beggar, no beggar, no beggar, sir!'"

Dickens, *Little Dorrit* (1857)

You seem to come like my own anger, my own malice, my own – whatever it is – I don't know what it is. But I am ill-used, I am ill-used, I am ill-used!

c. *The refrain.* Repetition of longer phrases is gentler on the ear when the phrases are spread apart, which also can enable them to serve as a kind of chorus, or burden, as when showing how different possibilities provoke the same reply.

Who is here so base that would be a bondman? If any, speak; for him have I offended. Who is here so rude that would not be a Roman? If any, speak; for him have I offended. Who is here so vile that will not love his country? If any, speak; for him have I offended. I pause for a reply.

Julius Caesar, 3, 2

There I have another bad match: a bankrupt, a prodigal, who dare scarce show his head on the Rialto; a beggar, that was us'd to come so smug upon the mart. Let him look to his bond. He was wont to call me usurer; let him look to his bond. He was wont to lend money for a Christian courtesy; let him look to his bond.

The Merchant of Venice, 3, 1

Methinks now this coined sun wears a ruddy face; but see! aye, he enters the sign of storms, the equinox! and but six months before he wheeled out of a former equinox at Aries! From storm to storm! So be it, then. Born in throes, 't is fit that man should live in pains and die in pangs! So be it, then! Here's stout stuff for woe to work on. So be it, then.

Melville, *Moby-Dick* (1851)

d. *Intermittent repetition of phrases.* A less rhythmic and more spontaneous effect can be had by circling back to the same or a nearly identical phrase less systematically. The speaker doesn't mean to offer a refrain; he just can't help saying the thing again and again.

Say not to me that it is *not* the lamp of lamps. I say to you it is. I say to you, a million of times over, it is. It is! I say to you that I will proclaim it to you, whether you like it or not; nay, that the less you like it, the more I will proclaim it to you.

Dickens, *Bleak House* (1853)

Pitt, speech in the House of Lords (1770)	I say we must necessarily undo these violent oppressive acts; they must be repealed – you will repeal them; I pledge myself for it, that you will in the end repeal them; I stake my reputation on it – I will consent to be taken for an idiot, if they are not finally repealed.
Macaulay, speech in the House of Commons (1842)	What could follow but one vast spoliation? One vast spoliation! That would be bad enough. That would be the greatest calamity that ever fell on our country. Yet would that a single vast spoliation were the worst!

e. *Emphasized repetition*, in which the speaker alerts the listener to it.

Henry, speech at the Second Revolutionary Congress of Virginia (1775)	There is no retreat but in submission and slavery! Our chains are forged! Their clanking may be heard on the plains of Boston! The war is inevitable – and let it come! I repeat it, sir, let it come!
Conrad, *Heart of Darkness* (1899)	When you have to attend to things of that sort, to the mere incidents of the surface, the reality – the reality, I tell you – fades.
Sheil, speech at Penenden Heath (1828)	False, I repeat it, with all the vehemence of indignant asseveration, utterly false is the charge habitually preferred against the religion which Englishmen have laden with penalties, and have marked with degradation.

5. EPANALEPSIS (*ep*-an-a-*lep*-sis) occurs when the same word or phrase is used at the beginning and end of a sentence or set of them – e.g., "The King is dead. Long live the King!" (or, in the original French, *Le Roi est mort. Vive le Roi!*). The usual effect is a sense of circuitry; the second instance of the repeated word completes a thought about it.

Julius Caesar, 1, 3	Cassius from bondage will deliver Cassius.
Madison, *Federalist* 51	Ambition must be made to counteract ambition.

Shakspeare will never be made by the study of
Shakspeare.

Emerson, *Self-Reliance*
(1841)

The minority gives way not because it is convinced
that it is wrong, but because it is convinced that it
is a minority.

Stephen, *Liberty, Equality,
Fraternity* (1873)

All buttoned-up men are weighty. All buttoned-up
men are believed in. Whether or no the reserved
and never-exercised power of unbuttoning, fasci-
nates mankind; whether or no wisdom is supposed
to condense and augment when buttoned up, and
to evaporate when unbuttoned; it is certain that
the man to whom importance is accorded is the
buttoned-up man.

Dickens, *Little Dorrit* (1857)

A prominent case of epanalepsis occurs in Brutus's speech
at the funeral of Julius Caesar, where the device is used
twice and then relaxed at the end – a useful idea (a pattern, then relief from it) considered more closely in later
chapters.

Romans, countrymen, and lovers! hear me for
my cause, and be silent, that you may hear:
believe me for mine honour, and have respect to
mine honour, that you may believe: censure me
in your wisdom, and awake your senses, that you
may the better judge.

Julius Caesar, 3, 2

6. *Special effects.*

a. *Repetition to suggest motion, action, or sound.*

But, sir, from the light in which he appears to hold
the wavering conduct of up, up, up – and down,
down, down – and round, round, round, – we are
led to suppose, that his real sentiments are not subject to vary, but have been uniform throughout.

Livingston, speech at New
York Ratifying Convention
(1788)

A good surgeon is worth a thousand of you. I have
been in surgeons' hands often, and have always

Richardson, *Clarissa* (1748)

found reason to depend upon their skill; but your art, Sir, what is it? – but to daub, daub, daub; load, load, load; plaster, plaster, plaster; till ye utterly destroy the appetite first, and the constitution afterwards, which you are called in to help.

Lamb, letter to Coleridge (1800)

My head is playing all the tunes in the world, ringing such peals! It has just finished the "Merry Christ Church Bells," and absolutely is beginning "Turn again, Whittington." Buz, buz, buz; bum, bum, bum; wheeze, wheeze, wheeze; fen, fen, fen; tinky, tinky, tinky; *cr'annch.*

    b. *Demands and exhortations.*

Ezekiel 33:11

[T]urn ye, turn ye from your evil ways; for why will ye die, O house of Israel?

Othello, 4, 1

Work on,
My medicine, work!

Dickens, *A Christmas Carol* (1843)

"Lead on!" said Scrooge. "Lead on! The night is waning fast, and it is precious time to me, I know. Lead on, Spirit!"

Melville, *Moby-Dick* (1851)

Stop snoring, ye sleepers, and pull. Pull, will ye? pull, can't ye? pull, won't ye? Why in the name of gudgeons and ginger-cakes don't ye pull? – pull and break something! pull, and start your eyes out!

    c. *To indicate identity or duplication.*

Richard III, 2, 4

And being seated, and domestic broils
Clean over-blown, themselves the conquerors
Make war upon themselves; brother to brother,
Blood to blood, self against self.

King John, 2, 1

Blood hath bought blood, and blows have
    answer'd blows;
Strength match'd with strength, and power
    confronted power;
Both are alike, and both alike we like.

[T]he contest between the rich and the poor is not a struggle between corporation and corporation, but a contest between men and men, – a competition, not between districts, but between descriptions.

Burke, *Reflections on the Revolution in France* (1791)

7. *Mixed themes.* Repetition itself can serve as a motif, with different uses of it combined in a short space to create a sort of reverberation. The second and different round of repetition reminds the ear of the first.

Ingenious men may assign ingenious reasons for opposite constructions of the same clause. They may heap refinement upon refinement, and subtlety upon subtlety, until they construe away every republican principle, every right sacred and dear to man.

Williams, speech at New York Ratifying Convention (1788)

For in tremendous extremities human souls are like drowning men; well enough they know they are in peril; well enough they know the causes of that peril; – nevertheless, the sea is the sea, and these drowning men do drown.

Melville, *Pierre* (1852)

Repetition at the Start:
ANAPHORA

ANAPHORA (a-*na*-pho-ra) occurs when the speaker repeats the same words at the start of successive sentences or clauses. This figure is a staple of high style, and so carries with it some risk of cliché; it gives an utterance the strong ring of oratory. Martin Luther King's "I have a dream" speech is known by that name because those words are repeated at the start of eight sentences in a row: a famous modern instance of anaphora.

Anaphora generally serves two principal purposes. Returning to the same words creates a hammering effect; the repeated language is certain to be noticed, likely to be remembered, and readily conveys strong feeling. Starting sentences with the same words also creates an involving rhythm. The rhythm may be good in itself, and it causes the ear to expect the pattern to continue. That expectation can then be satisfied or disrupted in various useful ways.

1. *Repetition of the subject with changes in the verb.* Anaphora is helpful for describing different things all done, or *to* be done, by the same subject. Often it also involves repetition of an auxiliary verb while the main verb changes; when used with the active voice in the first person, such constructions can produce a sense of inexorability:

Exodus 15:9

> The enemy said, I will pursue, I will overtake, I will divide the spoil; my lust shall be satisfied upon them; I will draw my sword, my hand shall destroy them.

Churchill, London radio broadcast (1940)

> But be the ordeal sharp or long, or both, we shall seek no terms, we shall tolerate no parley; we may show mercy – we shall ask for none.

Churchill's anaphora of future action – *we shall, we shall, we shall* – creates a sense of resolution that underscores the substance of what he is saying.

The same construction can be used passively, to describe a series of things all done *to* the same person:

> I say to you that if you rear yourself against it, you shall fall, you shall be bruised, you shall be battered, you shall be flawed, you shall be smashed.

Dickens, *Bleak House* (1853)

The anaphora gives the language a battering quality that again matches the underlying meaning.

Anaphora of this kind also can create a comprehensive sound, as when the speaker wishes to create a sense that all possibilities are covered (or all things but one):

> But madmen never meet. It is the only thing they cannot do. They can talk, they can inspire, they can fight, they can found religions; but they cannot meet.

Chesterton, *A Miscellany of Men* (1912)

> He's too delightful. If he'll only not spoil it! But they always *will*; they always do; they always have.

James, *The Ambassadors* (1903)

They always do, by itself, captures about the same literal meaning as the longer enumeration of past, present, and future; but the anaphora gives the result an exhaustive feel to go with the exhaustive substance.

2. *Repetition of the subject with different complements*, as when applying several modifiers to the same person or thing. Repeating the subject and verb gives each claim its own emphasis:

> Every man sees that he is that middle point whereof every thing may be affirmed and denied with equal reason. He is old, he is young, he is very wise, he is altogether ignorant.

Emerson, *Spiritual Laws* (1841)

The anaphora enables Emerson to independently affirm each statement and set it vividly against its contrary. The parallel nature of the claims is strengthened both by the repetition at the start (*he is . . . he is*) and by the omission of any conjunction at the end – a use of *asyndeton*, which has its own chapter later.

Here is a fine case of the same construction turned to the purpose of negation:

Burke, *Letter on the Proposals for Peace with the Regicide Directory of France* (1796)

I certainly should dread more from a wild-cat in my bedchamber than from all the lions that roar in the deserts behind Algiers. But in this parallel it is the cat that is at a distance, and the lions and tigers that are in our antechambers and our lobbies. Algiers is not near; Algiers is not powerful; Algiers is not our neighbor; Algiers is not infectious.

Anaphora also can heighten the contrast between affirmative and negative constructions when they are mixed:

Chesterton, *The Club of Queer Trades* (1905)

Why is it that the jolly old barbarians of this earth are always championed by people who are their antithesis? Why is it? You are sagacious, you are benevolent, you are well informed, but, Chadd, you are not savage.

Here is the same general idea, though without the explicit negative at the end:

Stevenson, *New Arabian Nights* (1882)

I shall lay this siege in form, Elvira; I am angry; I am indignant; I am truculently inclined; but I thank my Maker I have still a sense of fun.

The regularity of the anaphora at the start creates a stronger contrast at the end – not with a negative claim, but with an affirmative one that is different in tone from what has come before. The substance and the structure of the sentence both change direction.

3. *Repetition of the subject and verb with different objects, or phrases doing similar work.*

Dickens, *Bleak House* (1853)

They wanted wearing apparel, they wanted linen rags, they wanted money, they wanted coals, they wanted soup, they wanted interest, they wanted autographs, they wanted flannel, they wanted whatever Mr. Jarndyce had – or had not.

And now let me tell you we know all about the cheque – Soames's cheque. We know where you got it. We know who stole it. We know how it came to the person who gave it to you. It's all very well talking, but when you're in trouble always go to a lawyer.

Trollope, *The Last Chronicle of Barset* (1867)

In both cases repeating the subject and verb gives them a prominence they would lack if they appeared only at the start. Thus about the same substantive impression might be created in the second passage by listing the items serially (*we know where you got it, who stole it, and how it came...*), but repeating the subject and verb leaves *we know* ringing in the ears; it lays stress not just on the things known but on who knows them.

I can not forgive that judge upon the bench, or that governor in the chair of state, who has lightly passed over such offenses. I can not forgive the public, in whose opinion the duelist finds a sanctuary. I can not forgive you, my brethren, who till this late hour have been silent while successive murders were committed.

Nott, sermon at Albany (1804)

The anaphora makes each sentence a distinct pointing of the finger. The speaker points outward twice, then the hand turns toward the listener. The construction is used similarly here:

I was in mortal terror of the young man who wanted my heart and liver; I was in mortal terror of my interlocutor with the ironed leg; I was in mortal terror of myself, from whom an awful promise had been extracted. . . .

Dickens, *Great Expectations* (1861)

In both of these last cases, the listener gets involved in the repetition of subject and verb and perhaps isn't very struck by the objects to which they are attached – until the object is changed in a surprising way at the end of the last round.

4. *Changes in modifying language.* Various combinations of the elements so far considered – subject, verb, and complement – may be repeated, with changes just in the modifying words that follow them.

Dickens, *Hard Times* (1854)

He was goosed last night, he was goosed the night before last, he was goosed to-day. He has lately got in the way of being always goosed, and he can't stand it.

The principal uses of this construction are the same as those seen under our other recent headings. It can, as in the case just shown, make a condition sound pervasive or constant. Instead or in addition, the device can be used to set up a contrast between the early elements and an unexpected climax:

Johnson, in Boswell's *Life* (1791)

Sir, he was dull in company, dull in his closet, dull everywhere. He was dull in a new way, and that made many people think him GREAT.

The first sentence uses anaphora in the same way the previous passage from Dickens did: to drive home how relentlessly dull the subject was. But it also prepares the ear for the pleasure of the surprise ending.

Those are straightforward cases where identical statements are followed by modifiers that just change the time or place of their occurrence (*last night, the night before last, today*; or *in company, in his closet, everywhere*). But the same sort of construction can be used to enlarge on a theme in more elaborate ways.

Churchill, speech in the House of Commons (1936)

They have bought their knowledge, they have bought it dear, they have bought it at our expense, but at any rate let us be duly thankful that they now at last possess it.

And when this new principle – this new proposition that no human being ever thought of three years ago – is brought forward, I combat it as having an evil tendency, if not an evil design. I combat it as having a tendency to dehumanize the negro, to take away from him the right of ever striving to be a man. I combat it as being one of the thousand things constantly done in these days to prepare the public mind to make property, and nothing but property, of the negro in all the States of this Union.

Lincoln, debate with Stephen Douglas at Alton (1858)

This time the stem (*I combat it*) is short compared to the various elaborations attached to it. Repeating the stem helps prevent the action in the sentence from being lost in the long explanation of its rationale. The speaker's basic position becomes a kind of refrain.

A case of this sort of anaphora from scripture:

But woe unto you, scribes and Pharisees, hypocrites! for ye shut up the kingdom of heaven against men: for ye neither go in yourselves, neither suffer ye them that are entering to go in.

Woe unto you, scribes and Pharisees, hypocrites! for ye devour widows' houses, and for a pretence make long prayer: therefore ye shall receive the greater damnation.

Woe unto you, scribes and Pharisees, hypocrites! for ye compass sea and land to make one proselyte, and when he is made, ye make him twofold more the child of hell than yourselves.

Woe unto you, ye blind guides, which say, Whosoever shall swear by the temple, it is nothing; but whosoever shall swear by the gold of the temple, he is a debtor!

Matthew 23:13–16

5. *To elaborate on a single word.* A variation on the pattern just shown uses anaphora to state a subject repeatedly, with each round joined to a longer descriptive phrase afterwards.

Burke, speech on East India Bill (1783)

To whom then would I make the East-India Company accountable? Why, to parliament, to be sure; to parliament, from which their trust was derived; to parliament, which alone is capable of comprehending the magnitude of its object, and its abuse; and alone capable of an effectual legislative remedy.

Sheil, argument for the defense in the trial of John O'Connell (1843)

How, then, have we become enslaved? Alas! England, that ought to have been to us a sister and a friend – England, whom we have protected, and whom we do protect – England, at a period when, out of 100,000 of the seamen in her service, 70,000 were Irish, England stole upon us like a thief in the night, and robbed us of the precious gem of our liberty; she stole from us "that in which naught enriched her, but made us poor indeed."

Bright, *Principles of Foreign Policy* (1858)

And yet in all this we are told that there is something to create extreme alarm and suspicion; we, who have never fortified any places; we, who have not a greater than Sebastopol at Gibraltar; we, who have not an impregnable fortress at Malta, who have not spent the fortune of a nation almost in the Ionian Islands; we, who are doing nothing at Alderney; we are to take offence at the fortifications of Cherbourg!

In each of last two cases the anaphora postpones the action of the sentence while description of the subject is piled higher and higher, thus creating some suspense: what finally will be said about it? And in each case notice the contrast between the last statement made about the subject and all the ones that came before, which effectively served to set up the contrasting climax.

6. *Repeating descriptive language at the start*, as when several things share some important quality.

Dickens, *Great Expectations* (1861)

I thought it had the most dismal trees in it, and the most dismal sparrows, and the most dismal

cats, and the most dismal houses (in number half
a dozen or so), that I had ever seen.

Or perhaps the speaker wants instead to stress the common way in which various things are accomplished:

> I give this heavy weight from off my head
> And this unwieldy sceptre from my hand,
> The pride of kingly sway from out my heart;
> With mine own tears I wash away my balm,
> With mine own hands I give away my crown,
> With mine own tongue deny my sacred state,
> With mine own breath release all duty's rites:
> All pomp and majesty I do forswear....

Richard II, 4, 1

> By agitation Ireland became strong; by agitation
> she put down her bitter enemies; by agitation has
> conscience been set free; by agitation Irish freedom has been purchased; and by agitation it shall
> be secured.

O'Connell, speech in the
House of Commons (1830)

Or over what common period of time:

> It is the most grievous consequence of what we
> have done and of what we have left undone in the
> last five years – five years of futile good intentions,
> five years of eager search for the line of least resistance, five years of uninterrupted retreat of British
> power, five years of neglect of our air defenses.

Churchill, speech in the
House of Commons (1938)

Sometimes repeating a modifier is just a helpful way to
present action and link the elements of it together:

> Three machines – three horses – three flounderings
> – three turnings round – three splashes – three
> gentlemen, disporting themselves in the water like
> so many dolphins.

Dickens, *Sketches by Boz*
(1836)

> Now the dogs of war being let loose, began to lick
> their bloody lips; now Victory, with golden wings,
> hung hovering in the air; now Fortune, taking her

Fielding, *Tom Jones* (1749)

scales from her shelf, began to weigh the fates of Tom Jones, his female companion, and Partridge, against the landlord, his wife, and maid. . . .

The repeated *now* helps to unify the sentence; and naming the time in this way paints the picture more vividly, as if the author points to or conducts action occurring in the present and marks its pace. Fielding is having some fun here, as he often did, with a construction that was prominent in classical epic.

A variant of this theme is the modifying word stated repeatedly with various reasons for it appended afterwards. It much resembles a similar construction we saw at the end of section 3, above (the repeated noun with different language afterwards).

Grattan, speech in the Irish Parliament (1778)

I mentioned £80,000, the new expenses created by the last ministry; expenses memorable, because they happen to be equal to the whole amount of the new taxes; memorable, for they are a strain of profusion unparallelled; memorable, because men ashamed of that ministry on account of such expence endeavour to entail that expence upon the people. . . .

Douglass, speech at Rochester (1850)

I have shown that slavery is wicked – wicked, in that it violates the great law of liberty, written on every human heart – wicked, in that it violates the first command of the decalogue – wicked, in that it fosters the most disgusting licentiousness – wicked, in that it mars and defaces the image of God by cruel and barbarous inflictions – wicked, in that it contravenes the laws of eternal justice, and tramples in the dust all the humane and heavenly precepts of the New Testament.

Without the repetition the reader would become involved in the details of the reasoning, the statement of which would get farther and farther from the word it is all meant to explain. Returning to the word reminds the ear of the judgment being made, refreshes the listener's attention, and renews the passion in the utterance.

7. *Long stems*. In the examples seen so far, anaphora has usually meant just a short similarity at the start of successive sentences or clauses. The repeated language can go on longer, however, and so create a bit of suspense and surprise: the listener sits through almost the entire phrase a second time before learning how it will end differently.

> Was ever woman in this humour woo'd? *Richard III*, 1, 2
> Was ever woman in this humour won?

> The thing which is fundamentally and really   Chesterton, *Heretics* (1905)
> frivolous is not a careless joke. The thing which is
> fundamentally and really frivolous is a careless
> solemnity.

> Perhaps it may be our turn soon; perhaps it may   Churchill, speech at London
> be our turn now.   (1941)

8. *Miniatures*. Anaphora creates a distinctly energetic effect when applied at the start of several short phrases in a row.

> There is nothing simple, nothing manly, nothing   Burke, Speech on American
> ingenuous, open, decisive, or steady, in the pro-   Taxation (1774)
> ceeding, with regard either to the continuance or
> the repeal of the taxes.

Notice that the anaphora establishes a pattern (*nothing simple, nothing manly*) which is then relaxed (*nothing ingenuous, open, decisive, or steady*) – a classic pattern we will consider in more detail below. Here is a similar case from the same source:

> It is, indeed, a tax of sophistry, a tax of pedantry, a   Burke, Speech on American
> tax of disputation, a tax of war and rebellion, a tax   Taxation (1774)
> for anything but benefit to the imposers or satis-
> faction to the subject.

Burke attractively lengthens the parts as the sentence goes on: *pedantry* (three syllables), *disputation* (four), *war and rebellion* (five), and then the long finale. The anaphora provides a consistent anchor from which these extensions can depart.

Sterne, *Tristram Shandy*
(1760)

He was almost at his wit's end; – talked it over with her in all moods; – placed his arguments in all lights; – argued the matter with her like a christian, – like a heathen, – like a husband, – like a father, – like a patriot, – like a man: – My mother answered every thing only like a woman. . . .

This time the phrases marked by anaphora (*like a. . .*) are shorter than the phrases that come earlier in the sentence and the one that comes afterward. One effect of this is a kind of oscillation in the passage, as the phrases go from longer to shorter to long again; another effect is to add force to the phrases with anaphora, since they attract attention not only by the repetition at the start of them but also because they are so short. The anaphora is lightly resumed at the very end: setting the lone last instance of it (*like a woman*) against the multiple cases that came earlier helps to support the substantive point of the passage – the comparative narrowness of the mother's reply.

9. *Anaphora upon anaphora.* Repetition at the start can serve as a stylistic motif, with different words repeated in different ways that echo each other.

a. *Consecutive cases.* Here is a simple example in which one instance of anaphora (*your, your, your*) is immediately followed by another (*show, show, show*).

Burke, Speech on American
Taxation (1774)

They tell you, Sir, that your dignity is tied to it. I know not how it happens, but this dignity of yours is a terrible incumbrance to you; for it has of late been ever at war with your interest, your equity, and every idea of your policy. Show the thing you contend for to be reason, show it to be common sense, show it to be the means of attaining some useful end, and then I am content to allow it what dignity you please.

A more ambitious example, with four uses of anaphora in a single sentence:

> [A]h! if I could show you this! if I could show you these men and women, all the world over, in every stage of history, under every abuse of error, under every circumstance of failure, without hope, without help, without thanks, still obscurely fighting the lost fight of virtue, still clinging, in the brothel or on the scaffold, to some rag of honour, the poor jewel of their souls!

Stevenson, *Pulvis et Umbra* (1888)

When stacking anaphora in this way, pay attention again to the lengths of the repeated phrases. It is appealing to set off the regularity of the anaphora with variety in other respects, as when each batch of it differs in the length of its parts from the one before. The passage from Stevenson contains good examples: the middle use of it – *without hope, without help, without thanks* – uses shorter parts than the first (*under every. . .*) and last (*still obscurely fighting . . . still clinging. . .*). In the more common pattern, there are two rounds of anaphora rather than three; the first round consists of longer clauses, and the second of short ones:

> [Y]ou, Sir, who delight to utter execrations against the American commissioners of 1778, on account of their hostility to America; – you, Sir, who manufacture stage-thunder against Mr. Eden, for his anti-American principles; – you, Sir, whom it pleases to chaunt a hymn to the immortal Hamden; – you, Sir, approved of the tyranny exercised against America; – and you, Sir, voted 4,000 Irish troops to cut the throats of the Americans fighting for their freedom, fighting for your freedom, fighting for the great principle, *liberty*; but you found, at

Grattan, speech in the Irish Parliament (1783)

last (and this should be an eternal lesson to men of your craft and your cunning), that the King had only dishonoured you. . . .

The *you, Sir* clauses are the long uses of anaphora, and the *fighting for* clauses are the short ones – the sorts of miniatures we saw under the previous heading. The shorter second round of repetition creates a sense of acceleration and climax. Here is a similar case where anaphora again is used once with long pieces and then twice with short:

Orwell, *1984* (1949)

It was he who set the guards on to Winston and who prevented them from killing him. It was he who decided when Winston should scream with pain, when he should have a respite, when he should be fed, when he should sleep, when the drugs should be pumped into his arm. It was he who asked the questions and suggested the answers. He was the tormentor, he was the protector, he was the inquisitor, he was the friend.

b. *Embedded cases.* Uses of anaphora also can be embedded within one another, as in the previous example and as in the next case, where the first use of anaphora (*reduced.* . .) is suspended in the middle to make room for another (*power.* . .), but is resumed at the end:

Churchill, speech in the House of Commons (1938)

We have been reduced in those five years from a position of security so overwhelming and so unchallengeable that we never cared to think about it. We have been reduced from a position where the very word "war" was considered one which would be used only by persons qualifying for a lunatic asylum. We have been reduced from a position of safety and power – power to do good, power to be generous to a beaten foe, power to make terms with Germany, power to give her proper redress for her grievances, power to stop her arming if we chose, power to take any step in strength or mercy or justice which we thought right – reduced in five years from a position safe and unchallenged to where we stand now.

Or here, where the *in came . . . in they all came* constructions make way for *some shyly*, *some boldly*, etc., but then are brought back for the finish:

> In came the housemaid, with her cousin, the baker. In came the cook, with her brother's particular friend, the milkman. In came the boy from over the way, who was suspected of not having board enough from his master; trying to hide himself behind the girl from next door but one, who was proved to have had her ears pulled by her mistress. In they all came, one after another; some shyly, some boldly, some gracefully, some awkwardly, some pushing, some pulling; in they all came, any-how and everyhow.

Dickens, *A Christmas Carol* (1843)

10. *Regularity and relief*. An important technical question when using anaphora is how regular to make the repetition. Variety can be gained by abandoning the device at the end; the ear is pleased by the repetition, then pleased by the relief from it. The use of *flat* rather than *low* here is a good small example:

> [I]ts low gates and low wall and low roofs and low ditches and low sand-hills and low ramparts and flat streets, had not yielded long ago to the under-mining and besieging sea, like the fortifications children make on the sea-shore.

Dickens, *Little Dorrit* (1857)

The more common use of abandonment comes after a whole phrase has been repeated at the start of successive clauses or sentences, then is dropped for the last one.

> He had his plans for Poland and his plans for Nor-way. He had his plans for Denmark. He had his plans all worked out for the doom of the peaceful, trustful Dutch; and, of course, for the Belgians.

Churchill, London radio broadcast (1940)

Stevenson, *The Character of Dogs* (1884)

The day of an intelligent small dog is passed in the manufacture and the laborious communication of falsehood; he lies with his tail, he lies with his eye, he lies with his protesting paw; and when he rattles his dish or scratches at the door his purpose is other than appears.

The effect is a little like blowing up a balloon with short breaths and then letting it go; the repetition of words and structure accustoms the reader to regularity and compression, and the energy of that expectation is released into the last part of the sentence when the patterns are dropped.

Abandonment – or irregularity, to be more precise – is put to slightly different use in this celebrated passage of Churchill's:

Churchill, speech in the House of Commons (1940)

We shall go on to the end, we shall fight in France, we shall fight on the seas and oceans, we shall fight with growing confidence and growing strength in the air, we shall defend our Island, whatever the cost may be, we shall fight on the beaches, we shall fight on the landing grounds, we shall fight in the fields and in the streets, we shall fight in the hills; we shall never surrender. . . .

This moment in the speech is best-known for the repeated words themselves (*we shall fight. . .*), but notice what strength it gains from its internal variety. The parts separated by commas vary in size, lengthening fairly steadily until the middle, then starting shorter again, and then lengthening, and then shortening. The full form of the anaphora – *we shall fight* – comes and goes, both obviously (*we shall defend our island*; *we shall never surrender*) and in smaller ways (*in the fields and in the streets* – not *we shall fight in the fields, we shall fight in the streets*, etc.). These irregularities give the passage a greater sense of passion, of improvisation, and of the spontaneous outburst than it would have if the anaphora and repeated structure were more regular.

The anaphora also creates a repeated foundation onto which Churchill adds other kinds of variety – movement not only between different kinds of imagery (*seas and oceans . . . the air . . . the beaches*, etc.) but also between concrete images like those and the more abstract language at the start and end (*We shall go on to the end . . . we shall never surrender*). The passage taken as a whole illustrates very well the power of rhetorical technique to create an utterance of great force and utility; the substance of it could have been expressed concisely, and forgettably, in seven or eight words.

Repetition at the End:
EPISTROPHE

The most memorable moment – actually the only memorable moment – of the 1988 vice-presidential debate came when Dan Quayle, a young candidate for the office, suggested that he had as much experience as did John Kennedy before he was elected president. The reply of Quayle's opponent, Lloyd Bentsen, is still remembered by most who heard it and has passed into cultural currency among many who didn't: *Senator, I served with Jack Kennedy; I knew Jack Kennedy; Jack Kennedy was a friend of mine. Senator, you're no Jack Kennedy.* The substance of this riposte, like the substance of Churchill's line at the end of the last chapter, could have been said in many ways, most of which would have made no lasting impression. It owes its fame to EPISTROPHE (e-*pis*-tro-phee – sometimes also known as *antistrophe*): the repetition of a word or phrase at the end of a series of sentences or clauses. Notice that the repeated element, *Jack Kennedy*, is put at the front rather than the end of the third clause, then moved back to the end for the finish. The variety adds to the force of the device when it resumes.

The general purposes of epistrophe tend to be similar to those of anaphora, but the sound is different, and often a bit subtler, because the repetition does not become evident until each time a sentence or clause ends. Sometimes epistrophe also is easier to use, and it tends to be convenient on different occasions, because the parts of speech that most naturally go at the end of an English sentence or clause aren't the same as the ones that come most naturally at the start.

1. *Different actions, same objects.* Epistrophe is useful for describing various actions done by the same actor toward or concerning the same thing.

[T]o say nothing, to do nothing, to know nothing, and to have nothing, is to be a great part of your title, which is within a very little of nothing.

All's Well that Ends Well, 2, 4

They criticise every thing, analyse every thing, argue upon every thing, dogmatise upon every thing; and the bundle of your habits, feelings, humours, follies and pursuits is regarded by them no more than a bundle of old clothes.

Hazlitt, *Mr. Jeffrey* (1825)

And this right to live includes, and in fact is, the right to be what the child likes and can, to do what it likes and can, to make what it likes and can, to think what it likes and can, to smash what it dislikes and can, and generally to behave in an altogether unaccountable manner within the limits imposed by the similar rights of its neighbors.

Shaw, *A Treatise on Parents and Children* (1910)

In these last two cases the words repeated by the epistrophe may not be the ones most emphasized; rather, the device gives the verbs more emphasis by treating each of them as entitled to its own phrase, not just to a place on a list. This same construction also can be used, usually with fewer repetitions, just to unify claims and lend them euphony.

The constituency has judged me; it has elected me; I stand here with no legal disqualification upon me.

Bradlaugh, speech in the House of Commons (1881)

The sentence probably would be sound as a grammatical matter without the last two words, but they join the ending with the rest of the sentence and the process it describes. Epistrophe is helpful generally for thus driving home a progression through stages. The progression in that last example was literal: a march through events. But it also can be a progression through stronger *claims*:

Towards thee I roll, thou all-destroying but unconquering whale; to the last I grapple with thee; from hell's heart I stab at thee; for hate's sake I spit my last breath at thee.

Melville, *Moby-Dick* (1851)

2. *Same action, different doers or recipients*, as when the speaker means to describe several people all doing the same thing or meeting the same fate. In plainest form, the speaker simply attaches different subjects to the same verb.

Toombs, speech in the
Senate (1861)

We claim that the government, while the Constitution recognizes our property for the purposes of taxation, shall give it the same protection that it gives yours. Ought it not to be so? You say no. Every one of you upon the committee said no. Your senators say no. Your House of Representatives says no. Throughout the length and breadth of your conspiracy against the Constitution there is but one shout of no!

The usual effect of this pattern is a sense of comprehensiveness: everyone does (or doesn't do) the same thing, and the sameness of whatever is done is made more prominent than the doers of it.

Grattan, speech in the
House of Commons (1805)

The great preachers of our capital have not said so; Mr. Dunn, that meek spirit of the gospel, he has not said so; Mr. Douglass, in his strain of piety, morals, and eloquence, he has not said so; nor the great luminary himself; he who has wrung from his own breast, as it were, near £60,000, by preaching for public charities, and has stopped the mouth of hunger for public charities, and has stopped the mouth of hunger with its own bread, *he* has not said so.

Lincoln, debate with
Stephen Douglas at Peoria
(1854)

That perfect liberty they sigh for – the liberty of making slaves of other people, Jefferson never thought of, their own fathers never thought of, they never thought of themselves, a year ago.

The same construction can be put to passive use: those to whom something is done change, but the thing done to them stays the same, and is repeated at the end:

Death is Nature's remedy for all things, and why
not Legislation's? Accordingly, the forger was put
to Death; the utterer of a bad note was put to Death;
the unlawful opener of a letter was put to Death;
the purloiner of forty shillings and sixpence was
put to Death; the holder of a horse at Tellson's door,
who made off with it, was put to Death; the coiner
of a bad shilling was put to Death; the sounders of
three-fourths of the notes in the whole gamut of
Crime, were put to Death.

Dickens, *A Tale of Two Cities*
(1859)

3. *Changes in tense or mood.* The subject and the primary
action may stay the same, with variation only in the use
of the auxiliary verbs that go with them.

By the rejection of the bill, they seemed to declare,
that the House had been bought, was bought, and
should be bought again.

Grattan, speech in the Irish
Parliament (1792)

I have been faithful to you, and useful to you, and
I am attached to you. But I can't consent, and I
won't consent, and I never did consent, and I never
will consent to be lost in you.

Dickens, *Little Dorrit* (1857)

That example from Dickens is a double case of epistrophe;
the second sentence illustrates our current pattern. One
result of the device is to stress the occurrence of the action
at all times, but notice that he also weaves in language of
ability or obligation: not just *never did* and *never will* but
also *can't* and *won't*. The same general idea:

I do not know whether in all countries or in all
ages that responsibility could be maintained, but
I do say that here and now in this wealthy country
and in this scientific age it does in my opinion
exist, is not discharged, ought to be discharged,
and will have to be discharged.

Churchill, speech at Dundee
(1908)

4. *Things sharing the same quality,* which is repeated at the
end of every example.

Macaulay, *Hallam* (1828)

In the first place, the transaction was illegal from beginning to end. The impeachment was illegal. The process was illegal. The service was illegal. If Charles wished to prosecute the five members for treason, a bill against them should have been sent to a grand jury.

Chesterton, *Heretics* (1905)

The French Revolution is of Christian origin. The newspaper is of Christian origin. The anarchists are of Christian origin. Physical science is of Christian origin. The attack on Christianity is of Christian origin. There is one thing, and one thing only, in existence at the present day which can in any sense accurately be said to be of pagan origin, and that is Christianity.

In both of those examples the speaker is making a comprehensive claim – *illegal from beginning to end*, for example, or that everything except Christianity is of Christian origin. The epistrophe causes the pervasiveness to be felt more fully than it would if claimed once in simple form.

In another effective use of the same pattern, the speaker borrows a word offered by another – perhaps by an antagonist – and gives his own examples of its meaning. Irony or indignation are at home in these constructions.

Dickens, *A Christmas Carol* (1843)

"But you were always a good man of business, Jacob," faltered Scrooge, who now began to apply this to himself.

"Business!" cried the Ghost, wringing its hands again. "Mankind was my business. The common welfare was my business; charity, mercy, forbearance, and benevolence, were, all, my business. The dealings of my trade were but a drop of water in the comprehensive ocean of my business!"

Dickens, *David Copperfield* (1850)

"Mr. Micawber," said I, "what is the matter? Pray speak out. You are among friends."

"Among friends, Sir?" repeated Mr. Micawber;

and all he had reserved came breaking out of him. "Good Heavens, it is principally because I am among friends that my state of mind is what it is. What is the matter, gentlemen? What is not the matter? Villainy is the matter; baseness is the matter; deception, fraud, conspiracy, are the matter; and the name of the whole atrocious mass is – HEEP!"

[A]nd if I cannot say fie upon them, what shall I say of the men who, with these things of a constant and perpetual occurrence staring them in the face, talk to us of the immorality of the ballot, and tell us, forsooth, that it is an un-English proceeding. Un-English! . . . Fraud is indeed un-English; and dissimulation, and deception, and duplicity, and double-dealing, and promise-breaking, all, every vice akin to these vile things are indeed un-English; but tyranny, base, abominable tyranny, is un-English; hard-hearted persecution of poor fanatic wretches is un-English; crouching fear on one side, and ferocious menace and relentless savageness upon the other, are un-English! Of your existing system of voting these are the consequences.

Sheil, speech in the House of Commons (1843)

5. *Same general condition, different details*, as when the speaker means to apply several adjectives or adverbs to the same complement or object:

I hate to be poor, and we are degradingly poor, offensively poor, miserably poor, beastly poor.

Dickens, *Our Mutual Friend* (1865)

The divisions between uses of this pattern lie in about the same places as we have seen under other recent headings. Sometimes the effect is to stress the general condition over the detailed variations on it, as in the example just shown and here:

The tariff is a usurpation; it is a dangerous usurpation; it is a palpable usurpation; it is a deliberate usurpation.

Webster, Reply to Hayne (1830)

Webster, speech in the Senate (1836)

It might be presumptuous to say that I took a leading part, but I certainly took an early part, a decided part, and an earnest part, in rejecting this broad grant of three millions of dollars, without limitation of purpose or specification of object, called for by no recommendation, founded on no estimate, made necessary by no state of things which was known to us.

That example from Webster includes, after the epistrophe, an attractive use of *isocolon* – the use of consecutive phrases with a repeated structure (and not necessarily with repeated words, though in Webster's case the repeated *no* in the last three rounds is a little use of conduplicatio). We consider isocolon fully in a later chapter.

The speaker also may wish to make claims that are more distinct, and use the epistrophe at the end not to emphasize the repeated words for their own sake but to link the different claims in some way – perhaps for the sake of comparison, as here:

Churchill, speech in the House of Commons (1938)

That is the wisdom of the past, for all wisdom is not new wisdom.

Burke, Speech Relative to the Middlesex Election (1771)

That this House should have no power of expulsion is a hard saying. That this House should have a general discretionary power of disqualification is a dangerous saying. That the people should not choose their own representative, is a saying that shakes the Constitution. That this House should name the representative, is a saying which, followed by practice, subverts the constitution.

Notice that each of these last two examples varies the position of the repeated element, using it at the end of a phrase or sentence twice (the epistrophe) but then also using it in the middle of another phrase or two. In Burke's case the word *saying* is moved from the end of the first two sentences to the middle of the last two – which makes room for a fresh round of epistrophe with *constitution*.

6. *Different acts done in the same way*: a construction typically used to make the influence of a modifier seem pervasive.

I will buy with you, sell with you, talk with you, walk with you, and so following; but I will not eat with you, drink with you, nor pray with you.	*The Merchant of Venice*, I, 3

"You see me, young man; I never learned Greek, and I don't find that I have ever missed it. I have had a Doctor's cap and gown without Greek; I have ten thousand florins a year without Greek; I eat heartily without Greek; and, in short," continued he, "as I don't know Greek, I do not believe there is any good in it."	Goldsmith, *The Vicar of Wakefield* (1766)

[T]hey judge of us with a true knowledge of, and just deference for, our character – that a country enlightened as Ireland, chartered as Ireland, armed as Ireland, and injured as Ireland, will be satisfied with nothing less than liberty.	Grattan, speech in the Irish Parliament (1790)

I confided all to my aunt when I got home; and in spite of all she could say to me, went to bed despairing. I got up despairing, and went out despairing.	Dickens, *David Copperfield* (1850)

I look upon that enactment not as a law, but as a violence from the beginning. It was conceived in violence, is maintained in violence, and is being executed in violence.	Lincoln, letter to Joshua Speed (1855)

7. *Different conditions, identical outcome*: a useful construction when the speaker wishes to show emphatically that all roads lead to the same place.

When we call on you to abolish the fatal impost which keeps the country in paroxysm of excitement, you cry out, "the Church!" When we bid you rescue the country from the frightful litigation which turns our courts of justice into an arena for the combat of the political passions, you cry out, "the Church!" And when we implore you to ful-	Sheil, speech in the House of Commons (1837)

fill your contract at the Union, do redeem your pledge, given the emancipation, to extend to us British privileges, and grant us British institutions, you cry out, "the Church!"

Douglass, *My Bondage and My Freedom* (1855)

To ensure good behavior, the slaveholder relies on the whip; to induce proper humility, he relies on the whip; to rebuke what he is pleased to term insolence, he relies on the whip; to supply the place of wages, as an incentive to toil, he relies on the whip; to bind down the spirit of the slave, to imbrute and to destroy his manhood, he relies on the whip.

Thackeray, speech at New York (1852)

All children ought to love him. I know two that do, and read his books ten times for once that they peruse the dismal preachments of their father. I know one who, when she is happy, reads "Nicholas Nickleby"; when she is unhappy, reads "Nicholas Nickleby"; when she is tired, reads "Nicholas Nickleby"; when she is in bed, reads "Nicholas Nickleby"; when she has nothing to do, reads "Nicholas Nickleby"; and when she has finished the book, reads "Nicholas Nickleby" over again.

The pattern can be used to sketch a progression, with each possibility more extreme than the last but nevertheless leading to the same conclusion:

Poe, *The Pit and the Pendulum* (1843)

I had swooned; but still will not say that all of consciousness was lost. What of it there remained I will not attempt to define, or even to describe; yet all was not lost. In the deepest slumber – no! In delirium – no! In a swoon – no! In death – no! even in the grave all is not lost. Else there is no immortality for man.

Shaw, *Back to Methuselah* (1921)

He got a colony of mice, and cut off their tails. Then he waited to see whether their children would be born without tails. They were not, as Butler could have told him beforehand. He then cut off the children's tails, and waited to see whether the grandchildren would be born with at least rather short tails. They were not, as I could have told him beforehand. So with the patience and industry on which men of science pride themselves, he cut off the grandchildren's tails too, and waited, full of hope, for the birth of curtailed great-grandchildren. But their tails were quite up to the mark, as any fool could have told him beforehand.

8. *Anaphora and epistrophe.* Anaphora and epistrophe can complement each other. Alternating where the repetition is placed – at the beginning of a series of phrases, then at the end – may be used to create an appealing sense of balance.

> The things required for prosperous labor, prosperous manufactures, and prosperous commerce are three: first, liberty; secondly, liberty; thirdly, liberty – but these are not merely the same liberty, as I shall show you.

Beecher, speech at Liverpool (1863)

> The poor man buys simply for his body; he buys food, he buys clothing, he buys fuel, he buys lodging. His rule is to buy the least and the cheapest that he can. He goes to the store as seldom as he can – he brings away as little as he can – and he buys for the least he can.

Beecher, speech at Liverpool (1863)

> Think you that judgment waits till the doors of the grave are opened? It waits at the doors of your houses – it waits at the corners of your streets; we are in the midst of judgment – the insects that we crush are our judges – the moments we fret away are our judges – the elements that feed us, judge, as they minister – and the pleasures that deceive us, judge, as they indulge.

Ruskin, *Sesame and Lilies* (1865)

In those cases anaphora was followed by epistrophe. Here is the reverse sequence:

Churchill, London radio
broadcast (1940)

But all depends now upon the whole life-strength of the British race in every part of the world and of all our associated peoples and of all our well-wishers in every land, doing their utmost night and day, giving all, daring all, enduring all – to the utmost – to the end.

Anaphora and epistrophe also can be interlaced, as in this case where the middle phrase participates in both patterns:

O'Connell, speech at
Mullaghmast (1843)

No other principle makes a good soldier; conquer or die is the battle-cry for the good soldier; conquer or die is his only security. . . .

A classic form of transition from epistrophe to anaphora repeats a word at the end of the first two phrases, then moves it to the front of the phrases that come afterwards. The result is secure joinder of the two parts.

Grattan, speech in the
House of Commons (1812)

Gentlemen call for security; we call for security; we call for security against a policy which would make the British name in Ireland odious; we call for security against a policy which would make the British faith in Ireland equivocal; we call for security against a policy which would disinherit, disquality, and palsy a fourth part of the empire.

Dickens, *Little Dorrit* (1857)

My nephew, I introduce to you a lady of strong force of character, like myself – a resolved lady, a stern lady, a lady who has a will that can break the weak to powder: a lady without pity, without love, implacable, revengeful, cold as the stone, but raging as the fire.

Notice the two rounds of anaphora at the end of this last case; and notice throughout how the lengths of the units expand and contract – an important theme considered more fully in the chapter on isocolon.

9. *Uses of variety.* As with anaphora and other repetitive devices, the strongest uses of epistrophe sometimes are made by establishing the pattern and then abandoning it.

Thus it often is effective to repeat an ending a few times and then drop it in the concluding phrase; the finale is given a push because it releases the energy created by the earlier rounds of repetition.

> I will not parade the two old women, whose untimely and unseemly introduction into the dress-circle of diplomacy was hardly to have been expected of the high official whose name is at the bottom of this paper. They prove nothing, they disprove nothing, they illustrate nothing – except that a statesman may forget himself.

Holmes, *John Lothrop Motley: A Memoir* (1879)

> Slavery shrinks from the light; it hateth the light, neither cometh to the light, lest its deeds should be reproved.

Douglass, speech at London (1846)

> These are good reasons for remonstrating with him, or reasoning with him, or persuading him, or entreating him, but not for compelling him, or visiting him with any evil in case he do otherwise.

Stephen, *Liberty, Equality, Fraternity* (1873)

10. *Note on Lincoln's applications.* We have seen examples of Lincoln's use of epistrophe already, though not yet his most famous use of the device – probably the most famous instance of it in English:

> ... that this nation shall have a new birth of freedom, and that government of the people, by the people, for the people, shall not perish from the earth.

Lincoln, Gettysburg Address (1863)

He borrowed the idea partly from Daniel Webster.

> It is, Sir, the people's Constitution, the people's government, made for the people, made by the people, and answerable to the people.

Webster, Reply to Hayne (1830)

Lincoln was a master of epistrophe. Here he uses it in five or six different ways to make his consistency a rhetorical as well as a substantive fact:

Lincoln, letter to Horace
Greeley (1862)

If there be those who would not save the Union, unless they could at the same time save slavery, I do not agree with them. If there be those who would not save the Union unless they could at the same time destroy slavery, I do not agree with them. My paramount object in this struggle is to save the Union, and is not either to save or to destroy slavery. If I could save the Union without freeing any slave I would do it, and if I could save it by freeing all the slaves I would do it; and if I could save it by freeing some and leaving others alone I would also do that. What I do about slavery, and the colored race, I do because I believe it helps to save the Union; and what I forbear, I forbear because I do not believe it would help to save the Union. I shall do *less* whenever I shall believe what I am doing hurts the cause, and I shall do *more* whenever I shall believe doing more will help the cause. I shall try to correct errors when shown to be errors; and I shall adopt new views so fast as they shall appear to be true views.

Lincoln also made frequent use of a particular kind of epistrophe in which he repeated a word or phrase at the end of both halves of a sentence with little space between them.

Lincoln, letter to H.L. Pierce
(1859)

This is a world of compensation; and he who would be no slave must consent to have no slave.

Lincoln, letter to A.G.
Hodges (1864)

I could not take the office without taking the oath. Nor was it my view that I might take an oath to get power, and break the oath in using the power.

Lincoln, speech at Springfield (1858)

[T]he thing which determines whether a man is free or a slave is rather *concrete* than *abstract*. I think you would conclude that it was, if your liberty depended upon it, and so would Judge Douglas, if his liberty depended upon it.

The world will little note, nor long remember
what we say here, but it can never forget what they
did here.

Lincoln, Gettysburg Address
(1863)

Here as elsewhere, Lincoln's ear was influenced by the
King James Bible.

But if ye forgive not men their trespasses, neither
will your Father forgive your trespasses.

Matthew 6:15

And the land was not able to bear them, that they
might dwell together: for their substance was
great, so that they could not dwell together.

Genesis 13:6

Repetition at the Start and End:
SYMPLOCE

SYMPLOCE (most often pronounced *sim*-plo-see, though respectable sources don't always agree, and the more sensible pronunciation as a matter of etymology is *sim*-plo-kee) combines anaphora and epistrophe: words are repeated at the start of successive sentences or clauses, and other words are repeated at the end of them, often with just a small change in the middle. The nearly complete repetition lends itself to elegant effects. It also locks the speaker into a small number of possible patterns, so our treatment of them can be brief.

1. *Corrections; reversals of direction.* Symploce is useful for highlighting the contrast between correct and incorrect claims. The speaker changes the word choice in the smallest way that will suffice to separate the two possibilities; the result is conspicuous contrast between the small tweak in wording and the large change in substance. Some simple cases of correction, in which the symploce serves to emphasize a surprising change in direction:

Chesterton, *Orthodoxy* (1908)

> We do not need a censorship of the press. We have a censorship by the press.

Trollope, *The Prime Minister* (1876)

> I am not afraid of you; – but I am afraid for you.

The order may as easily be reversed: the correct statement followed by the incorrect one, which is negated:

Churchill, London radio broadcast (1940)

> We are fighting *by* ourselves alone; but we are not fighting *for* ourselves alone.

This construction also can emphasize the opposite nature of two claims, as here:

The madman is not the man who has lost his reason. The madman is the man who has lost everything except his reason.

Chesterton, *Orthodoxy*
(1908)

By keeping the statements parallel and nearly identical –
the same nouns and verbs in the same order, with a change
only in the words that relate them to each other – Chesterton causes the rhetoric to reflect the perfect reversal of
understanding he means to suggest in substance.

[T]he right honourable gentleman has in a very
ingenious manner twined and twisted the paragraph in question, to make it appear to be a libel;
and I hope that I may be allowed to try if I cannot
twine and twist it till it appears not to be a libel.

Flood, speech in the House
of Commons (circa 1764)

2. *Parallel elaboration.* Symploce can be used to make a
second statement elaborate on the first. The speaker offers
two claims, using the same vocabulary and structure for
each; a minor variation in the middle makes them distinct, but rhetorically as well as conceptually parallel.

Everything in the English government appears to
me the reverse of what it ought to be, and of what
it is said to be.

Paine, *The American Crisis*
(1783)

For he who does not love art in all things does not
love it at all, and he who does not need art in all
things does not need it at all.

Wilde, *The English Renaissance of Art* (1882)

He spoke with consummate ability to the bench,
and yet exactly as, according to every sound canon
of taste and ethics, the bench ought to be addressed.
He spoke with consummate ability to the jury, and
yet exactly as, according to every sound canon, that
totally different tribunal ought to be addressed.

Choate, eulogy for Daniel
Webster (1853)

This form of the device is often used to express continu-
ity despite a change in tense.

Dickens, *A Christmas Carol*
(1843)

"Let me leave it alone, then," said Scrooge. "Much good may it do you! Much good it has ever done you!"

Chesterton, *The Mad Official*
(1912)

I here challenge any person in his five wits to tell me what that woman was sent to prison for. Either it was for being poor, or it was for being ill. Nobody could suggest, nobody will suggest, nobody, as a matter of fact, did suggest, that she had committed any other crime.

3. *Extended uses*. Most of the examples so far have involved two claims with minor variations in the middle of them. More extended patterns also are possible, usually involving three or four parts. The typical idea then isn't to ring in a correction or twist on the first statement; it is to present a series of claims in a way that throws their commonality or connection into relief.

a. *Changes of a noun*; as when describing several things as similar or as meeting the same fate.

Dickens, *Little Dorrit* (1857)

In that room he found three gentlemen; number one doing nothing particular, number two doing nothing particular, number three doing nothing particular.

Dickens, *Our Mutual Friend*
(1865)

Everything about the Veneerings was spick and span new. All their furniture was new, all their friends were new, all their servants were new, their plate was new, their carriage was new, their harness was new, their horses were new, their pictures were new, they themselves were new, they were as newly married as was lawfully compatible with their having a bran-new baby. . . .

Those examples involve changes in the subject of the sentence; here is the same idea with a change made in the object:

Baker, speech in the Senate
(1861)

They will have their courts still; they will have their ballot-boxes still; they will have their elections still;

they will have their representatives upon this floor
still; they will have taxation and representation
still; they will have the writ of habeas corpus still;
they will have every privilege they ever had and all
we desire.

The general effect in all the cases just seen is similar. The
differences between the examples are made subordinate
to the points they have in common. That last passage could
as easily – probably more easily – have been written by
putting *still* closer to the middle of each clause (*they will
still have*, etc.); pushing it to the end lends the word more
weight and makes the statements seem more completely
parallel. And think a bit about the sound of the word. *Still*
is a single accented syllable ending with a liquid consonant – meaning, for our purposes, a consonant that is
made without friction and that can be sustained when it
is said, almost like a vowel (unlike, say, *ck*, which stops, or
p, which explodes). If *still* goes into the middle of a sentence it can easily be truncated, with its ending lost in the
movement to the next word. When it ends a sentence, *still*
gets sounded out more completely and it invites a little
pause afterwards. So the use of epistrophe gives the word
a more forceful sound as well as a more forceful placement.

b. *Changes of a modifier*; as when describing the same
thing several ways.

> They were not respectable people – they were not
> worthy people – they were not learned and wise
> and brilliant people – but in their breasts, all their
> stupid lives long, resteth a peace that passeth
> understanding!

Twain, *The Innocents Abroad*
(1869)

Each modifier gets its own clause, and the thing under
discussion is carved up into categories as the speaker goes
along. These constructions also tend to give the modifiers
more power than they would have had if strung on a list.
When most of the words in each clause are the same, the

stress in reading or speaking them falls hard on the changed adjective.

Dickens, *Hard Times* (1854)

I'll state the fact of it to you. It's the pleasantest work there is, and it's the lightest work there is, and it's the best-paid work there is.

Lloyd George, *International Honour* (1914)

I believe, in spite of recent events, there is as great a store of kindness in the German peasant as in any peasant in the world. But he has been drilled into a false idea of civilization, – efficiency, capability. It is a hard civilization; it is a selfish civilization; it is a material civilization.

The same theme is useful for comparing the same two things in different respects:

Dickens, *Hard Times* (1854)

I am a donkey, that's what *I* am. I am as obstinate as one, I am more stupid than one, I get as much pleasure as one, and I should like to kick like one.

c. *Changes of the verb*; as when describing the same person doing or not doing different things in the same way.

1 Corinthians 13:11

When I was a child, I spake as a child, I understood as a child, I thought as a child: but when I became a man, I put away childish things.

Sheil, speech in the House of Commons (1836)

He confiscates, as your fathers did; he banishes as they did; he debases as they did; he violates the instincts of human nature, and from the parent tears the child, as they did; and he inflicts upon a Catholic people a church alien to their national habits, feelings, and belief as you do.

Webster, argument in *Trustees of Dartmouth College v. Woodward* (1818)

[T]he legislature shall pass no act directly and manifestly impairing private property and private privileges. It shall not judge by act. It shall not decide by act. It shall not deprive by act. But it shall leave all these things to be tried and adjudged by the law of the land.

You knew what was going to happen. You intended
it to happen. You wanted it to happen. You are glad
it has happened; and it serves you right.

Shaw, *The Irrational Knot*
(1905)

4. *Independent statements followed by identical commen-*
taries; as when various deeds by the same actor lead to the
same outcome or judgment.

We are fond of talking about "liberty"; that, as we
talk of it, is a dodge to avoid discussing what is
good. We are fond of talking about "progress"; that
is a dodge to avoid discussing what is good. We are
fond of talking about "education"; that is a dodge
to avoid discussing what is good.

Chesterton, *Heretics* (1905)

The repetition of the verbal pattern matches the claim
that seemingly different acts serve the same purpose.

There is an agreement that the boards of accounts
and stamps should be united; that agreement they
violated. There is an agreement that the revenue
board should be confined to seven commission-
ers; that agreement they violate. There is a King's
letter, declaring that the salaries of the ordnance
shall be reduced; that declaration they violate. There
are principles and law against the sale of honours;
those principles and law they have violated.

Grattan, speech in the Irish
Parliament (1790)

Buonaparte, it seems, is to reconcile every thing by
the gift of a free constitution. He took possession
of Holland, he did not give her a free constitution;
he took possession of Spain, he did not give her a
free constitution; he took possession of Switzerland,
whose independence he had guaranteed, he did
not give her a free constitution; he took possession
of Italy, he did not give her a free constitution; he
took possession of France, he did not give her a
free constitution; on the contrary, he destroyed the
directorial constitution, he destroyed the consular
constitution, and he destroyed the late constitution, formed on the plan of England!

Grattan, speech in the
House of Commons (1815)

A related construction applies symploce to statements of an "if, then" character: again a variety of possibilities all come to the same result in sound and substance.

Disraeli, speech at Manchester (1872)

The Conservative party are accused of having no programme of policy. If by a programme is meant a plan to despoil churches and plunder landlords, I admit we have no programme. If by a programme is meant a policy which assails or menaces every institution and every interest, every class and every calling in the country, I admit we have no programme.

Chesterton, *The Aristocratic 'Arry* (1912)

If, living in Italy, you admire Italian art while distrusting Italian character, you are a tourist, or cad. If, living in Italy, you admire Italian art while despising Italian religion, you are a tourist, or cad. It does not matter how many years you have lived there.

5. *Lengthenings.* As with all other figures of repetition, the impact of symploce often is increased when it is combined with variety in the length or rhythm of the phrases involved. One possibility, familiar from earlier chapters, is to lengthen the last section. The repetition at the start and end continues, but the structure is varied:

Measure for Measure, 5, 1

That Angelo's forsworn, is it not strange?
That Angelo's a murderer, is't not strange?
That Angelo is an adulterous thief,
An hypocrite, a virgin-violator,
Is it not strange and strange?

Much Ado about Nothing, 4, 1

O, what men dare do! what men may do! what men daily do, not knowing what they do!

In this last case two types of variety are introduced in the last part: a longer syllable (*daily* instead of *dare* and *may*); and a longer separation between *what men* and the last word of the sentence. Both changes gently disrupt the expectations that the first two rounds of repetition had created.

> Is not the maintaining so numerous an army in time of peace to be condemned? Is not the fitting out so many expensive and useless squadrons to be condemned? Are not the encroachments made upon the Sinking Fund; the reviving the salt duty; the rejecting many useful bills and motions in Parliament, and many other domestic measures, to be condemned?

Pitt, speech in the House of Commons (1742)

By the time the third sentence arrives here, the listener has learned how the end of the pattern goes, so the speaker can afford to stack up more examples before getting there. Postponing the conclusion in this way makes it more climactic. This passage also illustrates a useful bit of technique in working with symploce: repeating the same grammatical structure within the middle part even as the words change. Here the use of gerunds mostly repeats (*the maintaining . . . the fitting out . . . the reviving . . . the rejecting*). This helps to sustain the sense of parallelism, especially when there is some distance between the repeated words at the beginning and end of each sentence.

6. *Abandonment.* Symploce also can be abandoned entirely and to good effect after it has conditioned the listener's expectations. We saw some examples in passing earlier in the chapter; here are a few others.

> He was there before the murder; he was there after the murder; he was there clandestinely, unwilling to be seen.

Webster, argument in the murder trial of John Francis Knapp (1830)

> [T]here is nothing in the way of your liberty except your own corruption and pusillanimity; and nothing can prevent your being free except yourselves. It is not in the disposition of England; it is not in the interest of England; it is not in her arms.

Grattan, speech in the Irish Parliament (1790)

Dickens, *Little Dorrit* (1857)

Mrs. Sparkler, lying on her sofa, looking through an open window at the opposite side of a narrow street over boxes of mignonette and flowers, was tired of the view. Mrs. Sparkler, looking at another window where her husband stood in the balcony, was tired of that view. Mrs. Sparkler, looking at herself in her mourning, was even tired of that view: though, naturally, not so tired of that as of the other two.

Chesterton, *The Crimes of England* (1915)

And if this Germanic sociology is indeed to prevail among us, I think some of the broad-minded thinkers who concur in its prevalence owe something like an apology to many gallant gentlemen whose graves lie where the last battle was fought in the Wilderness; men who had the courage to fight for it, the courage to die for it and, above all, the courage to call it by its name.

Notice that in these cases the repetition is sustained at the start of every clause straight through to the end. The abandonment comes just at the finish of the last part. The device also can be abandoned for a moment somewhere in the middle, as here:

Burke, argument in the impeachment trial of Warren Hastings (1788)

And, as to the man, is Mr. Hastings a man, against whom a charge of bribery is improbable? Why, he owns it. He is a professor of it. He reduces it into scheme and system. He glories in it.

Taking a break from the symploce (by ending a sentence with *scheme* and *system*) avoids monotony and also gives the harangue a more spontaneous sound. The speaker isn't trying too hard to hold to a pattern; he is too excited for that. Hastings later said of this speech, "For half an hour I looked at the orator in a reverie of wonder, and actually felt myself the most culpable man on earth."

Repeating the Ending at the Beginning:

ANADIPLOSIS

ANADIPLOSIS (a-na-di-*plo*-sis) is the use of the same language at the end of one sentence or clause and at the start of the next – an ABBC pattern. Probably the most famous example of it comes from a proverb popularized by Benjamin Franklin in *Poor Richard's Almanack* (1758):

> For want of a nail the shoe was lost, for want of a shoe the horse was lost; and for want of a horse the rider was lost; being overtaken and slain by the enemy, all for want of care about a horse-shoe nail.

1. *Chains of causation.* As that first example shows, anadiplosis is a natural device for describing causal progressions: each element is repeated, once as result of the prior cause and then again as cause of the next result.

> And not only so, but we glory in tribulations also; knowing that tribulation worketh patience;
> And patience, experience; and experience, hope:
> And hope maketh not ashamed; because the love of God is shed abroad in our hearts by the Holy Ghost which is given unto us.

Romans 6:3–5

The repeated elements make the links in the chain seem more secure and perhaps more inevitable. They strengthen the sense that one thing leads to another.

> For your brother and my sister no sooner met, but they looked; no sooner looked but they loved; no sooner loved but they sighed; no sooner sighed but they asked one another the reason; no sooner knew the reason but they sought the remedy: and in these degrees have they made a pair of stairs to marriage. . . .

As You Like It, 5, 2

O'Connell, speech in the
House of Commons (1831)

One party, then, was armed against the other – the armed party grew insolent – insolence led to scuffles, and scuffles ended in death.

James, *Washington Square*
(1881)

If she stands up for him on account of the money, she will be a humbug. If she is a humbug I shall see it. If I see it, I won't waste time with her.

The order can be reversed, too, so that the pattern becomes result–cause, result–cause, as here:

A Comedy of Errors, 1, 2

The meat is cold because you come not home;
You come not home because you have no
    stomach;
You have no stomach, having broke your fast;
But we, that know what 'tis to fast and pray,
Are penitent for your default to-day.

These patterns can then be abandoned at the end, which creates the favorable effects we have seen when considering variety in earlier chapters.

Johnson, *The Rambler* no. 21
(1750)

There is a general succession of events in which contraries are produced by periodical vicissitudes; labour and care are rewarded with success, success produces confidence, confidence relaxes industry, and negligence ruins that reputation which accuracy had raised.

Dickens, speech at London
(1855)

It came to pass that they were burnt in a stove in the House of Lords. The stove, overgorged with these preposterous sticks, set fire to the panelling; the panelling set fire to the House of Lords; the House of Lords set fire to the House of Commons; the two houses were reduced to ashes; architects were called in to build others; we are now in the second million of the cost thereof; the national pig is not nearly over the stile yet; and the little old woman, Britannia, hasn't got home to-night.

2. *Chains of reasoning.* Anadiplosis also may be used to describe chains of reasoning rather than causation.

BENEDICK. Only foul words; and thereupon I will kiss thee.

BEATRICE. Foul words is but foul wind, and foul wind is but foul breath, and foul breath is noisome; therefore I will depart unkissed.

Much Ado About Nothing, 5, 2

"To think better of it," returned the gallant Blandois, "would be to slight a lady; to slight a lady would be to be deficient in chivalry towards the sex; and chivalry towards the sex is a part of my character!"

Dickens, *Little Dorrit* (1857)

Man is born a predestined idealist, for he is born to act. To act is to affirm the worth of an end, and to persist in affirming the worth of an end is to make an ideal.

Holmes, speech at Harvard University (1911)

In the example from Holmes, and perhaps in all of these cases, the anadiplosis gives rhetorical backing to an implied form of argument in which the end point is reached through a series of identities: a is b, b is c – so a is c. A variation on this pattern strings together negatives. One cannot have x without y; one cannot have y without z – so by implication one cannot have x without z.

Society, dead or alive, can have no charm without intimacy, and no intimacy without interest in trifles which I fear Mr. Harrison would describe as "merely curious."

Balfour, speech at St. James University (1887)

ERNEST. . . . [S]urely you would admit that the great poems of the early world, the primitive, anonymous collective poems, were the result of the imagination of races, rather than the imagination of individuals?

GILBERT. . . . Not when they received a beautiful form. For there is no art where there is no style, and no style where there is no unity, and unity is of the individual.

Wilde, *The Critic as Artist* (1891)

Burke, *Thoughts on the Cause of the Present Discontents* (1770)

They believed that no men could act with effect who did not act in concert; that no men could act in concert who did not act with confidence; that no men could act with confidence who were not bound together by common opinions, common affections, and common interests.

3. *Ascension and climax.* Anadiplosis is a helpful tool for describing an ascent. Each repetition is accompanied by an increase in the scale of the thing under discussion.

Hamilton, speech at New York Ratifying Convention (1788)

We love our families more than our neighbors; we love our neighbors more than our countrymen in general.

Samuel Adams, speech at Philadelphia (1776)

The scale of officers, from the rapacious and needy commissioner to the haughty governor, and from the governor, with his hungry train, to perhaps a licentious and prodigal viceroy, must be upheld by you and your children.

In elaborate cases the result of this pattern is *climax*, a distinct rhetorical figure in which words increase in intensity or scale until finally reaching some sort of culmination. Climax and anadiplosis go well together, as shown in these examples that apply both devices to ascending states of mind:

Richard II, 5, 1

The love of wicked men converts to fear,
That fear to hate, and hate turns one or both
To worthy danger and deserved death.

Dickens, *Oliver Twist* (1838)

I know how cold formalities were succeeded by open taunts; how indifference gave place to dislike, dislike to hate, and hate to loathing, until at last they wrenched the clanking bond asunder. . . .

Poe, *The Imp of the Perverse* (1845)

The impulse increases to a wish, the wish to a desire, the desire to an uncontrollable longing, and the longing (to the deep regret and mortification of the speaker, and in defiance of all consequences) is indulged.

The repetition at the end of one part and the start of the next helps the reader feel the progress the speaker describes. Both feet come to rest on each stair before stepping to the next one. Anadiplosis also can help along ascension of a grander kind, as when the progression involves nature or religion.

> Now the quarry-discoverer is long before the stone-cutter; and the stone-cutter is long before the architect; and the architect is long before the temple; for the temple is the crown of the world.

Melville, *Pierre* (1852)

> There is no life in thee, now, except that rocking life imparted by a gentle rolling ship; by her, borrowed from the sea; by the sea, from the inscrutable tides of God.

Melville, *Moby-Dick* (1851)

> And let the kettle to the trumpet speak,
> The trumpet to the cannoneer without,
> The cannons to the heavens, the heaven to earth,
> "Now the king drinks to Hamlet."

Hamlet, 5, 2

Though less common, anadiplosis can also be used to walk through a hierarchy in the reverse direction – a descent, as shown here:

> The black Jehadia overawed the Arab army in the capital. The army in the capital dominated the forces in the provinces. The forces in the provinces subdued the inhabitants. The centralisation of power was assured by the concentration of military material.

Churchill, *The River War* (1899)

4. *Anadiplosis for emphasis*. Sometimes anadiplosis is not used for any substantive purpose of the kind just shown. The repetition just serves to improve the flow of the exposition, to emphasize the repeated word, and often to lend the utterance more feeling.

> Wherein is he good, but to taste sack and drink it? wherein neat and cleanly, but to carve a capon and

1 Henry IV, 2, 4

eat it? wherein cunning, but in craft? wherein crafty, but in villainy? wherein villanous, but in all things? wherein worthy, but in nothing?

Melville, *Mardi* (1849)

There, men were scourged; their crime, a heresy; the heresy, that Media was no demigod.

Webster, speech in the Senate (1836)

The bill, therefore, was lost. It was lost in the House of Representatives. It died there, and there its remains are to be found.

The passage from Webster is a double case of our current theme: *lost . . . lost* and *there . . . there.* The repeated use of the device creates a sense of gravity to go with the substance.

de Quincey, *Style* (1841)

But one man could not redeem a national dishonour. It *was* such, and such it was felt to be.

Dickens, *A Tale of Two Cities* (1859)

The beach was a desert of heaps of sea and stones tumbling wildly about, and the sea did what it liked, and what it liked was destruction.

Dickens, *A Christmas Carol* (1843)

"I wear the chain I forged in life," replied the Ghost. "I made it link by link, and yard by yard; I girded it on of my own free will, and of my own free will I wore it."

It is a useful exercise to mentally rewrite passages as they might have otherwise been composed and to ask what is gained and lost. This last passage from Dickens could have been written with anaphora (*of my own free will I girded it on, and of my own free will I wore it*) or epistrophe (*I girded it on of my own free will, and I wore it of my own free will*). Instead he uses anadiplosis to put the repetition on the inside rather than at the start or finish; this keeps the choices made by the speaker in the more prominent start and end positions, and so makes them strong while still stressing the common feature they share – the free will, which is repeated in succession. Anadiplosis also creates a different cadence than the other devices: a march up the hill and back down again. The verb phrases tumble out from the repeated middle parts as though by force of gravity, which makes a kind of match with the meaning.

That last passage also can be considered a type of *chiasmus*, of which more in its place.

5. *With anaphora*. Anadiplosis sometimes can be combined handsomely with anaphora. The most common technique moves from one of the devices to the other: the element repeated at the end and start – that is, the common word in the anadiplosis – is then repeated at the beginning of one or two more segments, creating a case of anaphora and thus varying the form of the repetition.

> She being none of your flesh and blood, your flesh and blood has not offended the King; and so your flesh and blood is not to be punish'd by him.

The Winter's Tale, 4, 4

> That ancient fabric which has been gradually reared by the wisdom and virtue of our fathers still stands. It stands, thanks be to God! solid and entire; but it stands alone, and it stands amid ruins.

Mackintosh, speech in the trial of Jean Peltier (1803)

The anaphora also can come before the anadiplosis, of course – or, as here, between two cases of it:

> I have no orders, but I have fears – fears that I will express, chafe as you may – fears that you may be consigning that young lady to something worse than supporting you by the labour of her hands, had she worked herself dead. These are my fears, and these fears I found upon your own demeanour.

Dickens, *Nicholas Nickleby* (1839)

A more exotic variation combines the two devices simultaneously by making the repeated element in the anadiplosis – the B in the ABBC pattern – itself a small case of anaphora:

> Ireland is not to be ruled by force. Indeed! It is to be ruled through Protestant jurors, and Protestant charges, and Protestant gaolers; but Protestant jurors, and Protestant charges, and Protestant

Sheil, argument for the defense in the trial of John O'Connell (1843)

gaolers, require that Protestant bayonets should sustain them, and that, with the discretion of the Home Office, the energy of the Horse Guards must be combined.

Repetition of the Root:

POLYPTOTON

POLYPTOTON (po-*lip*-toe-ton) means repeating the root of a word with a different ending.

1. *Reciprocity.* Polyptoton can be used with the active and passive forms of a verb to show how a single action may be done both by one and to one. Repeating the root of the word ties the wording of a sentence together in a way that suggests the same reciprocity as its substance.

Judge not, that ye be not judged.

Matthew 7:1

    I am a man
More sinn'd against than sinning.

King Lear, 3, 2

Let the people think they govern, and they will be governed.

Penn, *Some Fruits of Solitude* (1693)

Mrs. Montagu has dropped me. Now, sir, there are people whom one should like very well to drop, but would not wish to be dropped by.

Johnson, in Boswell's *Life* (1791)

It clearly would not be well for the world that we should always beat other nations and never be beaten.

Trollope, *North America* (1862)

Our knights are thinking only of the money they will make in ransoms: it is not kill or be killed with them, but pay or be paid.

Shaw, *Saint Joan* (1923)

If a League of peace-seeking peoples is set at nought, we must convert it into a League of armed peoples, too faithful to molest others, too strong to be molested themselves.

Churchill, speech at Manchester (1938)

2. *The actor and the act.* Polyptoton may be used to refer to the doer and the doing of an act, typically by using the

same root to build the subject and a verb form. The repetition snugly defines the actor by the act.

Richard II, 2, 1

With eager feeding food doth choke the feeder.

Webster, speech in the Senate
(1838)

I followed him; if I was seduced into error, or into unjustifiable opposition, there sits my seducer.

Like any repetitive device, polyptoton can, if used more than once, become a momentary motif.

Chesterton, *A Miscellany of Men* (1912)

I cannot understand why all solicitors did not leave off soliciting, all doctors leave off doctoring, all judges leave off judging, all benevolent bankers leave off lending money at high interest, and all rising politicians leave off having nothing to add to what their right honourable friend told the House about eight years ago.

Shaw, *A Treatise on Parents and Children* (1910)

In church, in the House of Commons, at public meetings, we sit solemnly listening to bores and twaddlers because from the time we could walk or speak we have been snubbed, scolded, bullied, beaten and imprisoned whenever we dared to resent being bored or twaddled at, or to express our natural impatience and derision of bores and twaddlers.

Hitting the reader over the head with the funny words a few times – or rather with the variations on the same root – creates a sense of redundancy and is a mild trespass on the reader's patience, which goes well with the meaning of Shaw's rant.

Polyptoton of this kind, with the verb set against a noun form of the same word, can also describe a turning of the tables.

Melville, *Moby-Dick* (1851)

The prophecy was that I should be dismembered; and – Aye! I lost this leg. I now prophesy that I will dismember my dismemberer.

But here I only remark the interesting fact that the conquered almost always conquer. Sparta killed Athens with a final blow, and she was born again. Sparta went away victorious, and died slowly of her own wounds.

Chesterton, *The Giant* (1909)

Again the substance of the point – here, the reversal of action – is made vivid by the close positioning of the similar words.

3. *Two nouns.* Some constructions similar to the ones just shown can be made by using different forms of the same noun to refer to actors and their characteristic activities or interests.

No man forgets his original trade: the rights of nations, and of kings, sink into questions of grammar, if grammarians discuss them.

Johnson, *Milton* (1794)

Such is the crime, and such is the criminal, which it is my duty in this debate to expose, and, by the blessing of God, this duty shall be done completely to the end.

Sumner, speech in the Senate (1856)

Naming the actor and the act with related words gives Sumner a chance to emphasize the damning root by saying it twice.

On any other occasion I should think myself justifiable in treating with silent contempt anything which might fall from that honorable member; but there are times when the insignificance of the accuser is lost in the magnitude of the accusation.

Grattan, speech in the Irish Parliament (1800)

In this example from Grattan, the repetition of the root (*accuser . . . accusation*) is artfully played off against the reversal of other words nearby (*insignificance . . . magnitude*).

We see the thief preaching against theft, and the adulterer against adultery. We have men sold to build churches, women sold to support the Gospel,

Douglass, *My Bondage and My Freedom* (1855)

and babes sold to purchase Bibles for the poor heathen!

Here polyptoton is used to support irony: the doer of the bad thing is the one speaking against it. Using the same root to describe them makes the oddity striking in language as well as concept; the identity between the speaker and that which he condemns is embedded in the sounds used to name them. Then the polyptoton is left behind, as Douglass moves in the second sentence to conduplicatio (*sold . . . sold . . . sold*) and a fresh round of isocolon, or repetition of structure.

Two nouns built from the same root also can be used to refer to the doer of an act and the person or other object to whom the act is done. The result is to stress their close and perhaps dependent nature:

Measure for Measure, 2, 2

The tempter or the tempted, who sins most, ha?

de Quincey, *System of the Heavens as Revealed by Lord Rosse's Telescopes* (1846)

Hence perhaps is explained, and not out of any self-oblivion from higher enthusiasm, a fact that often has occurred, of deer, or hares, or foxes, and the pack of hounds in pursuit, chaser and chased, all going headlong over a precipice together.

Chesterton, *Heretics* (1905)

When Byron divided humanity into the bores and bored, he omitted to notice that the higher qualities exist entirely in the bores, the lower qualities in the bored, among whom he counted himself.

Sometimes these constructions also express relations of superiority or priority, as when one party is subservient to another. The different endings on the words produce opposite roles for the players, the symmetry of which is stressed by the common root.

Burke, argument in the impeachment trial of Warren Hastings (1788)

We are all born in subjection – all born equally, high and low, governors and governed, in subjection to one great, immutable, preexistent law, prior to all our devices, and prior to all our contrivances. . . .

[I]t serves to modify the relations of human soci- | Poe, *Drake and Halleck*
ety – the relations of father and child, of master | (1850)
and slave, of the ruler and the ruled. . . .

Polyptoton with two nouns finally can serve as a neat way to refer to a possessor and the thing possessed.

For it is written, I will destroy the wisdom of the | 1 Corinthians 1:19
wise, and will bring to nothing the understanding
of the prudent.

I am for leaving England to the English, Scotland | O'Connell, speech at
to the Scotch; but we must have Ireland for the | Mullaghmast (1843)
Irish.

4. *Polyptoton to express variations in tense*, as when describing past or present action that will occur again. The identity of the root in each case emphasizes the identity of the past and future outcomes.

And I saw, and behold a white horse: and he that | Revelation 6:2
sat on him had a bow; and a crown was given unto
him: and he went forth conquering, and to conquer.

He took up an oar and, since he was to have the | James, *The Ambassadors*
credit of pulling, pulled. | (1903)

In so far as religion is gone, reason is going. | Chesterton, *Orthodoxy*
 | (1908)

The triple use of polyptoton to refer to past, present, and future is a classic construction for exhausting temporal possibilities, much like similar cases of epistrophe and symploce seen earlier in the book. It creates a strong sense of a single activity pursued continuously.

There is no measure more repugnant to the designs | Byron, speech in the House
and feelings of Bonaparte than Catholic emanci- | of Lords (1812)
pation; no line of conduct more propitious to his
projects than that which has been pursued, is pur-
suing, and, I fear, will be pursued towards Ireland.

"You're quite right, sir," interrupted the literary | Dickens, *Nicholas Nickleby*
gentleman, leaning back in his chair and exercising | (1839)

his toothpick. "Human intellect, sir, has progressed since his time, is progressing, will progress."

5. *Polyptoton with modifiers*, as when discussing different degrees of an adjective – the simple form and the comparative or superlative forms:

Dickens, *Bleak House* (1853)

The raw afternoon is rawest, and the dense fog is densest, and the muddy streets are muddiest near that leaden-headed old obstruction, appropriate ornament for the threshold of a leaden-headed old corporation, Temple Bar.

Parnell, speech in the House of Commons (1886)

During the last five years I know, sir, there have been very severe and drastic coercion bills; but it will require an even severer and more drastic measure of coercion now.

Conan Doyle, *The Great Boer War* (1900)

These were perhaps the finest natural warriors upon earth, marksmen, hunters, accustomed to hard fare and a harder couch.

A similar pattern pairs the simple and the absolute form of a modifier.

Brougham, speech in the House of Lords (1838)

For the vague, undefined, undefinable offense of insolence, thirty-nine lashes. . .

Emerson, *The American Scholar* (1837)

The human mind can not be enshrined in a person who shall set a barrier on any one side to this unbounded, unboundable empire.

Repeating the root here stresses not only how things are but that they could not be otherwise. Polyptoton using the adjective and noun form of the same root can likewise be used to describe a category (using the noun) and the most extreme members of it (using the adjective).

Stevenson, letter to Frances Sitwell (1873)

As I got down near the beach a poor woman, oldish, and seemingly, lately at least, respectable, followed me and made signs. She was drenched to the skin, and looked wretched below wretchedness.

[T]his is what the blood of the innocent Lamb of God, shed for the redemption of sinners, trampled upon by the vilest of the vile, insists upon.

Joyce, *A Portrait of the Artist as a Young Man* (1916)

Or polyptoton can be used with different forms of a modifier: the adjective and adverb closely paired. The most typical office of this construction is to show a match between act and response:

Unheedful vows may heedfully be broken; . . .

Two Gentlemen of Verona, 2, 6

    The noble Brutus
Hath told you Caesar was ambitious;
If it were so, it was a grievous fault,
And grievously hath Caesar answer'd it.

Julius Caesar, 3, 2

Antony's use of the common root makes the fault and the penalty sound congruent.

Trust men and they will be true to you; treat them greatly and they will show themselves great, though they make an exception in your favor to all their rules of trade.

Emerson, *Prudence* (1841)

Emerson uses polyptoton twice, or perhaps one and a half times: the words *trust* and *true* have distinct etymologies but share enough in their sense and sound to amount to a use of the device. *Greatly* and *great* are more exact examples of the present theme. Here is one more:

[A] species of fervour or intoxication, known, without doubt, to have led some persons to brave the guillotine unnecessarily, and to die by it, was not mere boastfulness, but a wild infection of the wildly shaken public mind.

Dickens, *A Tale of Two Cities* (1859)

6. *Polyptoton with modifier and verb*, as where the speaker wants to refer to the possibility of doing a thing and the actual doing of it.

I have never been able to love what was not lovable or hate what was not hateful out of deference for some general principle.

Conrad, *Some Reminiscences* (1912)

Henry, speech at Virginia
Ratifying Convention
(1788)

Let us suppose – for the case is supposable, possible, and probable – that you happen to deal those powers to unworthy hands. . . .

Lawrence, *Women in Love*
(1920)

It takes two people to make a murder: a murderer and a murderee. And a murderee is a man who is murderable. And a man who is murderable is a man who in a profound if hidden lust desires to be murdered.

The example from Lawrence manages to mix three nouns, a verb, and an adjective all with the same root, for a total of seven uses in a compressed space. The exaggerated use of the device creates a sense of playfulness.

Our current pattern also can be turned to an opposite purpose, as when referring to the doing of that which cannot be done. Polyptoton may then contribute to a sense of paradox.

Chesterton, *The Mystagogue*
(1912)

The honest man is he who is always trying to utter the unutterable, to describe the indescribable; but the quack lives not by plunging into mystery, but by refusing to come out of it.

Henry, speech at Virginia
Ratifying Convention
(1788)

I acknowledge it is difficult to form a constitution. But I have seen difficulties conquered which were as unconquerable as this.

Churchill, speech in the
House of Commons (1936)

The Government simply cannot make up their minds, or they cannot get the Prime Minister to make up his mind. So they go on in strange paradox, decided only to be undecided, resolved to be irresolute, adamant for drift, solid for fluidity, all-powerful to be impotent.

The last example provides an example of abandonment applied to polyptoton: Churchill uses the device to state his first two claims, then leaves it behind for the rest. The examples that don't use the rhetorical device sound better because they come after examples that do. The early repetition of roots (*decided* and *resolved*) reinforces the sense of paradox, which then continues in the remainder of the sentence; and after being hit with those two cases of polyptoton, the ear welcomes the relief that comes with *adamant* for *drift* and *solid* for *fluidity*.

7. *Polyptoton with modifier and noun.* Earlier we saw, in passing, an instance of polyptoton with adjectives and nouns: *wretched below wretchedness*, etc. Here is a closer look at pairings where noun and modifier match.

> They do not talk bookishly about clouds or stones, or pigs or slugs, or horses or anything you please. They talk piggishly about pigs; and sluggishly, I suppose, about slugs; and are refreshingly horsy about horses. They speak in a stony way of stones; they speak in a cloudy way of clouds; and this is surely the right way.

Chesterton, *Alarms and Discursions* (1910)

A more modest application:

> If we are only a commercial and manufacturing people, all must admit that commerce was thriving and that manufactures flourished.

Disraeli, speech on the Corn Laws (1846)

The effect is the now-familiar one: polyptoton stresses the match between traits and events.

> All one can say is, roughly, that the homelier the home, and the more familiar the family, the worse for everybody concerned.

Shaw, *A Treatise on Parents and Children* (1910)

In that example from Shaw, putting the two pairs next to each other produces euphony by varying the alliterated sounds.

> I had disgraced that name eternally. I had made it a low by-word among low people. I had dragged it through the very mire. I had given it to brutes that they might make it brutal, and to fools that they might turn it into a synonym for folly.

Wilde, *De Profundis* (1905)

Here as in earlier sections of the chapter, the same constructions can be turned around and used to describe mismatches: a thing doesn't have the quality one might associate with it, or isn't what it is said to be. It is another example of polyptoton to create paradox.

Mackintosh, speech in the trial of Jean Peltier (1803)	[T]hough deserted by the un-English government of England, they asserted their own ancient character, . . .
Chesterton, *The Man on Top* (1912)	It is the same with all the powerful of to-day; it is the same, for instance, with the high-placed and high-paid official. Not only is the judge not judicial, but the arbiter is not even arbitrary.
Chesterton, *Orthodoxy* (1908)	In short, oddities only strike ordinary people. Oddities do not strike odd people.

8. *Adjacent words*. Memorable cases of polyptoton can be achieved by putting the words with the same root – usually a verb and its object – side by side. Meeting the twin words in succession is arresting and amplifies their effect.

King John, 3, 1	All form is formless, order orderless.
All's Well that Ends Well, 4, 3	He hath out-villain'd villainy so far, that the rarity redeems him.
Hamlet, 3, 2	I would have such a fellow whipped for o'erdoing Termagant. It out-Herods Herod. Pray you avoid it.
Emerson, *Compensation* (1841)	Beware of too much good staying in your hand. It will fast corrupt and worm worms. Pay it away quickly in some sort.
Melville, *Moby-Dick* (1851)	They think me mad – Starbuck does; but I'm demoniac, I am madness maddened!
James, *The Ambassadors* (1903)	He had incurred the ridicule of having to have his explanation explained.
Churchill, speech in the House of Commons (1943)	These forces will be remorselessly applied to the guilty nation and its wicked leaders, who imag-

ined their superiority of air-power would enable them to terrorise and subjugate first all Europe and afterwards the world. They will be applied, and never was there such a case of the biter bitten.

Parallel Structure:

ISOCOLON

ISOCOLON (ai-so-*co*-lon), one of the most common and important rhetorical figures, is the use of successive sentences, clauses, or phrases similar in length and parallel in structure. An example familiar to the modern American ear was uttered by John Kennedy in his inaugural address of 1961:

> Let every nation know, whether it wishes us well or ill, that we shall pay any price, bear any burden, meet any hardship, support any friend, oppose any foe, in order to assure the survival and the success of liberty.

In some cases of isocolon the structural match may be so complete that the number of syllables in each phrase is the same; in the more common case the parallel clauses just use the same parts of speech in the same order. The device can produce pleasing rhythms, and the parallel structures it creates may helpfully reinforce a parallel substance in the speaker's claims. We have encountered isocolon a few times already, and here we also will see further examples of anaphora and other such repetitive devices familiar from earlier chapters. Repetition of structure and of words often go well together.

Isocolon, like anaphora, tends to mark an utterance as stylish and oratorical, so like all rhetorical devices – only more so – it has to be used with sensitivity to the occasion. An excessive or clumsy use of the device can create too glaring a finish and too strong a sense of calculation. Brutus's funeral oration in *Julius Caesar* is the classic example. The speech is eloquent, and makes constant use of isocolon (some examples appear below) – so constant that the result seems a little overpolished and off-putting, and sets up the audience to be carried away soon afterwards by Antony's speech, which has a less studied feel. (Antony's speech is full of guile, and for that matter full of rhetorical figures, but they are a bit subtler.)

1. *To make two claims about the same subject.* A common occasion for isocolon arises when the speaker wishes to make multiple claims about the same thing. For that purpose the doublet is useful: two statements with parallel structure.

> [A]t the last it biteth like a serpent, and stingeth like an adder.

Proverbs 23:32

> They who bow to the enemy abroad, will not be of power to subdue the conspirator at home.

Burke, *Letter on the Proposals for Peace with the Regicide Directory of France* (1797)

In both of these examples it is obvious enough how the parts of speech line up in the first and second halves of each passage. (In Burke's case: bow/subdue, enemy/conspirator, abroad/at home.) But observe also the identical rhythms. This is plainer in the line from Proverbs; here are the matching phrases in Burke's example with their accents highlighted: who *bow* to the *en*emy a*broad*, and sub*due* the con*spir*ator at *home*. In each phrase the same number of unstressed syllables lies between the stressed ones, making the result a very thorough instance of isocolon.

The more common use of the device lines up the parts of speech but not the accents, as here:

> He was a morose, savage-hearted, bad man: idle and dissolute in his habits; cruel and ferocious in his disposition.

Dickens, *The Pickwick Papers* (1837)

There is alignment in the last two phrases between the parts of speech, and also in the count of the syllables in the adjectives (*idle/cruel*; *dissolute/ferocious*). But there is some variation elsewhere, as in the length of the nouns at the end (*habits/disposition*) and in the arrangement of the stresses. This partial repetition doesn't make the result a less successful case of isocolon. As we have seen elsewhere, it often is rhetorically attractive to let variety in some elements serve as a counterpoint to repetition in others.

In each of the examples just shown, the speaker's parallel claims were consistent and pointed in the same direction. But one also can use isocolon to make comparisons and emphasize the contrast between two claims.

Congreve, *The Old Bachelor*, 5, 1 (1693)

Married in haste, we may repent at leisure.

Trollope, *North America* (1862)

Women of the class to which I allude are always talking of their rights, but seem to have a most indifferent idea of their duties.

Macaulay, *Sir James Mackintosh* (1835)

Judges, jurors, and spectators seemed equally indifferent to justice, and equally eager for revenge.

Emerson, *Worship* (1860)

The louder he talked of his honor, the faster we counted our spoons.

Churchill, radio broadcast to the United States (1938)

All-strong without, he is all-weak within.

The line from Emerson is another fairly complete case of isocolon, as it employs similar rhythms in each half. Both clauses use a pair of dactyls – that is, two rounds of syllables where a stressed one is followed by two that are not stressed: first, "the *loud*er he *talked* of his"; then, "the *fast*er we *count*ed our"). The rhythmic similarity of the two halves creates a felt sense of symmetry between the talking and its consequences. Notice, though, that the clauses end differently, the first with an unstressed syllable (*hon*or) and the second with a stressed one (*spoons*). The stressed ending draws the sentence to a firm close and, along with the concrete image (counting the spoons), it brings the sound of the sentence down to earth in a way that again matches its substance.

We will consider more extended uses of antithesis below.

2. *Triplets*. So far all of our examples have involved doublets. The repeated structure can be extended, naturally, to three elements or more. The arrangement of three par-

allel claims about the same subject creates a little sense of symmetry; the progress of the claims may be felt to have a beginning, middle, and end. Strictly speaking these are cases of *tricolon*, but the more precise term is fussy out of proportion to its utility.

> The notice which you have been pleased to take of my labours, had it been early, had been kind; but it has been delayed till I am indifferent, and cannot enjoy it; till I am solitary, and cannot impart it; till I am known, and do not want it.

Johnson, letter to the Earl of Chesterfield (1755)

> That this inhuman policy was a disgrace to the Colony, a dishonor to the Legislature, and a scandal to human nature, we need not at this enlightened period labor to prove.

Pinkney, speech in the Maryland State Assembly (1788)

> That "a little knowledge is a dangerous thing" is a saying which has now got currency as a proverb stamped in the mint of Pope's versification – of Pope who, with the most imperfect knowledge of Greek, translated Homer; with the most imperfect knowledge of the Elizabethan drama, edited Shakespeare; and with the most imperfect knowledge of philosophy, wrote the "Essay on Man."

Balfour, speech at St. Andrews University (1887)

> He remained fixed and determined, in principle, in measure, and in conduct. He practised no managements. He secured no retreat. He sought no apology.

Burke, Speech on American Taxation (1774)

Note that in this case from Burke we have two cases of isocolon, and indeed two triplets. Successive use of the device is another theme we consider in more detail later in the chapter.

3. *Isocolon to make parallel claims about different subjects.* We started with cases where isocolon is used to say various things about the same subject, because that is the most common and instinctive use of it. But the device can be used in other ways as well. It is helpful for making parallel

remarks about *different* subjects, as when various people are said to be doing various things, but the relationships between the actors and their activities are parallel.

Burke, *Reflections on the Revolution in France* (1791)

Kings will be tyrants from policy, when subjects are rebels from principle.

This example from Burke, like the first example he furnished near the start of this chapter, is a very pure case of isocolon. The two phrases on either side of the fulcrum word *when* have the same grammatical structure, the same number of syllables, and the same cadence. The more common examples, again, are parallel in the first way but allow some variety in the others.

Dickens, *Little Dorrit* (1857)

[T]he trials were made in the presence of a board of six, of whom two ancient members were too blind to see it, two other ancient members were too deaf to hear it, one other ancient member was too lame to get near it, and the final ancient member was too pig-headed to look at it.

Shaw, *Major Barbara* (1907)

The men snub the boys and order them about; the carmen snub the sweepers; the artisans snub the unskilled laborers; the foremen drive and bully both the laborers and artisans; the assistant engineers find fault with the foremen; the chief engineers drop on the assistants; the departmental managers worry the chiefs; and the clerks have tall hats and hymnbooks and keep up the social tone by refusing to associate on equal terms with anybody.

This use of isocolon need not be applied to the acts of different *people*; other parallel subjects will do as well.

Chesterton, *What's Wrong with the World* (1910)

The joy of battle comes after the first fear of death; the joy of reading Virgil comes after the bore of learning him; the glow of the sea-bather comes after the icy shock of the sea bath; and the success of the marriage comes after the failure of the honeymoon.

Notice that the parallelism is driven home here both by
the repeated structure of each part and the use of a common phrase – *comes after* – in each of them: a little case of
epimone. In the example from Dickens a moment ago, the
anchoring phrase was *ancient members were too*; in the case
from Shaw after that, there were no repeated words but
the verbs were all different ways of describing similar
sorts of activities: *snub* (three times), *find fault*, etc.

Chesterton liked constructions in which isocolon is
used to make parallel statements about different subjects.
He often used it to present examples of whatever claims
he made.

> In short, the democratic faith is this: that the most
> terribly important things must be left to ordinary
> men themselves – the mating of the sexes, the rear-
> ing of the young, the laws of the state.

Chesterton, *Orthodoxy*
(1908)

> When the pessimist looks at any infamy, it is to
> him, after all, only a repetition of the infamy of
> existence. The Court of Chancery is indefensible
> – like mankind. The Inquisition is abominable –
> like the universe.

Chesterton, *The Vote and the
House* (1908)

> A new philosophy generally means in practice the
> praise of some old vice. We have had the sophist
> who defends cruelty, and calls it masculinity. We
> have had the sophist who defends profligacy, and
> calls it the liberty of the emotions. We have had
> the sophist who defends idleness, and calls it art.

Chesterton, *The Methuse-
lahite* (1908)

4. *Isocolon with internal repetition of words.* A minor but
elegant chapter in the annals of isocolon belongs to the
repetition of words within the repetition of structure, so
that a pair in the first part matches a pair in the second.

> Then saith he unto them, Render therefore unto
> Caesar the things which are Caesar's; and unto
> God the things that are God's.

Matthew 22:21

Shaw, *A Treatise on Parents and Children* (1910)	The child at play is noisy and ought to be noisy: Sir Isaac Newton at work is quiet and ought to be quiet.

The repetition of words links elements that belong together; the repetition of structure invites comparison between the different pairs of elements. This construction also works well to describe cases where the pairs involve words that are mismatched rather than matched.

Dickens, *A Tale of Two Cities* (1859)	Having supposed that there was sense where there is no sense, and a laudable ambition where there is not a laudable ambition, I am well out of my mistake, and no harm is done.
Chesterton, *Heretics* (1905)	The aim of the sculptor is to convince us that he is a sculptor; the aim of the orator is to convince us that he is not an orator.

5. *Commands and instructions.* Isocolon is easily adapted to the imperative mood. The entries on a list of commands usually will have the same implied subject, which makes it easy to keep them parallel in structure.

Matthew 10:8	Heal the sick, cleanse the lepers, raise the dead, cast out devils: freely ye have received, freely give.
Churchill, speech at Manchester (1940)	Come then, let us to the task, to the battle, to the toil – each to our part, each to our station. Fill the armies, rule the air, pour out the munitions, strangle the U-boats, sweep the mines, plow the land, build the ships, guard the streets, succor the wounded, uplift the downcast, and honor the brave.

An enlargement on this pattern begins with rhetorical instructions to the listener, or invitations to make experiments, with the results then described in parallel form:

Julius Caesar, 1, 2	Brutus and Caesar: what should be in that "Caesar"?

Why should that name be sounded more than
    yours?
Write them together, yours is as fair a name;
Sound them, it doth become the mouth as well;
Weigh them, it is as heavy; conjure with 'em,
"Brutus" will start a spirit as soon as "Caesar."

If he could speak, he would say, Build temples: I will
lord it in their ruins; build palaces: I will inhabit
them; erect empires: I will inherit them; bury your
beautiful: I will watch the worms at their work;
and you, who stand here and moralize over me:
I will crawl over your corpse at the last.

Twain, *The Innocents Abroad* (1869)

6. *Dialogical applications*, in which the antagonist's claim
receives a reply in parallel form. If both speakers are using
the same device and the repartee is quick, the result is a
kind of banter; if just one of them uses it in reply to the
other, the result more likely is mockery.

QUEEN. Hamlet, thou hast thy father much
    offended.
HAMLET. Mother, you have my father much
    offended.
QUEEN. Come, come, you answer with an idle
    tongue.
HAMLET. Go, go, you question with a wicked
    tongue.

Hamlet, 3, 4

GLOUCESTER. Fairer than tongue can name thee,
    let me have
Some patient leisure to excuse myself.
LADY ANNE. Fouler than heart can think thee,
    thou canst make
No excuse current, but to hang thyself.

Richard III, 1, 2

"I do," said Scrooge. "Merry Christmas! What right
have you to be merry? What reason have you to be
merry? You're poor enough." "Come, then," returned
the nephew gaily. "What right have you to be

Dickens, *A Christmas Carol* (1843)

dismal? What reason have you to be morose? You're rich enough."

In non-literary life, an antagonist's claim is less likely to lend itself to a perfectly parallel riposte. But the speaker can compensate by restating the antagonist's position in a way that does lend itself to isocolon in reply:

Sheil, speech in the House of Commons (1843)

You think that the repealers of Ireland are conspicuously in the wrong; are you sure that you are yourselves conspicuously in the right?

Chesterton, *The Crimes of England* (1915)

Or when you say that the Belgians were so ignorant as to think they were being butchered when they weren't, we only wonder whether you are so ignorant as to think you are being believed when you aren't.

7. *Antithesis*, seen briefly earlier, is the juxtaposition of parallel but contrasting ideas or images. It is a rhetorical figure of its own, but usually appears with parallel phrasing as well – in other words, as a variety of isocolon.

a. *Serial uses of antithesis.*

Pitt, speech in the House of Commons (1743)

Our former minister betrayed the interests of his country by his pusillanimity; our present minister would sacrifice them by his Quixotism. Our former minister was for negotiating with all the world; our present minister is for fighting against all the world. Our former minister was for agreeing to every treaty, though never so dishonorable; our present minister will give ear to none, though never so reasonable.

Notice the multiple parallelisms. The first and second halves of each sentence are parallel to each other; and each sentence, taken in its entirety, is parallel to each of the other sentences in structure as well. In some cases repeated words help along the parallelism: *minister . . . minister* within each half of each sentence, and *present minister . . .*

former minister within each sentence of the whole passage. At other points the parallelism and antithesis are secured by the use of related but opposite words at comparable moments in the first and second parts of a sentence (*negotiating . . . fighting*; *dishonourable . . . reasonable*). A similar set of antitheses, with a similarly layered parallelism, is found in this passage from Frederick Douglass:

> What he most dreaded, that I most desired. What he most loved, that I most hated. That which to him was a great evil, to be carefully shunned, was to me a great good, to be diligently sought; and the argument which he so warmly urged, against my learning to read, only served to inspire me with a desire and determination to learn.

Douglass, *My Bondage and My Freedom* (1855)

Dickens made the serial antithesis a specialty.

> The mother looked young, and the daughter looked old; the mother's complexion was pink, and the daughter's was yellow; the mother set up for frivolity, and the daughter for theology.

Dickens, *Great Expectations* (1861)

> It was a trying morning; for there were a great many calls to make, and everybody wanted a different thing. Some wanted tragedies, and others comedies; some objected to dancing; some wanted scarcely anything else. Some thought the comic singer decidedly low, and others hoped he would have more to do than he usually had. Some people wouldn't promise to go, because other people wouldn't promise to go; and other people wouldn't go at all, because other people went.

Dickens, *Nicholas Nickleby* (1839)

> It was the best of times, it was the worst of times, it was the age of wisdom, it was the age of foolishness, it was the epoch of belief, it was the epoch of incredulity, it was the season of Light, it was the season of Darkness, it was the spring of hope, it was the winter of despair, we had everything before

Dickens, *A Tale of Two Cities* (1859)

us, we had nothing before us, we were all going
direct to Heaven, we were all going direct the other
way – in short, the period was so far like the present period, that some of its noisiest authorities
insisted on its being received, for good or for evil,
in the superlative degree of comparison only.

An antithesis can be also be made serial just at the front
end: instead of simply *y, not z*, the construction runs *x,
yes; and y, yes; but not z*. The emphasis is on the singular-
ity of the point that comes last.

Macaulay, speech in the
House of Commons (1843)

Even in our mirth, however, there is sadness; for it
is no light thing that he who represents the British
nation in India should be a jest to the people of
India. We have sometimes sent them governors
whom they loved, and sometimes governors whom
they feared; but they never before had a governor
at whom they laughed.

Chesterton, *Heretics* (1905)

A Frenchman can be proud of being bold and logical, and still remain bold and logical. A German
can be proud of being reflective and orderly, and
still remain reflective and orderly. But an Englishman cannot be proud of being simple and direct,
and still remain simple and direct.

b. *Not x but y constructions, and variants.*

Burke, *Reflections on the
Revolution in France* (1791)

His zeal is of a curious character. It is not for the
propagation of his own opinions, but of any opinions. It is not for the diffusion of truth, but for the
spreading of contradiction. Let the noble teachers
but dissent, it is no matter from whom or from
what.

de Quincey, *The Orphan
Heiress* (1859)

He, if any man ever did, realized the Roman poet's
description of being *natus rebus agendis* – sent into
this world not for talking, but for doing; not for
counsel, but for execution.

Isocolon and antithesis of this kind are helpful for describing causation: the cause of a thing is not *x*, but some alternative – perhaps the opposite of *x* (*not because ...but because*). These constructions usually start by anticipating an easy and obvious explanation for a thing, then twist its structure or vocabulary to reveal the actual reason for it. The true explanation is thrown into heightened relief when shown against the backdrop of a parallel but false one.

> If then that friend demand why Brutus rose against Caesar, this is my answer: – Not that I loved Caesar less, but that I loved Rome more.

Julius Caesar, 3, 2

> The Puritan hated bearbaiting, not because it gave pain to the bear, but because it gave pleasure to the spectators.

Macaulay, *The History of England* (1849)

> Encyclopædias are the growth of the last hundred years; not because those who were formerly students of higher learning have descended, but because those who were below encyclopædias have ascended.

de Quincey, *The Note Book of an English Opium Eater* (1855)

A nice variation occurs when the statements of the correct and incorrect causes of a thing borrow the same words used to describe the thing in the first place.

> The object of appending the name of a man to the name of a species is not to gratify the vanity of the man, but to indicate more precisely the species.

Strickland, letter to Charles Darwin (1849)

Man and *species* are named in the introductory clause, then repeated: *the vanity of the man ... more precisely the species*. Likewise *conservative* and *ideals* here:

> It was, in brief, that conservative ideals were bad, not because they were conservative, but because they were ideals.

Chesterton, *Heretics* (1905)

A related, interesting, and less common pattern: two related things are distinguished, and made the subject of an antithesis, because they have opposite causes. Again the master of the construction was Chesterton.

Chesterton, *Pope and the Art of Satire* (1903)

We might be angry at the libel, but not at the satire; for a man is angry at a libel because it is false, but at a satire because it is true.

Chesterton, *Heretics* (1905)

Men trust an ordinary man because they trust themselves. But men trust a great man because they do not trust themselves.

Chesterton, *Demagogues and Mystagogues* (1915)

The demagogue succeeds because he makes himself understood, even if he is not worth understanding. But the mystagogue succeeds because he gets himself misunderstood; although, as a rule, he is not even worth misunderstanding.

Chesterton, *Orthodoxy* (1908)

It is quite easy to see why a legend is treated, and ought to be treated, more respectfully than a book of history. The legend is generally made by the majority of people in the village, who are sane. The book is generally written by the one man in the village who is mad.

All of these cases are interesting in part because the claims they make may be less correct than they sound. The neat parallel way in which Chesterton makes his points gives them a ring of incontestability; the perfect rhetorical matching of the two claims lends some authority to them.

8. *The forced choice.* Isocolon may be used to present a situation as a choice between opposite possibilities stated in parallel fashion. (Sometimes the results also can be described as dilemmas.) The clean division used in these constructions has persuasive value. It invites a choice between the resulting alternatives rather than debate about where the division was made.

Julius Caesar, 3, 2

Had you rather Caesar were living and die all slaves, than that Caesar were dead, to live all free men?

In God's name, if it is absolutely necessary to declare either for peace or war, and the former can not be preserved with honor, why is not the latter commenced without delay?

Pitt, speech in the House of Lords (1778)

Lincoln made good use of this pattern, often reducing a conflict to two possible positions or outcomes.

One section of our country believes slavery is right, and ought to be extended, while the other believes it is wrong, and ought not to be extended. This is the only substantial dispute.

Lincoln, First Inaugural Address (1861)

Either the opponents of slavery will arrest the further spread of it, and place it where the public mind shall rest in the belief that it is in the course of ultimate extinction; or its advocates will push it forward, till it shall become alike lawful in all the States, old as well as new, North as well as South.

Lincoln, speech at Springfield (1858)

The pattern can be expanded by following a statement of the alternatives with a statement of their implications. The constructions thus follow this general model: *Either x or y. If x . . . If y . . .* This pattern lends itself to statement of a dilemma, in which either alternative leads to a similar or unappealing end.

But the proclamation, as law, either is valid or is not valid. If it is not valid it needs no retraction. If it is valid it cannot be retracted, any more than the dead can be brought to life.

Lincoln, letter to James Conkling (1863)

If any member of our party is guilty in that matter, you know it, or you do not know it. If you do know it, you are inexcusable for not designating the man and proving the fact. If you do not know it, you are inexcusable to assert it, and especially to persist in the assertion after you have tried and failed to make the proof.

Lincoln, speech at Cooper Institute (1860)

It was either necessary, or it was not, to pass your Coercion Bill. It was either necessary, or it was not,

Sheil, speech in the House of Commons (1834)

for the opponents of the Insurrection Act to put upon the statute-book a precedent for tyranny, and to supersede the tribunals of the country with the legislation of the Horse-Guards, and the judicature of the barrack yard. If it was unnecessary, it was detestable and atrocious; and if it was necessary for Lord Grey to introduce a bill which passed without dissent in the Lords, and which there were men who support ministers who declared that they would rather die than support it in that shape; if that was necessary, by whom was the necessity created?

The pattern can be extended beyond two alternatives.

Burke, Speech on Moving His Resolutions for Conciliation with the Colonies (1775)

[T]here are but three ways of proceeding relative to this stubborn spirit which prevails in your colonies and disturbs your government. These are, – to change that spirit, as inconvenient, by removing the causes, – to prosecute it, as criminal, – or to comply with it, as necessary.

A charming and kindred device is the review of categories and their occupants.

Chesterton, *Heretics* (1905)

The truth is, as I have said, that in this sense the two qualities of fun and seriousness have nothing whatever to do with each other, they are no more comparable than black and triangular. Mr. Bernard Shaw is funny and sincere. Mr. George Robey is funny and not sincere. Mr. McCabe is sincere and not funny. The average Cabinet Minister is not sincere and not funny.

Lamb, letter to Wordsworth (1816)

I have not bound the poems yet; I wait till people have done borrowing them. I think I shall get a chain and chain them to my shelves..., and people may come and read them at chain's length. For of those who borrow, some read slow; some mean to read but don't read; and some neither read nor

meant to read, but borrow to leave you an opinion of their sagacity.

9. *Successive cases of isocolon*. Different uses of isocolon
may be stacked, one after the other, so that parallel structure becomes a motif, just as we have seen that repetition
of words may become a motif.

All they ask we could readily grant if we thought slavery right; all we ask they could as readily grant, if they thought it wrong. Their thinking it right and our thinking it wrong is the precise fact upon which depends the whole controversy. Thinking it right, as they do, they are not to blame for desiring its full recognition, as being right; but thinking it wrong, as we do, can we yield to them?	Lincoln, speech at Cooper Institute (1860)
Ye cannot make us now less capable, less knowing, less eagerly pursuing of the truth, unless ye first make yourselves, that made us so, less the lovers, less the founders of our true liberty. We can grow ignorant again, brutish, formal and slavish, as ye found us; but you then must first become that which ye cannot be, oppressive, arbitrary and tyran-nous, as they were from whom ye have freed us.	Milton, *Areopagitica* (1660)
[I]f Catholic Spain, faithful Portugal, or the no less Catholic and faithful king of the one Sicily, (of which, by the by, you have lately deprived him,) stand in need of succour, away goes a fleet and an army, an ambassador and a subsidy, sometimes to fight pretty hardly, generally to negotiate very badly, and always to pay very dearly for our Popish allies.	Byron, speech in the House of Lords (1812)
You have had the House of Lords voted a nuisance. You have had the House of Commons kicked out in an ignominious manner by a military officer. You have had the Church completely sequestrated. All this has happened in England. But before a quarter of a century passed over, you returned to	Disraeli, speech to con-stituents (1842)

your old laws, your old habits, your old traditions, your old convictions.

The contrast between the longer descriptions of action at the start and the short account of the results at the end (and the repetition of words in the results – *your old …* *your old*) helps underscore the substance of Disraeli's claim: elaborate and varied events are met with a return to the same simple institutions.

Sheil, speech in the House of Commons (1835)

For what into all these affrighting perils are we to rush? For what into those terrific possibilities are we madly, desperately, impiously to plunge? For the Irish church! – the church of the minority, long the church of the state, never the church of the people – the church on which a faction fattens, by which a nation starves – the church from which no imaginable good can flow, but evil after evil in such black and continuous abundance has been for centuries, and is to this day, poured out – the church by which religion has been retarded, morality has been vitiated, atrocity has been engendered; which standing armies are requisite to sustain, which has lost England millions of her treasure, and Ireland torrents of her blood.

There are six distinct cases of isocolon in that last example (perhaps the precise number depends on how one counts) from an orator who evidently was so at home with the device that he sometimes seemed to use it about as instinctively as most people say the subject before the verb. Henry Grattan, another hero of Irish oratory, had the same gift. Successive isocolon was a staple of his speeches; he would use it to convey dudgeon, piling up parallel sets of epithets, accusations, or other such claims. The succession of matched clauses often conveyed a high pitch of feeling.

Grattan, speech in the Irish Parliament (1796)

This dreadful, this deadly, this wild, and this fatal proscription, when he is calling for volunteers to enroll in the service! What language, what denunciation, what dictation could France have suggested more opportune in time, more pregnant in disaffection, or more authoritative in mischief?

Do not tolerate that power which blasted you for a century, that power which shattered your loom, banished your manufacturers, dishonored your peerage, and stopped the growth of your people; do not, I say, be bribed by an export of woolen, or an import of sugar, and permit that power which has thus withered the land to remain in your country and have existence in your pusillanimity.

Grattan, speech in the Irish Parliament (1790)

But liberty, the foundation of trade, the charters of the land, the independency of Parliament, the securing, crowning, and the consummation of everything are yet to come. Without them the work is imperfect, the foundation is wanting, the capital is wanting, trade is not free, Ireland is a colony without the benefit of a charter, and you are a provincial synod without the privileges of a Parliament.

Grattan, speech in the Irish Parliament (1790)

A specialized instance of successive isocolon is recapitulation, in which the second round of the device repeats the words of the first.

As Caesar loved me, I weep for him; as he was fortunate, I rejoice at it; as he was valiant, I honour him: but, as he was ambitious, I slew him. There is tears for his love; joy for his fortune; honour for his valour; and death for his ambition.

Julius Caesar, 3, 2

On the contrary, no such complaint, no such report, and no such reference have existed; and this no complaint, and this no report, and this no reference, is a proof that government knew that the cause assigned was a vile pretence; too flimsy to be stated, and too ludicrous to be discussed.

Grattan, speech in the Irish Parliament (1790)

I never was rich before, I never was proud before, I never was happy before, I am rich in being taken

Dickens, *Little Dorrit* (1857)

by you, I am proud in having been resigned by you,
I am happy in being with you in this prison, as I
should be happy in coming back to it with you, if
it should be the will of GOD, and comforting and
serving you with all my love and truth.

The order of elements in the second round need not match
the order in the first; a change can relieve the listener
from what otherwise might be an excess of regularity.

Shaw, *Major Barbara* (1905)

What! no capacity for business, no knowledge of
law, no sympathy with art, no pretension to philosophy; only a simple knowledge of the secret
that has puzzled all the philosophers, baffled all
the lawyers, muddled all the men of business, and
ruined most of the artists: the secret of right and
wrong.

Mixing up the order of elements is especially helpful in
a case like this where the speaker is in an exclamatory
mood. The slight disorder is true to the usual course of
excited speech.

10. *Abandonment.* As with other devices, a speaker sometimes can disrupt the regularity of the isocolon to good
rhetorical effect. First and most obviously, the parallel
structure can simply be abandoned at the end. The
absence of the pattern creates a sense of release and brings
attention to the last phrase.

Matthew 13:13

Therefore speak I to them in parables: because
they seeing see not; and hearing they hear not, neither do they understand.

Adams, *Democracy* (1880)

If our age is to be beaten, let us die in the ranks. If
it is to be victorious, let us be first to lead the col-
umn. Anyway, let us not be skulkers or grumblers.

When the parallel structure is abandoned *and* the last
piece is lengthened, energy that had been contained in the
earlier, fixed forms is released and allowed to flow freely:

Nobody liked the Manchester School; it was endured as the only way of producing wealth. Nobody likes the Marxian school; it is endured as the
only way of preventing poverty. Nobody's real heart
is in the idea of preventing a free man from own-
ing his own farm, or an old woman from cultivat-
ing her own garden, any more than anybody's real
heart was in the heartless battle of the machines.

Chesterton, *What's Wrong with the World* (1910)

The first two sentences are each fifteen words long, have
comparable elements in the same order, and mostly use
the same language; they are classic cases of isocolon. The
last sentence likewise begins with *Nobody* but then veers
off; it turns out to be almost three times as long as the
other sentences and doesn't get resolved at the end in the
way they did. The departure from the structure of the first
two sentences releases some tension that was created by
the tight correspondence between them.

11. *Lengthening and shortening*. Variety and a sense of climax also can be had by lengthening or shortening the
parallel units while keeping the same structure at their
start and finish. To begin with instances where the
phrases are lengthened:

[T]here seemed to be nothing to support life,
nothing to eat, nothing to make, nothing to grow,
nothing to hope, nothing to do but die.

Dickens, *Little Dorrit* (1857)

America is false to the past, false to the present, and
solemnly binds herself to be false to the future.

Douglass, speech at
Rochester (1852)

Sometimes in these constructions the early parallel
phrases each end with a single word, for which the last
substitutes a *phrase*.

I fear, that we may before long see the tribunals
defied, the tax-gatherer resisted, public credit shaken,
property insecure, the whole frame of society has-
tening to dissolution.

Macaulay, speech in the
House of Commons (1831)

Shaw, *A Treatise on Parents and Children* (1910)

Teach a child to write and you teach it how to forge: teach it to speak and you teach it how to lie: teach it to walk and you teach it how to kick its mother to death.

The lengthening also can take a less abrupt form. The phrases with the repeated structure can simply get longer along the way, as here:

Dickens, *Hard Times* (1854)

Had he any prescience of the day, five years to come, when Josiah Bounderby of Coketown was to die of a fit in the Coketown street, and this same precious will was to begin its long career of quibble, plunder, false pretences, vile example, little service and much law? Probably not.

The progressive lengthening at the end creates a sense of expansion in the rhetoric – an unfurling quality. The effect is stronger when the parallel phrases are lengthened more steadily.

Phillips, *The Character of Napoleon* (1817)

At his touch, crowns crumbled, beggars reigned, systems vanished, the wildest theories took the color of his whim, and all that was venerable, and all that was novel, changed places with the rapidity of a drama.

Roosevelt, *On American Motherhood* (1905)

[E]asy divorce is now as it ever has been, a bane to any nation, a curse to society, a menace to the home, an incitement to married unhappiness and to immorality, an evil thing for men and a still more hideous evil for women.

Acceleration occurs when the parallel elements become shorter. Here the effect is contraction rather than expansion; as they decrease in length, the phrases come to a sharper point.

Shaw, *Man and Superman* (1903)

Marriage is to me apostasy, profanation of the sanctuary of my soul, violation of my manhood, sale of my birthright, shameful surrender, ignominious capitulation, acceptance of defeat.

The longest phrase, *profanation of the sanctuary of my soul*, comes early. It leads to the shorter matched pair *violation of my manhood* and *sale of my birthright*; then the still shorter *shameful surrender* – the fourth consecutive decrease in syllables. There is a slight uptick in length with *ignominious capitulation* and finally *acceptance of defeat*, so the acceleration is not perfectly regular. It is a trend from which we have some mild relief at the end. This might be considered a case in which two separate cases of isocolon are adjacent to one another, or as one case of isocolon that evolves in form – but there is no reason to bother about that difference.

> Eager faces strained round pillars and corners, to get a sight of him; spectators in back rows stood up, not to miss a hair of him; people on the floor of the court, laid their hands on the shoulders of the people before them, to help themselves, at anybody's cost, to a view of him – stood a-tiptoe, got upon ledges, stood upon next to nothing, to see every inch of him.

Dickens, *A Tale of Two Cities* (1859)

Again, we can view this last passage as a case where one round of isocolon – the three long clauses separated by semicolons – gives way to a new round of the device with shorter parts (*stood a-tiptoe*, etc.). Or those short phrases can be seen as an interruption that simply lengthens the last part before finally getting to the same finale once again: *of him*. (Perhaps it is best viewed as one case of isocolon embedded in another.) But the important point is only to notice how the sound of the short matched parts is more striking after just hearing a succession of longer ones.

12. *Oscillation*. A classic use of isocolon begins a passage with parallel elements of one length, then shortens them, then ends with a long phrase. Typically there is a modest bit of repeated structure at the start, consisting of phrases three or four words long apiece. Then comes a moment of compression where a few single words are strung together in a short series; then a longer, more elaborate

finish – perhaps using another parallel piece, or maybe just a longer concluding phrase that stands alone. These movements create a sense of rhetorical drama.

Melville, *Mardi* (1849)

Though we have discovered the circulation of the blood, men die as of yore; oxen graze, sheep bleat, babies bawl, asses bray – loud and lusty as the day before the flood. Men fight and make up; repent and go at it; feast and starve; laugh and weep; pray and curse; cheat, chaffer, trick, truckle, cozen, defraud, fib, lie, beg, borrow, steal, hang, drown – as in the laughing and weeping, tricking and truckling, hanging and drowning times that have been.

Dickens, *Great Expectations* (1861)

A man who had been soaked in water, and smothered in mud, and lamed by stones, and cut by flints, and stung by nettles, and torn by briars; who limped, and shivered, and glared and growled; and whose teeth chattered in his head as he seized me by the chin.

Beerbohm, *Diminuendo* (1895)

No pulse of life will escape me. The strife of politics, the intriguing of courts, the wreck of great vessels, wars, dramas, earthquakes, national griefs or joys; the strange sequels to divorces, even, and the mysterious suicides of land-agents at Ipswich – in all such phenomena I shall steep my exhaurient mind.

Churchill, speech at Harlow (1938)

Either Britain will rise again in her strength as a mighty, valiant nation, champion of lawful right, defender of human freedom, or she will collapse and be despoiled, plundered, mutilated, and reduced not merely to the rank of a second-rate country but to a dependent condition, a vassal status that I once heard Sir Edward Grey call "the conscript appendage to a stronger power."

Reversal of Structure:

CHIASMUS

A *CHIASMUS* (kai-*as*-mus) occurs when words or other elements are repeated with their order reversed. A well-known and relatively modern example here, as in the previous chapter, is from John Kennedy: *ask not what your country can do for you; ask what you can do for your country,* a saying which apparently evolved from the earlier appeal by Kennedy's boarding school headmaster to consider *not what Choate does for you, but what you can do for Choate,* and perhaps before that from a call by Oliver Wendell Holmes, Jr., *to recall what our country has done for each of us, and to ask ourselves what we can do for our country in return.* As we shall see, certain themes lend themselves especially well to expression in a chiasmus, and in some cases have been repeated in that form on many occasions.

Every chiasmus amounts to an ABBA pattern. In this example often attributed to Churchill, *war* fills the A role and *dishonor* the B role:

You were given the choice between war and dishonor.

You chose dishonor, and you will have war.

The pattern shown here explains the source of the word "chiasmus," which comes from the Greek letter χ (*chi*). Incidentally, Churchill probably never made the statement just shown, at least so far as any records show. What he did say in a letter of 1938 was this: *We seem to be very near the bleak choice between War and Shame. My feeling is that we shall choose Shame, and then have War thrown in a little later on even more adverse terms than at present.* So the authentic statement was a chiasmus, too, though a bit less pungent.

A chiasmus that reverses the same words, as in the examples mentioned thus far, calls attention to itself strongly and so has to be used with particular care. We will see many good examples of the device below, but in the hands of the typical modern politician a chiasmus often will sound disagreeably slick and perhaps even repulsive; one can hear the speaker stretching the substance of a claim in an unseemly effort to make it sound catchy. This is a hazard in the use of rhetorical figures generally. Stretching ideas to make them fit a scheme is bad practice for the obvious reason that it assigns the wrong priorities to substance and style; but it also is bad practice because the results tend to sound poor.

A chiasmus need not repeat the same words in reversed order. It can instead consist just of a structural reversal, with the two halves of the device using different words that do parallel work. (See, e.g., section 11 below.) These sorts of reversals create subtler effects, and so reduce the risk of the cloying impression just described. Some commentators call reversal of the same words *antimetabole* and reserve the term *chiasmus* for the reversals that are purely structural. In keeping with this book's preference for simple terminology and distaste for distinctions that aren't worth the bother for the typical user, we will call all these reversals by the same name – *chiasmus*; but the reader with a taste for jargon, a need for precision, or a fear of pedants is duly notified that more words are available.

As we move from devices that all involve repetition of some sort (in previous chapters) to devices that have other foundations and produce more complex effects, it often will be convenient to state their purposes in a more systematic manner. Thus the typical purposes of a good chiasmus:

a. The reversal of structure may reinforce the speaker's claim that there is a reversal or reciprocity of substance.

b. A chiasmus sounds convincing. It creates a closed loop that appears to leave no opening for dispute.

c. The reversal of sounds in a chiasmus is attractive,

memorable, and sometimes fascinating. Hearing the same words in opposite order, and finding that they still make sense (perhaps even more sense than before), is surprising, and at its best might seem to be a minor linguistic miracle; reversing the order of words in a sentence normally leads to gibberish, yet in a good chiasmus it actually seems illuminating, and meanwhile also produces the usual benefits of repeating words regardless of their order: emphasis, euphony, and sometimes attractive rhythm.

When one encounters a chiasmus in the wild, it usually looks like an outburst of verbal cleverness that would be hard to plan and create at home. But a chiasmus really isn't so hard to make deliberately. It just requires an instinct for the occasions that serve as fertile ground for its use. Much of this chapter thus is organized around those occasions – some types of meanings and intentions that most readily lend themselves to a reversed rhetorical structure.

1. *The chiasmus to describe reversals of action*. These tend to be uses that express a sense similar to *on the contrary* or *it's the other way around*. We begin with cases of reversed control, as when influence flows in an unexpected direction between two points. This pattern is often used to refute a superficial impression or contradict a commonplace.

> Men need not trouble to alter conditions, conditions will so soon alter men. The head can be beaten small enough to fit the hat.

Chesterton, *What's Wrong with the World* (1910).

> Be a little careful about your Library. Do you foresee what you will do with it? Very little to be sure. But the real question is, What it will do with you.

Emerson, *Journal* (1873)

A common occasion for this sort of chiasmus can arise when one speaks of the government and the governed, laws and those affected by them, etc.

> For as in absolute governments the King is law, so in free countries the law ought to be King; and there ought to be no other.

Paine, *Common Sense* (1776)

Chesterton, *Thoughts around Koepenick* (1915)

In short, we do not get good laws to restrain bad people. We get good people to restrain bad laws.

Churchill, speech at Paris (1936)

We live in countries where the people own the Government and not in countries where the Government owns the people.

As noted in the introduction to this chapter, a chiasmus can occur when the structure of a statement is reversed but not all the words are the same. The simplest examples arise where one of the words in the first part gets replaced by a different form (e.g., a pronoun) in the second.

Brutus no. 11 (1788)

The legislature must be controlled by the constitution, and not the constitution by them.

Lincoln, letter to A.G. Hodges (1864)

In telling this tale I attempt no compliment to my own sagacity. I claim not to have controlled events, but confess plainly that events have controlled me.

Churchill, speech in the House of Commons (1943)

We shape our buildings, and afterwards our buildings shape us.

In all these cases the A element in the ABBA pattern consists of two different words that point to the same meaning, while the B element consists of the same word. Of course the pattern can be reversed as well, with the A element the same while the B changes form:

Sterne, *Tristram Shandy* (1760)

But this is neither here nor there – why do I mention it? – Ask my pen, – it governs me, – I govern not it.

And in some cases the nouns change in form enough that none of the words in the ABBA structure are literally repeated, though the verb typically will be:

Thoreau, *Walden* (1854)

We do not ride on the railroad; it rides upon us.

Franklin, *Poor Richard's Almanack* (1734)

He does not possess wealth; it possesses him.

We have been considering cases of reversed control. A related use of the chiasmus can describe reversals of *causation*: normally one would expect A to be done because of в, but instead в is done because of а. Sometimes in these cases one wants to describe misplaced priorities, as where the reasons for a decision are subordinated to the wish that it come out a particular way.

People do not seem to talk for the sake of expressing their opinions, but to maintain an opinion for the sake of talking.

Hazlitt, *On Coffee-House Politicians* (1821)

When the pay is not given for the sake of the work, but the work found for the sake of the pay, inefficiency is a matter of certainty. . . .

Mill, *Principles of Political Economy* (1848)

I do not mean that they choose what is customary, in preference to what suits their own inclination. It does not occur to them to have any inclination, except for what is customary.

Mill, *On Liberty* (1859)

2. *The chiasmus to suggest reciprocity*. These uses express a sense similar to *and vice versa*. A standard application is to reciprocal prospects for action or aggression.

England finds that she cannot conquer America, and America has no wish to conquer England.

Paine, *The American Crisis* (1783)

The assertion of that sentiment is our sure protection; for no person will attack us, and we will attack nobody.

O'Connell, speech at Mullaghmast (1843)

Bearing this in mind, and seeing that sectionalism has since arisen upon this same subject, is that warning a weapon in your hands against us, or in our hands against you?

Lincoln, speech at Cooper Institute (1860)

The reversal or reciprocity in a chiasmus can involve neglect or other forms of passivity.

He sometimes leaves them in the lurch, and is sometimes left in the lurch by them.

Hazlitt, *Mr. Brougham* (1825)

Is he so eager for money as to be indifferent to revenge? Or so eager for revenge as to be indifferent to money?

Macaulay, *Madame D'Arblay* (1843)

Dickens, *A Tale of Two Cities* (1859)	I am a disappointed drudge, sir. I care for no man on earth, and no man on earth cares for me.

Or the chiasmus can describe reciprocal prospects for relationship or exchange.

Franklin, *Dangers of a Settled Bureaucracy* (1787)	[T]here will always be a party for giving more to the rulers, that the rulers may be able, in return, to give more to them.
Churchill, speech at Cambridge (1939)	[I]n the pass to which things have come, we stand at least as much in need of the aid of France as the French do of the aid of Britain.

Though not quite a matter of exchange, this is as good a spot as any for inclusion of a prominent related chiasmus:

Matthew 7:12	Therefore all things whatsoever ye would that men should do to you, do ye even so to them: for this is the law and the prophets.

3. *The chiasmus to describe matches and mismatches.* These uses typically express a sense similar to *each has what the other wants.*

Swift, *Gulliver's Travels* (1726)	Sometimes our neighbors want the things which we have, or have the things which we want; and we both fight, till they take ours or give us theirs.
Jefferson, letter to Benjamin Hawkins (1803)	[A] coincidence of interests will be produced between those who have lands to spare, and want other necessaries, and those who have such necessaries to spare, and want lands.
Dickens, *Nicholas Nickleby* (1839)	She has youth, you have money. She has not money, you have not youth. Tit for tat – quits – a match of Heaven's own making!

Those are examples of a match between quite concrete needs, but a chiastic matching also can occur in a more abstract way:

Thy name well fits thy faith; thy faith thy name.

Cymbeline, 4, 2

Suit the action to the word, the word to the action; with this special observance, that you o'erstep not the modesty of nature.

Hamlet, 2, 2

A Frenchman must be always talking, whether he knows any thing of the matter or not; an Englishman is content to say nothing, when he has nothing to say.

Johnson, in Boswell's *Life* (1791)

The same constructions also can be used to describe a mismatch. A chiasmus can help bring out the irony in such a case.

Affections, like the conscience, are rather to be led than drawn; and, it is to be feared, they that marry where they do not love, will love where they do not marry.

Fuller, *The Holy State and the Profane State* (1642)

"Oh! sir," answered Jones, "it is as possible for a man to know something without having been at school, as it is to have been at school and to know nothing."

Fielding, *Tom Jones* (1749)

Our former minister thought of nothing but negotiating when he ought to have thought of nothing but war; the present minister has thought of nothing but war, or at least its resemblance, when he ought to have thought of nothing but negotiation.

Pitt, speech in the House of Commons (1743)

It appears to me, that Huggins has ball without powder, and Warton powder without ball.

Johnson, in Boswell's *Life* (1791)

It is a capital mistake to theorize before one has data. Insensibly one begins to twist facts to suit theories, instead of theories to suit facts.

Conan Doyle, *A Scandal in Bohemia* (1891)

It's an epitome of life. The first half of it consists of the capacity to enjoy without the chance; the last half consists of the chance without the capacity.

Twain, letter to Edward Dimmitt (1901)

4. *Relationships between sets.* These uses often express variants on the idea that *all x's are y's, but not all y's are x's.*

Poe, *The Murders in the Rue Morgue* (1841)

The analytical power should not be confounded with ample ingenuity; for while the analyst is necessarily ingenious, the ingenious man is often remarkably incapable of analysis.

Shaw, *Major Barbara* (1905)

For me there is only one true morality; but it might not fit you, as you do not manufacture aerial battleships. There is only one true morality for every man; but every man has not the same true morality.

Burke, Speech on Moving His Resolutions for Conciliation with the Colonies (1775)

If you do not succeed, you are without resource: for, conciliation failing, force remains; but, force failing, no further hope of reconciliation is left.

Lincoln, letter to James Hackett (1863)

Those comments constitute a fair specimen of what has occurred to me through life. I have endured a great deal of ridicule, without much malice; and have received a great deal of kindness not quite free from ridicule. I am used to it.

5. *The chiasmus to state identities.*

Macbeth, I, I

Fair is foul, and foul is fair,
Hover through the fog and filthy air.

Keats, *Ode on a Grecian Urn* (1820)

Beauty is truth, truth beauty, – that is all
Ye know on earth, and all ye need to know.

Emerson, *Representative Men* (1850)

Plato is philosophy, and philosophy, Plato. . . .

6. *Dialogical applications.* In the chapter on isocolon we saw how that device may be used in dialogue: a reply can employ the same structure as the principal claim. Comparable use can be made of a chiasmus, resulting in a tidy riposte.

2 Henry IV, I, 2

CHIEF JUSTICE. You have misled the youthful prince.
FALSTAFF. The youthful prince hath misled me.

LIGARIUS.... What's to do?

BRUTUS. A piece of work that will make sick men whole.

LIGARIUS. But are not some whole that we must make sick?

BRUTUS. That must we also.

Julius Caesar, 2, 1

SHIRLEY.... I wouldn't have your conscience, not for all your income.

UNDERSHAFT. I wouldn't have your income, not for all your conscience, Mr. Shirley.

Shaw, *Major Barbara* (1905)

As also noted before, real life tends not to cooperate as well as the literary examples just shown might suggest; an antagonist's claim does not often lend itself to a comeback with a nicely reversed structure. One should savor such chances when they arise. In the meantime, this inconvenience can be overcome by restating the claim in a way that admits of a chiastic reply.

If he asks me why I introduce what he calls paradoxes into a philosophical problem, I answer, because all philosophical problems tend to become paradoxical.

Chesterton, *Heretics* (1905)

If I say "a peasant saw a ghost," I am told, "But peasants are so credulous." If I ask, "Why credulous?" the only answer is – that they see ghosts.

Chesterton, *Orthodoxy* (1908)

7. *Chesterton's specialties.* As those last examples show, the chiasmus was a device well suited to Chesterton's view of the world. He believed that modern thought constantly had things backward. Chesterton thus made a specialty of the chiasmus, and put it to some distinctive and innovative uses that the student of the device should note at least briefly. One was the flipped pair, in which different sorts of people are compared by showing their reversed relationships to elements presented in chiastic form.

Chesterton, *What's Wrong with the World* (1910)	The old hypocrite, Tartuffe or Pecksniff, was a man whose aims were really worldly and practical, while he pretended that they were religious. The new hypocrite is one whose aims are really religious, while he pretends that they are worldly and practical.
Chesterton, *Heretics* (1905)	Before long the world will be cloven with a war between the telescopists and the microscopists. The first study large things and live in a small world; the second study small things and live in a large world.
Chesterton, *Heretics* (1905)	This is shown in the odd mistake perpetually made about Cecil Rhodes. His enemies say that he may have had large ideas, but he was a bad man. His friends say that he may have been a bad man, but he certainly had large ideas.

Another Chestertonian favorite was the use of the chiasmus to play with definitions of words.

Chesterton, *Orthodoxy* (1908)	Pragmatism is a matter of human needs; and one of the first of human needs is to be something more than a pragmatist.
Chesterton, *Heretics* (1905)	Mr. McCabe thinks that I am not serious but only funny, because Mr. McCabe thinks that funny is the opposite of serious.
Chesterton, *On Running After One's Hat* (1908)	An inconvenience is only an adventure wrongly considered; an adventure is an inconvenience rightly considered.

8. *The chiastic play on words*, which may create a clever impression, mild amusement, or, in excess, annoyance.

Lincoln, debate with Stephen Douglas at Ottawa (1858)	[A]nything that argues me into his idea of perfect social and political equality with the negro is but a specious and fantastic arrangement of words, by which a man can prove a horse-chestnut to be a chestnut horse.
Melville, *Moby-Dick* (1851)	Signs and wonders, eh? Pity if there is nothing wonderful in signs, and significant in wonders!

I wasted time, and now doth time waste me. *Richard II*, 5, 5

9. *The emphatic chiasmus*, in which the reversal of words conveys no new information or idea, but repeats the original claim.

Varlet, thou liest; thou liest, wicked varlet! *Measure for Measure*, 2, 1

A most beastly place. Mudbank, mist, swamp, and work; work, swamp, mist, and mudbank. Dickens, *Great Expectations* (1861)

Fool and coward! Coward and fool! Tear thyself open, and read there the confounding story of thy blind doltishness! Melville, *Pierre* (1852)

[F]rom beginning to end, no grievance is mentioned except connected with slavery, – it is slavery, slavery, slavery, from the beginning to the end. Cobden, speech at Rochdale (1863)

10. *The multiple chiasmus*, in which the device becomes a repeating theme.

Woe unto them that call evil good, and good evil; that put darkness for light, and light for darkness; that put bitter for sweet, and sweet for bitter! Isaiah 5:20

The shepherd seeks the sheep, and not the sheep the shepherd; but I seek my master, and my master seeks not me: therefore, I am no sheep. *The Two Gentlemen of Verona*, 1, 1

[F]ormer ministers, I say, have put questions to us; we beg to put questions to them. They desired to know by what authority this nation has acted. This nation desires to know by what authority they have acted. Grattan, speech in the Irish Parliament (1782)

At present it is not we that silence the Press; it is the Press that silences us. It is not a case of the Commonwealth settling how much the editors shall say; it is a case of the editors settling how much the Commonwealth shall know. Chesterton, *Limericks and Counsels of Perfection* (1915)

I am not by nature bond to you, or you to me. Nature does not make your existence depend Douglass, Letter to My Old Master, Thomas Auld (1855)

upon me, or mine to depend upon yours. I cannot
walk upon your legs, or you upon mine. I cannot
breathe for you, or you for me; I must breathe for
myself, and you for yourself.

Dickens, *Nicholas Nickleby*
(1839)

There were the same unimpeachable masters and
mistresses in want of virtuous servants, and the
same virtuous servants in want of unimpeachable
masters and mistresses, and the same magnificent
estates for the investment of capital, and the same
enormous quantities of capital to be invested in
estates, and, in short, the same opportunities of all
sorts for people who wanted to make their fortunes.

11. *The structural chiasmus*. We have seen that a chiasmus
may occur without repetition of all the words involved.
The repetition and reversal may be structural, as when it
involves grammatical elements or parts of speech that different words are used to fill. Here are some more dramatic
examples where the changes between the first and second
parts of the chiasmus do more than just switch in a pronoun. The final effects here tend to be subtler than the
ones shown so far. They work especially well when the different words occupying the symmetrical positions are
opposites or otherwise related in a way that makes the
structural reversal clear.

Isaiah 28:15

We have made a covenant with death, and with
hell are we at agreement; ...

Measure for Measure, 2, 1

Some rise by sin, and some by virtue fall.

Gladstone, speech at Green-
wich (1871)

England is a great lover of liberty; but of equality
she never has been so much enamoured.

Kingsley, *Hereward* (1886)

Out, siren, with fairy's face and tail of fiend, and
leave the husband with his wife!

Stevenson, *Treasure Island*
(1883)

Watch him as we pleased, we could do nothing to
solve it; and when we asked him to his face, he
would only laugh if he were drunk, and if he were

sober deny solemnly that he ever tasted anything
but water.

It is for us, the living, rather, to be dedicated here   Lincoln, Gettysburg Address
to the unfinished work which they who fought   (1863)
here have thus far so nobly advanced. It is rather for
us to be here dedicated to the great task remaining before us. . . .

This last example contains a plain enough chiasmus –
though widely spaced – in *dedicated here* and *here dedicated*. But there also is a subtler, structural one: *unfinished
work* and *task remaining*.

But O, what damned minutes tells he o'er   *Othello* 3, 3
Who dotes, yet doubts; suspects, yet strongly loves!

Here *dotes* and *loves* are the A elements, because they are
verbs of affection; *doubts* and *suspects* are the B elements.

12. *The phonetic chiasmus*. A chiasmus also may be based
just on the sound or length of the words involved.
A famous example is the opening line of Coleridge's
Kubla Khan (1816):

In Xanadu did Kubla Khan
A stately pleasure-dome decree. . . .

The B element is the last syllable of *Xanadu* and the first
syllable of *Kubla,* which share the same long vowel sound.
The A elements are the syllables before and after those B
elements: *Xana* and . . . *a Khan.*
    Lincoln made use of a phonetic chiasmus in the Gettys-
burg Address:

Four score and seven years ago our fathers brought
forth on this continent a new nation, conceived in
liberty. . . .

Continent and *conceived* are the A elements; *new* and *nation*
are the B elements – an alliterative chiasmus. A similar
phonetic chiasmus appears a few sentences later: *The*

*world will little note, nor long remember what we say here,
but it can never forget what they did here.*

The chiasmus is . . . *little note, nor long. . .* , followed by
isocolon and also the kind of epistrophe that Lincoln
liked best (we saw this passage earlier in the chapter on
that subject).

A chiasmus can be based not only on the sounds in
the words but on their type, or feel.

Matthew 6:13

And lead us not into temptation, but deliver us
from evil. . . .

The A elements are *lead* and *evil*, which are short Saxon
words. The B elements are *temptation* and *deliver*, which
are longer Romance words – in other words, they came
into English, however indirectly, from Latin rather than
from Germanic sources. But you need not know anything
about etymology to appreciate the chiastic effect, which
is that the inner words and the outer words *sound* different. The transition through the long words reinforces the
plea. A somewhat similar use of the device is found in
this passage:

Churchill, speech in the
House of Commons (1940)

. . . our Empire beyond the seas, armed and guarded
by the British Fleet, would carry on the struggle,
until, in God's good time, the New World, with all
its power and might, steps forth to the rescue and
the liberation of the old.

The A elements are *New World* and *old*, which are related
in sense and in type. The B elements are the doublets
power and might and *rescue and liberation*.

We now are in position to appreciate a new aspect of
another passage from Churchill that we saw for a different purpose in the chapter on anaphora:

Churchill, London radio
broadcast (1940)

But be the ordeal sharp or long, or both, we shall
seek no terms, we shall tolerate no parley; we may
show mercy – we shall ask for none.

Notice the light chiasmus: the A elements are the mono-syllabic *seek no terms* at the start and *ask for none* at the finish. The B elements are the polysyllabic *parley* and *mercy*.

13. *The chiasmus paired with repetition of words.* As we have seen, one rhetorical device often can be used alongside others to create distinctive effects. The chiasmus in particular often sits well next to other figures that involve repetition rather than reversal; the combination of the two themes creates a rhetorically rich sound. Here, first, are instances of the chiasmus adjacent to anaphora – the repetition of words at the start of consecutive phrases.

> Thus, by quartering ill policy upon ill principles, they have frequently promoted the cause they designed to injure, and injured that which they intended to promote.

Paine, *The American Crisis* (1783)

> Mr. Merdle's right hand was filled with the evening paper, and the evening paper was full of Mr. Merdle. His wonderful enterprise, his wonderful wealth, his wonderful Bank, were the fattening food of the evening paper that night.

Dickens, *Little Dorrit* (1857)

The chiasmus paired with epistrophe, or repetition at the end of consecutive phrases:

> One woman is fair, yet I am well; another is wise, yet I am well; another virtuous, yet I am well; but till all graces be in one woman, one woman shall not come in my grace.

Much Ado about Nothing, 2, 3

> What shall I learn of beans or beans of me? I cherish them, I hoe them, early and late I have an eye to them; and this is my day's work.

Thoreau, *Walden* (1854)

> There is no such thing as backing a winner; for he cannot be a winner when he is backed. There is no such thing as fighting on the winning side; one fights to find out which is the winning side.

Chesterton, *What's Wrong with the World* (1910)

14. *Chiasmus alongside isocolon*. Powerful combinations also can be had by pairing a chiasmus with a case of isocolon. The chiasmus can create a little appetite for regular repetition of structure which the isocolon then satisfies. The chiasmus creates a loop; the isocolon pulls it straight.

Grattan, speech in the Irish Parliament (1794)

They are both incendiaries; the one would destroy government to pay his court to liberty; the other would destroy liberty to pay his court to government: but the liberty of the one would be confusion, and the government of the other would be pollution.

Dickens, *Bleak House* (1853)

Equity sends questions to law, law sends questions back to equity; law finds it can't do this, equity finds it can't do that. . . .

Chesterton, *What's Wrong with the World* (1910)

Men have not got tired of Christianity; they have never found enough Christianity to get tired of. Men have never wearied of political justice; they have wearied of waiting for it.

The same contrast between repetition and reversal can be had by putting the isocolon first, of course:

Chesterton, *The Prehistoric Railway Station* (1909)

Even mere bigness preached in a frivolous way is not so irritating as mere meanness preached in a big and solemn way. People buy the *Daily Mail*, but they do not believe in it. They do believe in the *Times*, and (apparently) they do not buy it.

Now some examples of isocolon paired with the *structural* chiasmus.

Churchill, *Savrola* (1900)

Death comes early to such men, whose spirits are so wrought that they know rest only in action, contentment only in danger, and in confusion find their only peace.

Sheil, argument for the defense in the trial of John O'Connell (1843)

Gamblers denounce dice – drunkards denounce debauch – against immoralities let wenchers rail.

In these last cases the same structure is repeated twice and then reversed in the last round. In the passage from Churchill, for example, the conditions (*only in action . . . only in danger*) are put at the end of the first two phrases, creating a case of isocolon; then comes the chiastic reversal at the end, where *in confusion* arrives first. The reversal provides relief from the pattern set up earlier, and lets the sentence come to rest with a strong word.

> Our principle is simply this; uniformity where you can have it; diversity where you must have it; but in all cases certainty.

Macaulay, speech in the House of Commons (1833)

This sentence from Macaulay begins as a case of isocolon, as the "uniformity" and "diversity" clauses are parallel in structure. Notice that those clauses also use epistrophe. But then the last clause abandons both the epistrophe and the isocolon in favor of a structural chiasmus: the phrase describing the occasion – *in all cases* – comes first, and the subject – *certainty* – is pushed to last, into emphatic position at the end of the sentence.

> [T]he captain made his advances in form, the citadel was defended in form, and at length, in proper form, surrendered at discretion.

Fielding, *Tom Jones* (1749)

Again the first two phrases employ isocolon; they are structurally the same. And again they also are cases of epistrophe, since they end with the same words (*in form*) after the different actions described. These regularities allow a graceful reversal in the last part of the sentence, which inverts the structure and also moves the repeated word (*form*) from the end to the beginning. Here are three more examples of the pattern.

> They must sting like wasps, revenge like wasps, hold altogether like wasps, build like wasps, work hard like wasps, rob like wasps; then, like the wasps, they will be the terror of all around, and kill and eat all their enemies.

Kingsley, *Superstition* (1867)

Grattan, speech in the
House of Commons (1808)

Let me ask them, is an exclusion from the two Houses of Parliament nothing? from the shrievalty nothing? from the privy-council nothing? from the offices of state nothing? from the Bank nothing? Is it nothing to be censured, schooled and suspected?

Macaulay, speech in the
House off Commons (1831)

We saw – who did not see? – great defects in the first bill. But did we see nothing else? Is delay no evil? Is prolonged excitement no evil? Is it no evil that the heart of a great people should be made sick by deferred hope?

Grattan's passage starts as a case of symploce (*from . . . nothing, from . . . nothing*); then the *nothing* is moved to the front of the last sentence: a reversal of structure and abandonment of the symploce, resulting in a kind of rhetorical punctuation to help complete the point. The example from Macaulay follows an identical pattern.

Inversion of Words:

ANASTROPHE

ANASTROPHE (a-*na*-stro-phee) (sometimes considered synonymous with *hyperbaton* – accent on the second syllable) occurs when words appear in unexpected order. In English, anastrophe typically means a departure from the conventional *subject*, *verb*, *object* word order, or movement of a modifier into an unexpected place. This device used to be strongly associated with Shakespeare; for today's student, anastrophe is more likely to bring to mind the Yoda character in the *Star Wars* movies. Some applications of the device create an archaic sound, but it still has a number of powerful rhetorical uses. Some standard purposes of reversed word order:

a. The unexpected placement of words calls attention to them. Pushing a word into an especially early or late position often creates emphasis in itself; then the emphasis is still greater because the ordering mildly violates the reader's expectations.

b. Inversion may put words in an order that creates an attractive rhythm.

c. Inversion may compress a meaning into fewer words.

d. Inversion sometimes causes the full meaning of a sentence to become clear only late in its progress; this bit of suspense makes the finish more climactic when it arrives.

1. *The object comes first.* A classic form of anastrophe moves the object, or words doing similar work, to the front of the sentence.

BOLINGBROKE. I thought you had been willing to resign.

Richard II, 4, 1

KING RICHARD. My crown I am; but still my
griefs are mine.

Burke, *On Conciliation with
the Colonies* (1775)

[T]he general character and situation of a people
must determine what sort of government is fitted
for them. That point nothing else can or ought to
determine.

Trollope, *North America*
(1862)

Many women, having received their lessons in walking from a less eligible instructor, do move in this
way, and such women this unfortunate little lady
has been instructed to copy.

Anastrophe of this and other kinds can be repeated to
energetic effect.

Johnson, letter to James
MacPherson (1775)

I thought your book an imposture; I think it an
imposture still. For this opinion I have given my
reasons to the publick, which I here dare you to
refute. Your rage I defy.

Four sets of words in this passage come in at least slightly
unexpected places that make them more emphatic: *still*,
for this opinion, *here*, and *your rage*. Notice how each of
these movements strengthens the ends of the phrases involved. Compare the rhythm, for example, of *I still think
it an imposture* and *I think it an imposture still*. Moving the
little word still to the finish causes the sentence to end
with a stressed syllable; the fist comes down with the
period at the end. Apart from its rhythmic merits, moving
still to the end emphasizes the word because it arrives late.
    In the second sentence, compare the endings of *which
I dare you to refute here*, which Johnson might have used,
and the actual *which I here dare you to refute*. This time
moving the little word earlier is the strengthening step,
since it leaves behind a strong word – the verb, and the
upshot of the sentence – at the end. This ordering also
gives the phrase a lightly iambic rhythm (ba-*bum* ba-*bum*
ba-*bum* ba-*bum*). In the last sentence, inverting *your rage*
and *I defy* adds some life to both phrases; they would lie

flatter if Johnson had used ordinary sentence structure. The ordering also has a more substantive advantage. The sentences in the passage generally create the feeling of a duel; they all are about oppositions between *I* and *my* vs. *you* and *yours*. The inversion at the end causes the parting shot to be *I defy* rather than *your rage*. It gives Johnson the last word.

The inverted language also may consist of more extended phrases than we have yet seen.

> How we disposed of our eggs and figs, I defy you, or the Devil himself, had he not been there (which I am persuaded he was), to form the least probable conjecture. . . .

Sterne, *Tristram Shandy* (1760)

> Whether he is since dead, I cannot say; the world do not so much as know that he ever lived!

Hazlitt, *On Genius and Common Sense* (1821)

> What effects a daily increasing familiarity with the scaffold, and with death upon it, wrought in France in the Great Revolution, everybody knows.

Dickens, *Capital Punishment* (1846)

This passage from Dickens illustrates another frequent consequence of inversion. Normal English word order gives the reader early notice of what a sentence is going to mean: the subject and verb usually come near the start, leaving the remainder of the sentence to convey details. The line that Dickens wrote unfolds differently. The principal subject and verb do not arrive until the last two words. A sentence of this kind – one that is grammatically incomplete until the end, and whose full meaning may not appear until then – is called *periodic*. Sentences that make their meaning clear as they go along, and that might have been stopped at various points in their progress without grammatical objection, are called *loose*. A loose style tends to be easier to follow, of course, because it makes fewer demands on the reader's attention; when reading a periodic sentence, you have to keep the early words in mind until their significance is finally cleared up by the last ones. Indeed, speakers of English are so used to loose sentences that they tend to be baffled when they first meet languages like German or Latin where the verb often comes at the end. How inconvenient not to know what the point of a sentence will be until it is done! But as many of the examples in this chapter show, there are advantages to the delay. The suspense about what the sentence will say creates energy that may be released in emphatic and satisfying fashion at the finish.

An especially common use of our current pattern moves a prepositional phrase to an early position.

Swift, A Sermon on the Causes of the Wretched Condition of Ireland (c. 1720)	From these two nurseries, I say, a great number of our servants come to us, sufficient to corrupt all the rest.
Hamilton, speech at New York Ratifying Convention (1788)	The influence of these is as powerful as the most permanent conviction of the public good; and against this influence we ought to provide.
Sheil, speech in the House of Commons (1835)	He could not go to the root of the evil; and although he now expresses a strong disrelish for ecclesiastical abuses, of that disrelish while he was in office he gave no very unequivocal evidence. . . .
Melville, *Moby-Dick* (1851)	In life but few of them would have helped the whale, I ween, if peradventure he had needed it; but upon the banquet of his funeral they most piously do pounce.

Moving *upon the banquet of his funeral* to the front of the second clause keeps it parallel with the first one, which, in a very mild inversion, puts the modifier (*in life*) early. It also allows the sentence to end with *they most piously do pounce*, which is a stronger finish – culminating with action, with a stressed syllable, and with a bit of exploding alliteration at the same time. Ending with *his funeral* would have lost those advantages.

Boswell, *Life of Johnson* (1791)	To such unhappy chances are human friendships liable.

Notice that after placing the prepositional phrase at the start, Boswell then inverts the subject and verb, too – *are human friendships liable*, not *human friendships are liable*. Here is another case of the same pair of inversions:

> [B]ut in every other light, and from every other cause, is war inglorious and detestable.

Paine, *The American Crisis* (1783)

Finally, notice the force that can be achieved when anastrophe of this kind is put into the service of a negative claim.

> But his unbiased opinion, his mature judgment, his enlightened conscience, he ought not to sacrifice to you, to any man, or to any set of men living.

Burke, Speech to the Electors of Bristol (1774)

> Sir, it is because I will not become a mere nominal minister of his creation – it is because I disdain to become the puppet of that right honorable gentleman – that I will not resign; neither shall his contemptuous expressions provoke me to resignation; my own honor and reputation I never will resign.

Pitt, speech in the House of Commons (1784)

This last example includes several different inversions. Putting the *it is because* clauses early creates a strong build-up to the point that follows from them – *I will not resign* – and so makes the negative more emphatic. If those last words had come early in the sentence, the *because* clauses would have been less interesting; they would just explain a result that the reader already had heard about. Then there is an inversion in the last clause: the object comes first. Notice again the various consequences when compared with the conventional order: *I never will resign my own honor and reputation*. In the inverted version the words moved earlier are lent additional power; but so, in another way, is *never*, since now the run-up to that word makes it more climactic once it is reached. And the rearrangement preserves a certain parallelism – a bit of epistrophe in which all the clauses end with *resign* or a variant.

2. *The reversal of a noun and its modifier.* In English, unlike, say, French and Spanish, it is conventional to put an adjective before the noun it modifies: *the ugly barn*, not *the barn ugly*. (Modifying *phrases* do routinely come after the noun: *the barn that was ugly*.) Flipping the noun and modifier thus can increase the force attached to them. These reversals also tend to create a strong sense of heightened language.

Burke, *On Conciliation with the Colonies* (1775)

[A]ll reasoning concerning our mode of treating them must have this proportion as its basis, or it is a reasoning weak, rotten, and sophistical.

Putting the adjectives at the finish, instead of ending with *reasoning*, gives them the sound of an open-ended cascade, which otherwise would have been stopped by the noun.

Churchill, London radio broadcast (1940)

The association of interest between Britain and France remains. The cause remains. Duty inescapable remains.

Carlyle, *Model Prisons* (1850)

Stupidity intellectual and stupidity moral (for the one always means the other, as you will, with surprise or not, discover if you look) had borne this progeny. . . .

de Quincey, *The Note Book of an English Opium Eater* (1855)

[A]nd then Nemesis will be at his heels with ruin perfect and sudden.

Exclamatory uses:

Romeo and Juliet, 3, 2

Did ever dragon keep so fair a cave?
Beautiful tyrant! fiend angelical!

Melville, *Mardi* (1849)

Woman unendurable: deliver me, ye gods, from being shut up in a ship with such a hornet again.

Beerbohm, *Ho-Tei* (1909)

Monster immensurable! What belt could inclip you? What blade were long enough to prick the heart of you?

3. *The inverted complement.* A complement – or more precisely a "subject complement" – is a word or phrase

that describes or renames the subject of a sentence, and comes after a linking verb (generally a form of the verb *to be*, though some commentators would expand the list). This sounds a bit complicated but usually is simple in practice. In the sentence *The man is happy*, the word *happy* is a complement. Anastrophe can be used to reverse that order and give more prominence to the modifier:

> Happy the man who can take books leisurely, like a soaking rain, and not inquire too curiously for the amount of fertilizer they contain.

Holmes, letter to Harold Laski (1929)

The linking verb is implied (*happy* [*is*] *the man*); Holmes thus combines anastrophe with ellipsis, or the omission of words – a device we will consider in a later chapter.

> Blessed are the poor in spirit: for theirs is the kingdom of heaven.
> Blessed are they that mourn: for they shall be comforted.
> Blessed are the meek: for they shall inherit the earth.

Matthew 5:3–5

> Some one called Omar "the sad, glad old Persian." Sad he is; glad he is not, in any sense of the word whatever.

Chesterton, *Heretics* (1905)

> True it is, that philosophy makes us wiser, but Christianity makes us better men.

Fielding, *Tom Jones* (1749)

> Certain it is that they do not see it as we see it.

Lincoln, speech at New Haven (1860)

Longer cases, in which the early complement consists of a phrase rather than a word:

> [S]uch constant irreconcilable enemies to science are the common people.

Swift, *Gulliver's Travels* (1726)

> "Yes, my dear sir," said he, "it is but too true; I have it on good authority – a gone church – a lost church – a ruined church – a demolished church is the Church of England. Toleration to dissenters! oh, monstrous!"

Borrow, *Lavengro* (1851)

Conan Doyle, *The Missing Three-Quarter* (1904)	"An outspoken, honest antagonist is the doctor," said Holmes.

Melville made fine use of this pattern.

Melville, *Moby-Dick* (1851)	Take off thine eye! more intolerable than fiends' glarings is a doltish stare!
Melville, *Moby-Dick* (1851)	Ex officio professors of Sabbath breaking are all whalemen.
Melville, *Moby-Dick* (1851)	How could one look at Ahab then, seated on that tripod of bones, without bethinking him of the royalty it symbolized? For a Khan of the plank, and a king of the sea, and a great lord of Leviathans was Ahab.

These constructions are strong because they turn what would otherwise be a pouring out into a pouring in. Instead of a single entity spawning a multitude of qualities or comparisons, a multitude of qualities and comparisons modify a thing that is named only after the build-up is complete. It is like the difference between watching someone put on a disguise and watching someone take it off. The latter is more dramatic.

4. *Adverbs.* In conventional English word order, adverbs come after the verbs they modify: *he ran quickly*. Anastrophe can give the adverb a harder push by placing it earlier.

Paine, *The American Crisis* (1783)	Truly may we say, that never did men grow old in so short a time!
Jefferson, letter to Washington (1784)	I hope our country will of herself determine to cede still further to the meridian of the mouth of the great Kanhaway. Further she cannot govern; so far is necessary for her own well being.
Churchill, speech in the House of Commons (1941)	Thus far then have we travelled along the terrible road we chose at the call of duty.

Well is it known that ambition can creep as well as soar.

Burke, *On the Proposals for Peace with the Regicide Directory of France* (1797)

Constructions with *never* are a standard use of this pattern.

Never did philosopher speak more correctly, and I only wonder that so wise a remark could have existed so many ages, and mankind not have laid it more to heart.

Irving, *Knickerbocker's History of New York* (1809)

I find, my lords, I have undesignedly raised a laugh; never did I less feel merriment.

Curran, argument in the trial of Mr. Justice Johnson (1805)

Never to those blood-stained accursed hands will the future of Europe be confided.

Churchill, speech at London (1941)

5. *The early verb.*

[W]hatever other business he has to attend to, waking or sleeping, breathe he must, or die he will.

Melville, *Moby-Dick* (1851)

But it was natural that he should gradually allow himself to be over-persuaded by Clennam, and should yield. Yield he did.

Dickens, *Little Dorrit* (1857)

[T]he long night of barbarism will descend, unbroken even by a star of hope, unless we conquer, as conquer we must; as conquer we shall.

Churchill, London radio broadcast (1940)

Forcing the verb to an early position can give rise to constructions that are awkward – though perhaps lovably so, from the standpoint of a connoisseur.

On the very second day (I date from the day of horrors), as is usual in such cases, there were a matter of twenty people, I do think, supping in our room; they prevailed on me to eat with them (for to eat I never refused).

Lamb, letter to Coleridge (1796)

Well may mankind shriek, inarticulately anathematising as they can. There are actions of such emphasis that no shrieking can be too emphatic for them. Shriek ye; acted have they.

Carlyle, *The French Revolution* (1837)

6. *Negation.* We have seen the force that anastrophe can add to denials or other negative claims in general. We also should not omit these other old-fashioned constructions that are useful for expressing negatives of more particular kinds.

Acts 3:6

Then Peter said, Silver and gold have I none; but such as I have give I thee.

Dickens, *David Copperfield* (1850)

Throat she had none; waist she had none; legs she had none, worth mentioning. . . .

The inverted negative also can be put to good use in the imperative mood.

King Lear, 1, 1

Peace, Kent!
Come not between the dragon and his wrath.

Paine, *The American Crisis* (1783)

Say not when mischief is done, that you had not warning, and remember that we do not begin it, but mean to repay it.

Carlyle, *The French Revolution* (1837)

They menace him, level muskets at him, he yields not; they hold up Feraud's bloody head to him, with grave stern air he bows to it, and yields not.

de Quincey, *Style* (1841)

Then, again, another delusion, by which all parties disguise the truth, is, the absurd belief that, not being read at present, a book may, however, be revived hereafter. Believe it not!

Hawthorne, *The Scarlet Letter* (1850)

Yet fear not for him! Think not that I shall interfere with Heaven's own method of retribution, or, to my own loss, betray him to the gripe of human law.

Lincoln, speech at Republican State Convention of Illinois (1856)

[W]hen they have made things of all the free negroes, how long, think you, before they will begin to make things of poor white men? Be not deceived. Revolutions do not go backward.

7. *With isocolon.* Anastrophe may be combined with isocolon. The result is a set of parallel and inverted parts,

sometimes with repeated words. To this pairing we owe one of the better sentences that Dickens wrote, and some fine moments from others as well.

My opinion of the coal trade on that river is, that it may require talent, but that it certainly requires capital. Talent, Mr. Micawber has; capital, Mr. Micawber has not.	Dickens, *David Copperfield* (1848)
What the white whale was to Ahab, has been hinted; what, at times, he was to me, as yet remains unsaid.	Melville, *Moby-Dick* (1851)
How far the sacrifice is necessary, has been shown. How far the unsacrificed residue will be endangered, is the question before us.	Madison, Federalist 45 (1788)
Fondly do we hope, fervently do we pray, that this mighty scourge of war may speedily pass away.	Lincoln, Second Inaugural Address (1865)
Let all the guaranties those fathers gave it be not grudgingly, but fully and fairly maintained. For this Republicans contend, and with this, so far as I know or believe, they will be content.	Lincoln, speech at Cooper Institute (1860)

Constructions with *more* and *less*:

More than that we ought not to look for, and less than that heaven has not yet suffered us to want.	Paine, *The American Crisis* (1783)
[W]e shall give a very good account of ourselves. More than that it would be boastful to say. Less than that it would be foolish to believe.	Churchill, London radio broadcast (1941)

Like other forms of isocolon, of course, this kind need not be limited to two parts.

Of that Constitution I was the author; in that Constitution I glory; and for it the honorable gentleman should bestow praise, not invent calumny.	Grattan, speech in the Irish Parliament (1800)
After having combated calumnies the most atrocious, sophistries the most plausible, and perils the	Phillips, speech at Dublin (undated)

most appalling, that slander could invent, or ingenuity devise, or power array against you, I at length
behold the assembled rank and wealth and talent
of the Catholic body offering to the legislature
that appeal which cannot be rejected. . . .

8. *With chiasmus*. Putting a clause with anastrophe next
to one with a conventional word order is an easy way to
create a chiasmus.

Paine, *The American Crisis*
(1783)

How you may rest under this sacrifice of character
I know not; but this I know, that you sleep and rise
with the daily curses of thousands upon you. . . .

The A or outer elements in the chiasmus are the long
phrases describing what he knows or doesn't know; the
B or inner elements are *I know*.

Churchill, speech in the
House of Commons (1940)

We abate nothing of our just demands; not one jot
or tittle do we recede.

The outer elements are the verbs – *abate* and *recede*; the
inner elements are *nothing of our just demands* and *not one
jot or tittle*.

Sheil, argument for the
defense in the trial of John
O'Connell (1843)

They may be mistaken – they may be blinded by
strong emotions – but corrupt they cannot be.

The outer elements are *be*; the inner elements are the
adjectives – *blinded* and *corrupt*.

Melville, *The Confidence-Man*
(1857)

In short, as in appearance he seemed a dog, so now,
in a merry way, like a dog he began to be treated.

Lincoln, debate with
Stephen Douglas at Peoria
(1854)

Less than this our fathers could not do, and more
they would not do. Necessity drove them so far,
and farther they would not go.

Thoreau, *A Week on the Con-
cord and Merrimack Rivers*
(1849)

Nothing more strikingly betrays the credulity of
mankind than medicine. Quackery is a thing universal, and universally successful.

Universal and *universally* are the B elements (a little use of polyptoton); the A elements are *thing* and *successful*. If those latter words seem too unalike to form the outer parts of a chiasmus – and perhaps they are – then consider it a mere case of anadiplosis.

Using Extra Conjunctions:
POLYSYNDETON

POLYSYNDETON (po-ly-*sin*-de-tahn) is the repeated use of conjunctions. It can serve several useful ends.

a. Polysyndeton may be used to create rhythm. *A and B and C and D* may produce a regular and useful cadence where *A, B, C, and D* had none to speak of.

b. Polysyndeton also regulates the pace of an utterance. Inserting extra conjunctions can slow a statement down by drawing out the process of saying it. But it also can speed an utterance up, as when all the conjunctions suggest excitability and urgency. The result depends on the context.

c. Polysyndeton can create the impression that the speaker is making up the meaning as the utterance goes along. A normal list of items with commas between most of them and an *and* only before the last one requires the speaker to know when the list is coming to an end, since just before the end is the one and only place where the *and* goes. Putting an *and* after every item suggests that the speaker doesn't have a plan of this kind; each item on the list might be the last or might not, depending on how many more things occur to the speaker. The resulting sound of artlessness may enhance the speaker's credibility.

d. In the most common case of polysyndeton the speaker uses "and" to connect items in a series, rather than separating them with commas. The result is to emphasize every one of the items singly; each is entitled to particular mention rather than burial in a list.

e. Sometimes the repeated use of conjunctions also serves to emphasize the large *number* of items the speaker names.

f. Polysyndeton is an important device for building

loose sentences: an extra conjunction may attach a thought to the end of a clause or sentence where it was not expected, thus creating possibilities for surprise and interest.

When learning to use polysyndeton it helps to understand both the consequences of the device and some of the situations that especially tend to call for it. Some of the examples shown below are thus grouped roughly by the effects the device creates (emphasis of each item in a list, emphasis of their numerosity, etc.); others are grouped according to occasions on which the device is used (to review explanations, as an aid to abuse, etc.). Efforts to group cases of polysyndeton by their effects have to be approximate because those effects sometimes overlap: the items named are each emphasized singly *and* their numerosity is made more impressive, and so on. But it at least is possible to point to cases where one of those results is more prominent than the others.

1. *To emphasize each item.* We start with some cases in which the most important consequence is to give force to each member of a list.

a. *Applications to nouns.*

> Suppose a civil companion, or a led captain, should, instead of virtue, and honour, and beauty, and parts, and admiration, thunder vice, and infamy, and ugliness, and folly, and contempt, in his patron's ears.

Fielding, *Joseph Andrews* (1742)

> Thus, then, though Time be the mightiest of Alarics, yet is he the mightiest mason of all. And a tutor, and a counselor, and a physician, and a scribe, and a poet, and a sage, and a king.

Melville, *Mardi* (1849)

In this last example, adding a conjunction before every item gives the second sentence a strong cadence that it otherwise would lack. Polysyndeton turns some of the phrases, and particularly the last two – *and a sage, and a king* – from monosyllables into anapests (in other words, units with two unstressed syllables followed by a stressed one). The result is almost too musical for its own good, but in any event it is a strong illustration of the effect that polysyndeton can have on rhythm.

b. *Applications to action.* Conjunctions may be used to connect verbs or verb phrases – typically three of them – lending individual weight to each and creating a heightened sense of activity.

Hawthorne, *English Note-books* (1856)

We talked about the position of men of letters in England, and they said that the aristocracy hated and despised and feared them. . . .

Conan Doyle, *The Great Boer War* (1900)

They niggled and quibbled and bargained until the State was left as a curious hybrid thing such as the world has never seen.

Lincoln, speech at Cooper Institute (1860)

We stick to, contend for, the identical old policy on the point in controversy which was adopted by our fathers who framed the Government under which we live; while you with one accord reject and scout and spit upon that old policy, and insist upon substituting something new.

Curran, speech in defense of Archibald Rowan (1794)

Shall they be found, let me ask you, in the accursed bands of imps and minions that bask in their disgrace, and fatten upon their spoils, and flourish upon their ruin?

c. *Applications to modifiers.* Setting off every modifier with its own conjunction gives an extra push to each of them, and may also add an air of exasperation to their recital.

Boswell, *Life of Johnson* (1791)

It is weak, and contemptible, and unworthy, in a parent to relax in such a case. It is sacrificing general advantage to private feelings.

Twain, *A Tramp Abroad* (1880)

A German daily is the slowest and saddest and dreariest of the inventions of man.

[Y]ou will find every question which he has asked me more fairly and boldly and fully answered than he has answered those which I put to him.

Lincoln, debate with Stephen Douglas at Freeport (1858)

Men, she perceives, are clumsy, and talk loud, and have no drawing-room accomplishments, and are rude; and she proceeds to model herself on them.

Beerbohm, *The Decline of the Graces* (1909)

And you can seldom get through even a whole paragraph without being monotonous, or irrelevant, or unintelligible, or self-contradictory, or broken-minded generally. If you have something to teach us, teach it to us now.

Chesterton, *The Crimes of England* (1915)

2. *Narration*. Polysyndeton lends a sense of motion to a narrative, and in long cases can give the action a breathless or headlong quality.

He went to church, and walked about the streets, and watched the people hurrying to and fro, and patted children on the head, and questioned beggars, and looked down into the kitchens of houses, and up to the windows, and found that everything could yield him pleasure.

Dickens, *A Christmas Carol* (1843)

[T]hen the rushing *Pequod*, freighted with savages, and laden with fire, and burning a corpse, and plunging into that blackness of darkness, seemed the material counterpart of her monomaniac commander's soul.

Melville, *Moby-Dick* (1851)

I fumed and sweated and charged and ranted till I was hoarse and sick and frantic and furious; but I never moved him once – I never started a smile or a tear!

Twain, *How the Author Was Sold in Newark* (1869)

He was going to travel! I never had been away from home, and that word "travel" had a seductive charm for me. Pretty soon he would be hundreds and hundreds of miles away on the great plains and deserts, and among the mountains of the Far

Twain, *Roughing It* (1872)

West, and would see buffaloes and Indians, and prairie dogs, and antelopes, and have all kinds of adventures, and may be get hanged or scalped, and have ever such a fine time, and write home and tell us all about it, and be a hero.

3. *Completeness.* Sometimes a list is meant to sound comprehensive: everything is covered. Polysyndeton can add to that sense of completeness; it suggests that the speaker is laboring a little to mention all the possibilities.

Thoreau, *Walden* (1854)

Of a life of luxury the fruit is luxury, whether in agriculture, or commerce, or literature, or art.

Dickens, *Great Expectations* (1861)

No one seemed surprised to see him, or interested in seeing him, or glad to see him, or sorry to see him, or spoke a word, except that somebody in the boat growled as if to dogs, "Give way, you!" which was the signal for the dip of the oars.

Reed, speech in the House of Representatives (1894)

I regret this the less because I know that many a philosopher has put the world into a nutshell only to find that the nutshell contained a world in which nobody ever lived, or moved, or had his being, and consequently a world which was of no human account.

The same pattern can be applied to list a series of places, and thus to suggest all places.

Melville, *Moby-Dick* (1851)

Then tossing both arms, with measureless imprecations he shouted out: "Aye, aye! and I'll chase him round Good Hope, and round the Horn, and round the Norway Maelstrom, and round perdition's flames before I give him up."

Dickens, *Great Expectations* (1861)

It was a run indeed now, and what Joe called, in the only two words he spoke all the time, "a Winder." Down banks and up banks, and over gates, and splashing into dikes, and breaking among coarse rushes: no man cared where he went.

The sense of completeness may be clinched by following the items on the list with a more general gesture toward everything in their class.

> I do not see why they should not enjoy every fundamental right in their property, and every original substantial liberty, which Devonshire, or Surrey, or the county I live in, or any other county in England, can claim. . . .

Pitt, speech in the House of Lords (1777)

> Hitherto we have considered aristocracy chiefly in one point of view. We have now to consider it in another. But whether we view it before or behind, or sideways, or any way else, domestically or publicly, it is still a monster.

Paine, *The Rights of Man* (1791)

> Is it so bad then to be misunderstood? Pythagoras was misunderstood, and Socrates, and Jesus, and Luther, and Copernicus, and Galileo, and Newton, and every pure and wise spirit that ever took flesh. To be great is to be misunderstood.

Emerson, *Self-Reliance* (1841)

The broad statement also can go in advance of the particulars that illustrate it.

> And every living substance was destroyed which was upon the face of the ground, both man, and cattle, and the creeping things, and the fowl of the heaven; and they were destroyed from the earth: and Noah only remained alive, and they that were with him in the ark.

Genesis 7:23

> All sensuality is one, though it takes many forms; all purity is one. It is the same whether a man eat, or drink, or cohabit, or sleep sensually.

Thoreau, *Walden* (1854)

> The man who does nothing cuts the same sordid figure in the pages of history, whether he be cynic, or fop, or voluptuary.

Roosevelt, *Citizenship in a Republic* (1910)

4. *Numerosity.* Polysyndeton is useful for suggesting not only that a list is complete, but that it is wide-ranging –

that it contains many items, to which more probably could be added. It creates the sound of a speaker going on and on, with the implication that he could keep doing so.

Burke, *Reflections on the Revolution in France* (1791)	Who, born within the last forty years, has read one word of Collins, and Toland, and Tindal, and Chubb, and Morgan, and that whole race who called themselves Freethinkers? Who now reads Bolingbroke? Who ever read him through?
Burke, speech in the House of Commons (1780)	But the deluded people of France are like other madmen, who, to a miracle, bear hunger, and thirst, and cold, and confinement, and the chains and lash of their keeper, whilst all the while they support themselves by the imagination that they are generals of armies, prophets, kings, and emperors.
Shaw, *A Treatise on Parents and Children* (1910)	That Consciousness of Consent which, even in its present delusive form, has enabled Democracy to oust tyrannical systems in spite of all its vulgarities and stupidities and rancors and ineptitudes and ignorances, would operate as powerfully among children as it does now among grown-ups.
Wodehouse, *The Coming of Bill* (1920)	There had been cigars and clothes and dinners and taxi-cabs and all the other trifles which cost nothing but mount up and make a man wander beyond the bounds of his legitimate income.
Orwell, *As I Please* (1947)	I doubt whether Petronius, or Chaucer, or Rabelais, or Shakespeare would remain un-bowdlerised if our magistrates and police were greater readers.
Thoreau, *Walden* (1854)	I did not use tea, nor coffee, nor butter, nor milk, nor fresh meat, and so did not have to work to get them; again, as I did not work hard, I did not have to eat hard, and it cost me but a trifle for my food; but as he began with tea, and coffee, and butter, and milk, and beef, he had to work hard to pay for them....

5. *Ad nauseam*. Items separated by conjunctions can become tiring to the ear. The power of polysyndeton to thus fatigue the reader can be used not to suggest completeness or even mere numerosity but to make the number of items on a list seem tiresome. Some applications to things:

> Are the decorations of temples an expenditure less worthy a wise man than ribbons, and laces, and national cockades, and petit maisons, and petit soupers, and all the innumerable fopperies and follies in which opulence sports away the burden of its superfluity?

Burke, *Reflections on the Revolution in France* (1791)

> And I am sure that I never read any memorable news in a newspaper. If we read of one man robbed, or murdered, or killed by accident, or one house burned, or one vessel wrecked, or one steamboat blown up, or one cow run over on the Western Railroad, or one mad dog killed, or one lot of grasshoppers in the winter – we never need read of another.

Thoreau, *Walden* (1854)

> The law talks about rights, and duties, and malice, and intent, and negligence, and so forth, and nothing is easier, or, I may say, more common in legal reasoning, than to take these words in their moral sense, at some state of the argument, and so to drop into fallacy.

Holmes, *The Path of the Law* (1897)

The same pattern can be applied to actions. We saw a few moments ago how polysyndeton can lend liveliness to a narrative of events. When the device is pushed a bit further in the way we are considering now, it instead creates a sense of endlessness; for this effect it helps to keep the connected verbs short as well as to make them numerous.

> It's about nothing but costs now. We are always appearing, and disappearing, and swearing, and interrogating, and filing, and cross-filing, and

Dickens, *Bleak House* (1853)

arguing, and sealing, and motioning, and referring, and reporting, and revolving about the Lord Chancellor and all his satellites, and equitably waltzing ourselves off to dusty death, about costs.

Twain, *My Autobiography* (1907)

We discussed, and discussed, and discussed, and disputed and disputed and disputed; at any rate, he did, and I got in a word now and then when he slipped a cog and there was a vacancy.

Shaw, *A Treatise on Parents and Children* (1910)

[B]oth legislators and parents and the paid deputies of parents are always inhibiting and prohibiting and punishing and scolding and laming and cramping and delaying progress and growth instead of making the dangerous places as safe as possible and then boldly taking and allowing others to take the irreducible minimum of risk.

6. *To start sentences.* Starting sentences or other sorts of independent clauses with conjunctions is too common to warrant general discussion, but using the technique in successive sentences has some consequences worth noting.

a. *The Biblical voice.* The best-known use of this pattern is found in the Bible, and indeed it is so familiar there that any somber and repeated use of *And* at the start of sentences, especially to narrate developments in a story, tends to echo the Biblical voice.

Genesis 1:23–24

And God said, Let the earth bring forth the living creature after his kind, cattle, and creeping thing, and beast of the earth after his kind: and it was so.

    And God made the beast of the earth after his kind, and cattle after their kind, and every thing that creepeth upon the earth after his kind: and God saw that it was good.

Poe, *The Masque of the Red Death* (1842)

And now was acknowledged the presence of the Red Death. He had come like a thief in the night. And one by one dropped the revellers in the blood-bedewed halls of their revel, and died each in the despairing posture of his fall. And the life of the ebony clock went out with that of the last of the gay. And the flames of the tripods expired. And Darkness and Decay and the Red Death held illimitable dominion over all.

And they bore him away unresisting.

    "Thus perish the ungodly," said Pani to the shuddering pilgrims.

    And they quitted the temple, to journey toward the Peak of Ofo.

Melville, *Mardi* (1849)

b. *To suggest excitability.*

God bless me, what horrid women I saw; I never knew what a plain-looking race it was before. I was sick at heart with the looks of them. And the children, filthy and ragged! And the smells! And the fat black mud!

Stevenson, letter to Frances Sitwell (1876)

And he's five years younger than she! And he's got nothing but his curacy! And he's a celibate!

Trollope, *The Way We Live Now* (1875)

Anyone, I tell you, would have flung himself upon that research. And I worked three years, and every mountain of difficulty I toiled over showed another from its summit. The infinite details! And the exasperation! A professor, a provincial professor, always prying. 'When are you going to publish this work of yours?' was his everlasting question. And the students, the cramped means! Three years I had of it –

Wells, *The Invisible Man* (1897)

c. *To suggest a flow of events.* Twice already we have seen polysyndeton used to give one shading or another to a narrative of action. Now we consider a third idea: polysyndeton in the same circumstances but to start separate sentences. Finishing a sentence and then repeatedly restarting with a conjunction lends an account a staccato quality, and makes each development seem an independent event. It also suggests heightened feeling in the speaker, as new points come to mind too quickly to be integrated into a longer and more carefully constructed sentence.

Scott, *Ivanhoe* (1819)

"Our master was too ready to fight," said the Jester; "and Athelstane was not ready enough, and no other person was ready at all. And they are prisoners to green cassocks, and black visors. And they lie all tumbled about on the green, like the crab-apples that you shake down to your swine. And I would laugh at it," said the honest Jester, "if I could for weeping." And he shed tears of unfeigned sorrow.

Poe, *The Premature Burial* (1844)

At length the slight quivering of an eyelid, and immediately thereupon, an electric shock of a terror, deadly and indefinite, which sends the blood in torrents from the temples to the heart. And now the first positive effort to think. And now the first endeavor to remember. And now a partial and evanescent success. And now the memory has so far regained its dominion, that, in some measure, I am cognizant of my state.

Dickens, *Bleak House* (1853)

I have forgotten to mention – at least I have not mentioned – that Mr. Woodcourt was the same dark young surgeon whom we had met at Mr. Badger's. Or that Mr. Jarndyce invited him to dinner that day. Or that he came. Or that when they were all gone and I said to Ada, "Now, my darling, let us have a little talk about Richard!" Ada laughed and said –

7. *Loose sentences.* A loose sentence, as explained in the chapter on anastrophe, is one that can be stopped at various points with no grammatical trouble but that keeps going. A greater than expected use of conjunctions can make a sentence unusually loose; not only *could* the sentence have been stopped earlier, but one might have expected it to have stopped. Typically this sense of unexpected extension occurs because the ear expects an *and*

to come just once and signal a winding down of the sentence; but then comes another one, and perhaps still another. The device thus can lend a sentence a feeling of spontaneity by suggesting that the speaker is making it up as he goes, tacking on thoughts without calculation.

> "He is not my Lord Castlewood," says Beatrix, "and he knows he is not; he is Colonel Francis Esmond's son, and no more, and he wears a false title; and he lives on another man's land, and he knows it."

Thackeray, *The History of Henry Esmond* (1852)

> We think it is good for the world, good for the Jews, and good for the British Empire, and it is also good for the Arabs dwelling in Palestine, and we intend it to be so.

Churchill, speech at Jerusalem (1921)

An extra *and* may help make the last clause or two in a sentence seem to be an afterthought – a last little dash of description or explanation that the speaker has to mention before leaving off.

> I thought it hard, I own, that there should be so many of them; my lord, and the court, and the jury, and the counsellors, and the witnesses, all upon one poor man, and he too in chains.

Fielding, *Tom Jones* (1749)

> Would that he consumed his own smoke! for his smoke is horrible to inhale, and inhale it you must, and not only that, but you must live in it for the time.

Melville, *Moby-Dick* (1851)

Polysyndeton can create a related but slightly different effect when a sentence seems to have spent itself but the speaker turns out not to be done. The piece tacked onto the end isn't quite an afterthought; it's just a little push beyond where the ear expected to go.

> Both parties deprecated war, but one of them would *make* war rather than let the nation survive, and the other would *accept* war rather than let it perish, and the war came.

Lincoln, Second Inaugural Address (1865)

The sentence from Lincoln feels about finished after *perish*, because the parallelism between the claims has been made complete. But it isn't finished; and adding the last burst or gasp unexpectedly at the end gives it a dash of force. We have seen earlier in the book some cases where it is evident that the King James Bible influenced Lincoln's ear. The passage just shown is probably another example. Compare it to this:

Luke 17:27

They did eat, they drank, they married wives, they were given in marriage, until the day that Noe entered into the ark, and the flood came, and destroyed them all.

8. *Stringed alternatives*. A similar device adds alternatives to a series (the repeated *or*) to prolong a sentence. The repetition of *or* tends to create the sound of thought occurring, rather than of prior thought being recorded, as more alternatives keep coming to the speaker's mind.

Baker, speech in the Senate
(1861)

Shall one battle determine the fate of an empire? or the loss of one thousand men, or twenty thousand; or one hundred million dollars, or five hundred million dollars? In a year's peace, in ten years, at most, of peaceful progress, we can restore them all.

Conan Doyle, *The White Company* (1891)

Yet, if for an instant he lay the cross aside, or if he fail to journey to Pitt's Deep, where it is ordered that he shall take ship to outland parts, or if he take not the first ship, or if until the ship be ready he walk not every day into the sea as far as his loins, then he becomes outlaw, and I shall forthwith dash out his brains.

Thackeray, *The History of Henry Esmond* (1852)

It was my lord's custom to fling out many jokes of this nature, in presence of his wife and children, at meals – clumsy sarcasms which my lady turned many a time, or which, sometimes, she affected not to hear, or which now and again would hit their mark and make the poor victim wince (as you

could see by her flushing face and eyes filling with
tears), or which again worked her up to anger and
retort, when, in answer to one of these heavy bolts,
she would flash back with a quivering reply.

9. *Pairings between items.*

[H]e acts absurdities even in his views; such as
drinking more, when he is drunk already; picking
up a common woman, without regard to what she
is or who she is, whether sound or rotten, clean or
unclean, whether ugly or handsome, whether old
or young, and so blinded as not really to distinguish.

Defoe, *Moll Flanders* (1722)

They went quietly down into the roaring streets,
inseparable and blessed; and as they passed along
in sunshine and shade, the noisy and the eager, and
the arrogant and the froward and the vain, fretted
and chafed, and made their usual uproar.

Dickens, *Little Dorrit* (1857)

If you are ready to leave father and mother, and
brother and sister, and wife and child and friends,
and never see them again – if you have paid your
debts, and made your will, and settled all your
affairs, and are a free man – then you are ready for
a walk.

Thoreau, *Walking* (1862)

10. *To review explanations.* We turn now to a few substantive occasions for which polysyndeton is especially suited.
We have seen that the device can stress the number of
possibilities on a list. A classic application of this usage is
to enumerate possible explanations for something. Each
candidate is given its own moment of consideration, and
perhaps again the use of *or* between all of them can make
it sound as though the speaker is generating the ideas as
he goes.

[A]nd one thing after another made my wife give
Besse warning to be gone, which the jade, whether
out of fear or ill-nature or simplicity I know not,

The Diary of Samuel Pepys
(1664)

but she took it and asked leave to go forth to look a place, and did. . . .

Curran, speech in defense of Archibald Rowan (1794)

England is marked by a natural avarice of freedom which she is studious to engross and accumulate, but most unwilling to impart, whether from any necessity of policy, or from her weakness, or from her pride, I will not presume to say; but that so is the fact you need not look to the east or to the west – you need only look to yourselves.

Dickens returned to this construction many times.

Dickens, *Nicholas Nickleby* (1839)

Newman fell a little behind his master, and his face was curiously twisted as by a spasm; but whether of paralysis, or grief, or inward laughter, nobody but himself could possibly explain.

Dickens, *American Notes* (1842)

Now, it is every night the lurking-place of a ghost: a shadow: – a silent something, horrible to see, but whether bird, or beast, or muffled human shape, he cannot tell.

Dickens, *Dombey and Son* (1848)

Her mother sat mowing, and mumbling, and shaking her head, but whether angrily or remorse-fully, or in denial, or only in her physical infirmity, did not appear.

11. *As an aid to abuse.* Polysyndeton is a natural way to add energy to a rant, and to name-calling in particular. In addition to lending emphasis to each of a series of epithets, it can create the sense that the speaker is grasping in the heat of the moment for ever more impressive insults, tossing each aside in favor of a new and better one as he goes.

Twelfth Night, 5, 1

Will you help? – an ass-head, and a coxcomb, and a knave, a thin-faced knave, a gull?

Melville, *Moby-Dick* (1851)

"No, sir; not yet," said Stubb, emboldened, "I will not tamely be called a dog, sir."

"Then be called ten times a donkey, and a mule,

and an ass, and begone, or I'll clear the world of
thee!"

For he is, by heaven, the most self-satisfied, and the
shallowest, and the most coxcombical and utterly
brainless ass!

Dickens, *Bleak House* (1853)

It is not mixed monarchy, with parts happily tem-
pered, and so forth, the cant of grave and superan-
nuated addresses; but a rank, and vile, and simple,
and absolute government, rendered so by means
that make every part of it vicious and abominable. . . .

Grattan, speech in the Irish
Parliament (1792)

12. *To enumerate horrors*, which are stressed singly and so
made to seem numerous and vivid.

It was not by persecution, but despite of it –
despite of imprisonment, and exile, and spoliation,
and shame, and death, despite the dungeon, the
wheel, the bed of steel, and the couch of fire – that
the Christian religion made its irresistible and
superhuman way.

Sheil, speech in the House
of Commons (1848)

I had supposed, Mr. President, that the question,
whether a gentleman shall lie or murder or torture, depended on his sense of his own character,
and not on his opinion of his victim.

Hoar, speech in the Senate
(1902)

If here and there an individual refuses to be docile,
ten docile persons will beat him or lock him up
or shoot him or hang him at the bidding of his
oppressors and their own.

Shaw, *A Treatise on Parents
and Children* (1910)

13. *Polysyndeton with other figures*. We conclude with a
glance at the effects achieved by combining polysyndeton
with other devices.

a. *With anaphora.*

The chuckle with which he said this, and the
chuckle with which he paid for the Turkey, and the

Dickens, *A Christmas Carol*
(1843)

chuckle with which he paid for the cab, and the chuckle with which he recompensed the boy, were only to be exceeded by the chuckle with which he sat down breathless in his chair again, and chuckled till he cried.

Dickens, *Bleak House* (1853)

"No, no, my dear friend. No, no, Mr. George. No, no, no, sir," remonstrates Grandfather Smallweed, cunningly rubbing his spare legs. "Not quite a dead halt, I think. He has good friends, and he is good for his pay, and he is good for the selling price of his commission, and he is good for his chance in a lawsuit, and he is good for his chance in a wife, and – oh, do you know, Mr. George, I think my friend would consider the young gentleman good for something yet?"

Forster, *A Room with a View* (1908)

"And mess with typewriters and latch-keys," exploded Mrs. Honeychurch. "And agitate and scream, and be carried off kicking by the police. And call it a Mission – when no one wants you! And call it Duty – when it means that you can't stand your own home! And call it Work – when thousands of men are starving with the competition as it is! And then to prepare yourself, find two doddering old ladies, and go abroad with them."

b. *With epistrophe or symploce.*

Dickens, *Hard Times* (1854)

I am a Coketown man. I am Josiah Bounderby of Coketown. I know the bricks of this town, and I know the works of this town, and I know the chimneys of this town, and I know the smoke of this town, and I know the Hands of this town.

Shaw, *A Treatise on Parents and Children* (1910)

And there is no logical reason why I should do for a child a great many little offices, some of them troublesome and disagreeable, which I should not do for a boy twice its age, or support a boy or girl when I would unhesitatingly throw an adult on his own resources. But there are practical reasons, and sensible reasons, and affectionate reasons for all these illogicalities.

Aside from higher considerations, charity often operates as a vastly wise and prudent principle – a great safeguard to its possessor. Men have committed murder for jealousy's sake, and anger's sake, and hatred's sake, and selfishness' sake, and spiritual pride's sake; but no man that ever I heard of, ever committed a diabolical murder for sweet charity's sake.

Melville, *Bartleby, the Scrivener* (1853)

c. *With isocolon.*

A man who had been soaked in water, and smothered in mud, and lamed by stones, and cut by flints, and stung by nettles, and torn by briars; who limped, and shivered, and glared and growled; and whose teeth chattered in his head as he seized me by the chin.

Dickens, *Great Expectations* (1861)

This is a fine example of both polysyndeton and isocolon; it illustrates in particular the idea of *oscillation* introduced at the end of the isocolon chapter – the grow-and-shrink effect in which the author varies the length of the clauses, starting with a set of parallel long ones, then using a batch of parallel shorter ones, and finally finishing with a long clause. Here is another case of polysyndeton used with oscillating isocolon:

And on top of it all, society lives! People go and come, and buy and sell, and drink and dance, and make money and make love, and seem to know nothing and suspect nothing and think of nothing; and iniquities flourish, and the misery of half the world is prated about as a "necessary evil", and generations rot away and starve, in the midst of it, and day follows day, and everything is for the best in the best of possible worlds.

James, *The Figure in the Carpet* (1896)

Like Dickens a moment ago, James piles up parallel clauses, but also lengthens and then shortens them (and then lengthens and shortens them again) to create rhetorical drama. The passage illustrates, at the same time, the *ad nauseam* effect of polysyndeton seen earlier in this chapter, and notice as well some other consequences of the device. The subjects change during the passage (from *people* to *iniquities*, and then *generations*, etc.), but the conjunctions hold the passage together as one thought, both by enabling it to be said as a single sentence and by running a common verbal thread through it from start to finish. The sentence also uses another idea familiar from earlier in the book. In the chapter on anaphora we saw an example from Churchill where one case of anaphora was embedded within another; here we find a similar idea with polysyndeton, as the multiple *ands* are used to connect not only the principal items listed but also items on a list within the list (*know nothing and suspect nothing and think of nothing*).

Leaving Out Conjunctions:
ASYNDETON

ASYNDETON (ah-*sin*-de-tahn) means leaving out a conjunction where it might have been expected. Neil Kinnock used the device (along with isocolon, anaphora, and alliteration) when he said in 1976, *The House of Lords must go – not be reformed, not be replaced, not be reborn in some nominated life-after-death patronage paradise, just closed down, abolished, finished.* Some classic purposes of asyndeton:

a. The omission of the conjunction is irregular and unexpected, and thus can create a moment of emphasis.

b. The omission suggests that each of the items has independent force. Polysyndeton (the use of more conjunctions than might have been expected) has a similar effect, and for a similar reason: with both devices, the items in a series are all treated the same way; either all are connected by conjunctions or none are.

c. Omitting conjunctions may suggest that the items mentioned are restatements of one another, or that each is a substitute for the last, rather than a list of independent entries.

d. The connection of items by commas alone may emphasize the close relationship between them.

e. The omission of conjunctions can create a sense of acceleration. The conjunctions left out would have served as a mild brake against the accumulation of words or phrases that instead flow freely.

f. Omitting conjunctions may, in certain cases, improve the music of the sentence – again, as polysyndeton also does. In a case of polysyndeton the repeated conjunctions establish a rhythm; with asyndeton the words alone have to do the work.

g. The omission of conjunctions may create a mood of solemnity. It also risks seeming mannered. The reader may conclude that a few of the examples in this chapter would have been improved by avoiding the device.

Some commentators distinguish between various species of this device: the use of commas without conjunctions to connect single words (*articulus* or *brachylogia*) or clauses (*asyndeton*). The distinctions are not useful enough to employ here.

1. *Nouns and noun phrases.*

Emerson, *The American Scholar* (1837)

Drudgery, calamity, exasperation, want, are instructors in eloquence and wisdom.

Beerbohm, *Zuleika Dobson* (1911)

Admiration, homage, fear, he had sown broadcast.

The same pattern may be employed with phrases.

Churchill, London radio broadcast (1940)

We seek to beat the life and soul out of Hitler and Hitlerism. That alone, that all the time, that to the end.

This use of a conjunction at the end of this last passage would have spoiled the rhythm of it and diminished the sense of unity between the claims.

Henry, Speech at Virginia Ratifying Convention (1788)

The rights of conscience, trial by jury, liberty of the press, all your immunities and franchises, all pretensions to human rights and privileges, are rendered insecure, if not lost, by this change, so loudly talked of by some, and inconsiderately by others.

Here use of a conjunction before the last item – making it *and all pretensions* – would have caused Henry's enumeration to sound finite and contained; the *and* would have made the last item sound like the concluding item on his list. Leaving out the conjunction makes it sound as though he is just reeling off examples, with some of them (especially the last) perhaps restatements of others or inclusive of them, and without any sense that the last thing mentioned is the last he *could* mention. The same general effect occurs in the next two examples.

> There we meet the slime of hypocrisy, the varnish of courts, the cant of pedantry, the cobwebs of the law, the iron hand of power.

Hazlitt, *Mr. Gifford* (1825)

> The Innkeeper, hat in hand in the yard, swore to the courier that he was blighted, that he was desolated, that he was profoundly afflicted, that he was the most miserable and unfortunate of beasts, that he had the head of a wooden pig.

Dickens, *Little Dorrit* (1857)

Asyndeton with phrases often is used with other devices at the same time, as we shall see several times in this chapter. Note this in the examples just shown: the passage from Hazlitt combines asyndeton with isocolon (phrases with similar structure). The passages from Dickens and Churchill use some anaphora (the repetition of language at the start of successive clauses). Henry's case uses a bit of both, along with a dash of ellipsis (see chapter 12).

2. *Modifiers.* It is common enough to string several modifiers together without a conjunction when they come before a noun: *the accursed, cruel, diabolical American war* (from a passage to be examined later in the book). But when the adjectives appear *after* the noun, a conjunction is more customary at the end, so its omission is more striking:

> How can its administration be any thing else than a succession of expedients temporizing, impotent, disgraceful?

Hamilton, Federalist 37 (1787)

> Of a sudden, and all at once, there came wafted over the ocean from the strange vessel (which was now close upon us) a smell, a stench, such as the whole world has no name for – no conception of – hellish – utterly suffocating – insufferable, inconceivable.

Poe, *The Narrative of Arthur Gordon Pym of Nantucket* (1838)

Again, the asyndeton suggests that the words on the list aren't separate items – that they have a cumulative quality in which each adds to the last but also might partly displace it, as if better, stronger words keep occurring to the speaker.

Asyndeton of this kind can be paired attractively with exclamations. Omitting the conjunction adds to the sense of feeling and emphasis that the punctuation mark also suggests, as shown in these examples (both of which also use epistrophe):

Grattan, speech in the House of Commons (1812)

[Y]ou cannot do it; your good sense and your good feelings forbid it; the feelings of your countrymen forbid it; – it is an interdict, horrible, unnatural, impossible!

Twain, letter to W. D. Howells (1878)

Munich did seem the horriblest place, the most desolate place, the most unendurable place! – and the rooms were so small, the conveniences so meagre, and the porcelain stoves so grim, ghastly, dismal, intolerable!

3. *Verbs and combinations.*

Burke, Speech on Moving His Resolutions for Conciliation with the Colonies (1775)

It is the spirit of the English Constitution, which, infused through the mighty mass, pervades, feeds, unites, invigorates, vivifies every part of the empire, even down to the minutest member.

Poe, *The Black Cat* (1843)

My immediate purpose is to place before the world, plainly, succinctly, and without comment, a series of mere household events. In their consequences, these events have terrified – have tortured – have destroyed me.

The effect is the now familiar one: leaving out any conjunctions tends to suggest that each word (*terrified, tortured, destroyed*) adds to or perhaps improves upon the previous one; the speaker thinks better of each word uttered and substitutes a stronger choice.

Observe again how asyndeton, when used to link

phrases, may be joined naturally to other devices involving repetition of words or of structure. With anaphora:

> Repeal the Missouri Compromise, repeal all compromises, repeal the Declaration of Independence, repeal all past history, you still cannot repeal human nature.

Lincoln, debate with Stephen Douglas at Peoria (1854)

> But, in a larger sense, we cannot dedicate, we cannot consecrate, we cannot hallow this ground.

Lincoln, Gettysburg Address (1863)

These both are cases where sense and style would suffer obvious damage by use of a conjunction where convention would call for it.

4. *Independent clauses*. Asyndeton also can be used to link entire independent clauses that might have stood by themselves as sentences – the "comma splice" despised by many grammarians but which has rhetorical value when used judiciously; much of its value arises precisely because it violates grammatical convention. Indeed, one has to be especially cautious in using this pattern because some people mistakenly regard it as an error wherever it occurs. In stuffy settings it should be avoided outright, and in all events it should be reserved for occasions where the writer has established rhetorical credibility, and so can expect the pattern to be viewed as a stylistic decision rather than a blunder.

Notice that unlike most of the devices in this book, this use of asyndeton exists mostly for the eye rather than the ear. In writing, one can see the comma; when the same words are spoken, the presence of a period or semicolon may be inferred.

a. *To express contrast*.

> Society is produced by our wants, and government by our wickedness; the former promotes our happiness *positively* by uniting our affections, the latter *negatively* by restraining our vices. The one encourages intercourse, the other creates distinctions.

Paine, *Common Sense* (1776)

Chesterton, *Orthodoxy* (1908)	My acceptance of the universe is not optimism, it is more like patriotism.
Orwell, *A Hanging* (1931)	This man was not dying, he was alive just as we were alive.

b. *To make parallel statements about the same subject or object.*

Ecclesiastes 2:10	And whatsoever mine eyes desired I kept not from them, I withheld not my heart from any joy; for my heart rejoiced in all my labour. . . .
Holmes, *The Common Law* (1881)	A man who has used a way ten years without title cannot sue even a stranger for stopping it. He was a trespasser at the beginning, he is nothing but a trespasser still.
Orwell, *The Lion and the Unicorn* (1941)	Another is that, as Europeans go, the English are not intellectual. They have a horror of abstract thought, they feel no need for any philosophy or systematic "world-view."

c. *To enlarge.* The first statement in the pair is general; the second elaborates, illustrates, or states an implication.

Stevenson, *My First Book: "Treasure Island"* (1894)	I think little of these, they are trifles and details; and no man can hope to have a monopoly of skeletons or make a corner in talking birds.
Wells, *Social Panaceas* (1912)	Our situation is an intricate one, it does not admit of a solution neatly done up in a word or a phrase.
Fowler, *The King's English* (1930)	[T]he reader will indulgently remember that to correct a bad sentence satisfactorily is not always possible; it should never have existed, that is all that can be said.

d. *More than two clauses.*

Irving, *Tales of a Traveler* (1822)	I hated my uncle, I hated the monks, I hated the convent in which I was immured.

"My friends," says Mr. Chadband with his perse-
cuted chin folding itself into its fat smile again as
he looks round, "it is right that I should be hum-
bled, it is right that I should be tried, it is right that
I should be mortified, it is right that I should be
corrected."

Dickens, *Bleak House* (1853)

I appeal to your charity, I appeal to your generosity, I appeal to your justice, I appeal to your
accounts, I appeal, in fine, to your purse.

Stevenson, letter to his
father (1866)

The present arrangement is not convenient, it is
not cheap, it is not free from danger, it is not only
not perfect but is so much the reverse that we
could hardly find words to express our sense of its
awkwardness if we could look upon it with new
eyes, or as the cuckoo perhaps observes it.

Butler, *On Memory as a Key
to the Phenomena of Heredity*
(1882)

Death and sorrow will be the companions of our
journey; hardship our garment; constancy and
valor our only shield. We must be united, we must
be undaunted, we must be inflexible.

Churchill, speech in the
House of Commons (1949)

5. *Asyndeton as an aid to invective.*

[I]nstead of what was but just now the delight and
boast of the creation, there will be cast out in the
face of the sun a bloated, putrid, noisome carcass,
full of stench and poison, an offence, a horror, a
lesson to the world.

Burke, speech in the House
of Commons (1785)

Sir, this is a picture so horrid, so wretched, so
dreadful, that I need no longer dwell upon it.

Henry, speech at Virginia
Ratifying Convention (1788)

We have seen that sometimes asyndeton is useful for string-
ing words together when each is stronger than the last;
leaving out conjunctions suggests that each word displaces
the weaker one that came before. This can be a helpful
technique when delivering epithets in ascending order.

Yet this is the unnatural caprice, this the injustice,
the gross, the foul, the outrageous, the monstrous,

Brougham, speech in the
House of Lords (1838)

the incredible injustice of which we are daily and hourly guilty toward the whole of the ill-fated African race.

Shaw, *Man and Superman* (1903)

Stuff! lunacy! There is a rascal in our midst, a libertine, a villain worse than a murderer; and we are not to learn who he is!

6. *Asyndeton with other devices.*

a. *With polysyndeton.* Sometimes good effects can be obtained by following asynedeton with polysyndeton or vice versa. The omission of conjunctions may create a subtle appetite for them which polysyndeton then satisfies, or the other way around. To begin with cases where the asyndeton comes first:

Brougham, speech in the House of Lords (1838)

The time has come, the trial has been made, the hour is striking; you have no longer a pretext for hesitation, or faltering, or delay.

Spencer, speech at Birmingham (1884)

From a national and imperial point of view, you need never be alarmed at the dangers of one-man power so long as the House of Lords endures. Be he minister, be he capitalist, be he demagog – be he Mr. Gladstone, or Mr. Chamberlain, or even Mr. Schnadhorst – against that bulwark of popular liberty and civil order he will dash himself in vain.

Grattan, speech in the Irish Parliament (1790)

There is no object which a course of corrupt government will not finally ruin – morality, constitution, commerce, manufacture, agriculture, industry. A corrupt minister issues forth from his cabinet like sin and death, and senates first wither under his footsteps; then he consumes the treasury, and then he corrupts the capital, and the different forms of constitutional life, and the moral system; and, at last, the whole island is involved in one capacious curse from shore to shore, from nadir to the zenith.

Now the reverse order: polysyndeton, then asyndeton (and then, perhaps, polysyndeton again):

Where men are not acquainted with each other's principles, nor experienced in each other's talents, nor at all practised in their mutual habitudes and dispositions by joint efforts in business; no personal confidence, no friendship, no common interest, subsisting among them; it is evidently impossible that they can act a public part with uniformity, perseverance, or efficacy.

Burke, *Thoughts on the Cause of the Present Discontents* (1770)

b. *Asyndeton with anaphora or epistrophe.*

They are men; it is saying nothing worse of them; many of them are but ill informed in their minds, many feeble in their circumstances, easily overreached, easily seduced.

Burke, Speech on a Bill for Shortening the Duration of Parliaments (1780)

The repeal of the sacred Missouri Compromise has installed the weapons of violence: the bludgeon, the incendiary torch, the death-dealing rifle, the bristling cannon – the weapons of kingcraft, of the inquisition, of ignorance, of barbarism, of oppression.

Lincoln, Speech at Republican State Convention (1856)

The short modifying phrase, repeated thrice with the same start, without conjunctions, and with a different ending each time, is a classic and sonorous pattern:

The absolute monarchy was at an end. It breathed its last, without a groan, without struggle, without convulsion.

Burke, *Reflections on the Revolution in France* (1789)

Some idea, some fancy, takes possession of the brain; and however ridiculous, however distressing, however ruinous, haunts us by a sort of fascination through life.

Hazlitt, *On the Past and Future* (1821)

c. *Asyndeton with isocolon.*

Oh God! what could I do? I foamed – I raved – I swore!

Poe, *The Tell-Tale Heart* (1843)

He would make it a rule of political action for the people and all the departments of the government.

Lincoln, speech at Springfield (1858)

I would not. By resisting it as a political rule, I disturb no right of property, create no disorder, excite no mobs.

Beerbohm, *A Home-coming*
(1909)

Of her everything is redolent. She it is that has cut the thick stale sandwiches, bottled the bitter beer, brewed the unpalatable coffee.

Leaving Out Words:

ELLIPSIS

AN *ELLIPSIS* (el-*lip*-sis) is an omission of expected words, with various of these consequences:

a.   An ellipsis involves the audience in an utterance; the reader or listener fills in the missing language, consciously or not.

b.   Missing words sometimes are a small surprise. The result may be a moment of emphasis on whatever was omitted.

c.   The omission of words can create a sense of brevity, energy, and elegance.

d.   Often an ellipsis occurs because a later phrase borrows a word from an earlier one. The effect of this can be to tie the two phrases together more snugly and strengthen the felt link between them.

1.   *The omitted noun.* The simplest case of an omitted noun occurs when it simply is lopped off the end of a sentence or clause, leaving behind an adjective with nothing explicit to modify. The reader fills in the missing word by borrowing it from earlier in the sentence. In the following case, *better* is the adjective left behind at the end; the unwritten word it modifies is *plan*.

> In short, had you cast about for a plan on purpose to enrich your enemies, you could not have hit upon a better.

Paine, *The American Crisis* (1783)

Notice that this usage can make the adjective at the end sound a bit like a noun of its own.

> "The greater idiot ever scolds the lesser," muttered Ahab, advancing.

Melville, *Moby-Dick* (1851)

Thoreau, *A Week on the Con-cord and Merrimack Rivers* (1849)

It often happens that the sicker man is the nurse to the sounder.

Chesterton, *A Glimpse of My Country* (1909)

It may be a strange sight to see the blind leading the blind; but England provides a stranger. England shows us the blind leading the people who can see.

Conan Doyle, *The Six Napoleons* (1904)

No, I have never seen this face which you show me in the photograph. You would hardly forget it, would you, sir, for I've seldom seen an uglier.

With the possessive:

Trollope, *The Eustace Diamonds* (1873)

To be alone with the girl to whom he is not en-gaged is a man's delight; to be alone with the man to whom she is engaged is the woman's.

Chesterton, *What's Wrong with the World* (1910)

They do not want their own land; but other people's.

In the cases just shown, the missing words (*delight* and *land*) are borrowed from earlier in the sentence – from the ends of the previous clauses in each case. But some-times an omitted word can just be filled in by the reader. The next two examples are like this. They are so collo-quial that they barely seem to qualify as cases of ellipsis, but in both cases another word could have been added comfortably at the end, and in both of them the result would have been a weakening.

Stoker, *Dracula* (1897)

You think to baffle me, you – with your pale faces all in a row, like sheep in a butcher's.

Chesterton, *The Toy Theatre* (1909)

I run after Jones with a hatchet, and if he turns round and tries to get rid of me the only possible explanation is that he has a very small balance at his banker's.

Even when it is clear enough what the omitted word would *mean*, it may not be perfectly what the word would *be*. Thus one could mentally insert various words at the end of those last two examples, but the open-ended way they are written doesn't make the meaning any less clear; and meanwhile ending the sentences with particular words might have weakened them by making the image too specific for its own good.

Here, finally, is a related interesting way of ending a sentence: with a transitive verb – in other words, a verb that normally takes an object. When the sentence suddenly ends and no object has appeared, the reader is left at the edge of a cliff. Imagination fills in the rest.

> Empire has happened to them and civilisation has happened to them as fresh lettuces come to tame rabbits. They do not understand how they got, and they will not understand how to keep.

Wells, *An Englishman Looks at the World* (1914)

> If I falsify in this, you can convict me. The witnesses live, and can tell.

Lincoln, letter to John Hardin (1846)

> Most of them would probably say to us, "Let us alone, *do* nothing to us, and *say* what you please about slavery." But we do let them alone – have never disturbed them – so that, after all, it is what we say which dissatisfies them. They will continue to accuse us of doing, until we cease saying.

Lincoln, speech at Cooper Union (1860)

In this last example, *doing* and *saying* are gerunds – in other words, they are forms of verbs acting as nouns – so we fudge a bit by considering the passage here. It is included now anyway because it involves the same basic ideas as the other cases just shown: ending a sentence with verb forms that cry out for some further words to complete the thought, but that the speaker declines to supply.

2. *The omitted verb*. Here we begin with cases where the verb is missing from the middle of a clause. Typically it is borrowed by implication from earlier in the sentence. Some with a taste for terminology would prefer to call this type of ellipsis a *zeugma*, though that term is sometimes given wider meaning as well (on which see Lanham's *Handlist of Rhetorical Terms*).

Richard II, 1, 1	Good uncle, let this end where it begun; We'll calm the Duke of Norfolk, you your son.
Melville, *Moby-Dick* (1851)	Now, the grand distinction between officer and man at sea, is this – the first lives aft, the last forward.
Lincoln, debate with Stephen Douglas at Peoria (1854)	Slavery is founded in the selfishness of man's nature – opposition to it in his love of justice.
Dickens, *Little Dorrit* (1857)	How young she seemed to him, or how old he to her; or what a secret either to the other, in that beginning of the destined interweaving of their stories, matters not here.

A pithy application of this pattern reduces the second part to two words.

Julius Caesar, 3, 1	As fire drives out fire, so pity pity....
Macbeth, 1, 2	DUNCAN. Dismay'd not this our captains, Macbeth and Banquo? CAPTAIN. Yes, as sparrows eagles, or the hare the lion.
Sterne, *Tristram Shandy* (1760)	As war begets poverty; poverty peace....

Sometimes replacing lost words with a comma improves clarity and cadence.

King Lear, 2, 1	By his authority I will proclaim it, That he which finds him shall deserve our thanks, Bringing the murderous coward to the stake; He that conceals him, death.
Burke, *Thoughts on the Cause of the Present Discontents* (1770)	Resistance to power has shut the door of the House of Commons to one man; obsequiousness and servility, to none.

Notice how the dropped phrase (*have shut the door...*) leaves behind a more compact and powerful wording. It also makes the contrast Burke that wants to draw – *to one ... to none* – sharper by keeping those opposites closer together. Separating them with another round of *have shut the door of the House of Commons* would weaken the sentence by delaying the point with a bunch of words that don't add anything for the reader.

> The dull distinguish only races or nations, or at most classes, but the wise man, individuals.

Thoreau, *A Week on the Concord and Merrimack Rivers* (1849)

Again, the ellipsis keeps *individuals* snug with the words to which it is compared – *races, nations,* and *classes.*

> But at best, the greatest reviewers but prey on my leavings. For I am critic and creator; and as critic, in cruelty surpass all critics merely, as a tiger, jackals.

Melville, *Mardi* (1849)

> [S]ince then, they have gradually taken their road in life – we, ours – and we have held no correspondence.

Dickens, *A Tale of Two Cities* (1859)

> You can always tell an old soldier by the inside of his holsters and cartridge boxes. The young ones carry pistols and cartridges; the old ones, grub.

Shaw, *Arms and the Man* (1898)

Verbs or verb phrases may also be omitted from the end of a clause rather than the middle. Again the speaker relies on the listener to borrow words from earlier in the sentence – perhaps one, or perhaps quite a few – and to tack them onto the end.

> Out of the trunk, the branches grow; out of them, the twigs.

Melville, *Moby-Dick* (1851)

> And this is the eternal law. For, Evil often stops short at itself and dies with the doer of it; but Good, never.

Dickens, *Our Mutual Friend* (1865)

> Actors who can't act believe in themselves; and debtors who won't pay.

Chesterton, *Orthodoxy* (1908)

3. *The omission of subject and verb.* We turn to more substantial omissions: cases where the subject and verb are left out of a second clause, with the listener expected to borrow them from the first. Sometimes such omissions,

despite seeming large as a grammatical matter, flow easily and place little strain on the audience.

Webster, speech in the Senate (1848)

Liars by nature, they are treacherous and faithless to their friends, cowardly and cringing to their enemies. . . .

Emerson, *The American Scholar* (1837)

Books are the best of things, well used; abused, among the worst.

Shaw, *Maxims for Revolutionists* (1903)

Do not love your neighbor as yourself. If you are on good terms with yourself, it is an impertinence; if on bad, an injury.

Burke, Speech on Moving His Resolutions for Conciliation with the Colonies (1775)

I really think that for wise men this is not judicious, for sober men not decent, for minds tinctured with humanity not mild and merciful.

Notice that in each case the words left out (*they are*, *you are*, *this is*) have little power; the omission of them leaves behind a higher density of strong language. The omissions are especially easy on the ear when the verb they leave out is some form of *to be*, such as *are* or *is* in the examples just shown. But sometimes other simple verbs can be dropped easily enough as well, such as *have* in these cases:

Lamb, letter to Wordsworth (1830)

Here we have nothing to do with our victuals but to eat them, with the garden but to see it grow, with the tax-gatherer but to hear him knock, with the maid but to hear her scolded.

Livingston, speech at New York Ratifying Convention (1788)

With regard to the sword and the purse, I could have no conception of Congress keeping a sword, and the states using it; of Congress using a purse, and the states keeping it; of Congress having power, and the states exercising it.

Observe the parallel structure of the clauses in each case, which helps the reader keep track of the meaning despite the missing words.

The risk of strain on the reader becomes a bit greater

when two separate pieces of a clause are left out and borrowed from earlier.

> Navigation is not the final cause of astronomy, nor telegraphy of electro-dynamics, nor dyeworks of chemistry.

Balfour, speech at St. Andrews University (1887)

This works reasonably well. The second and third clauses each borrow twice from the first: *is*, and *the final cause*. The first of those borrowings is very slight, so the result flows and the omissions leave behind strong words.

> What we call knowledge is often our positive ignorance; ignorance our negative knowledge.

Thoreau, *Walking* (1862)

> If ye love wealth better than liberty, the tranquility of servitude than the animating contest of freedom – go from us in peace.

Samuel Adams, speech at Philadelphia (1776)

Each of these last two cases involves double ellipses that are substantial. In the example from Thoreau, *what we call* and *is often* are both omitted in the second clause and borrowed from the first. In the example from Adams, the same is true of *if ye love* and *better*. Both of these examples teeter on the edge of excess; especially in the second passage, the omission of the words can cause some readers a moment of slight confusion (but it was, after all, a speech, and perhaps the ellipsis is easier to hear than to read).

To return to an idea introduced a moment ago, double omissions of this kind hold up better when they are aided by repetition of words or structure. The repetition helps to orient the reader and make the meaning obvious even with some words left out. Punctuation to show where the omission came may help, too. These examples illustrate both points:

> Give almost any man I know ten pounds, and he will impose upon you to a corresponding extent; a thousand pounds – to a corresponding extent; ten thousand pounds – to a corresponding extent. So great the success, so great the imposition.

Dickens, *Little Dorrit* (1857)

Emerson, *Circles* (1841)

New arts destroy the old. See the investment of capital in aqueducts made useless by hydraulics; fortifications, by gunpowder; roads and canals, by railways; sails, by steam; steam by electricity.

4. *Omissions that anticipate what is yet to come*. Almost all the examples so far have omitted words in a later part of a sentence because they already were used in an earlier part and so can be borrowed by implication. But the reverse pattern also is possible: an omission that borrows in advance from later in the sentence. The amount borrowed mustn't be large, and the delay in repayment can't be long.

Burke, *Thoughts on the Cause of the Present Discontents* (1770)

It was soon discovered, that the forms of a free, and the ends of an arbitrary Government, were things not altogether incompatible.

Clinton, speech at New York Ratifying Convention (1788)

That gentleman may wish for a consolidated, I wish for a federal republic.

Dickens, *A Christmas Carol* (1843)

External heat and cold had little influence on Scrooge. No warmth could warm, no wintry weather chill him.

Lincoln, debate with Stephen Douglas at Springfield (1858)

Wise counsels may accelerate, or mistakes delay it, but, sooner or later, the victory is sure to come.

5. *Ellipsis with isocolon* – a pattern we have seen a few times already, but worth a moment of attention to itself.

Hamilton, Federalist 18 (1787)

By his intrigues and bribes he won over to his interests the popular leaders of several cities; by their influence and votes, gained admission into the Amphictyonic council; and by his arts and his arms, made himself master of the confederacy.

Burke, speech at Bristol (1780)

We knew beforehand, or we were poorly instructed, that toleration is odious to the intolerant, freedom to oppressors, property to robbers, and all kinds and degrees of prosperity to the envious.

To him, your celebration is a sham; your boasted liberty, an unholy license; your national greatness, swelling vanity; your sounds of rejoicing are empty and heartless; your denunciations of tyrants, brass-fronted impudence; your shouts of liberty and equality, hollow mockery; your prayers and hymns, your sermons and thanksgivings, with all your religious parade and solemnity, are to him mere bombast, fraud, deception, impiety, and hypocrisy – a thin veil to cover up crimes which would disgrace a nation of savages.

Douglass, speech at Rochester (1852)

As earlier examples have shown, this construction was a favorite of Emerson's.

The priest becomes a form; the attorney, a statute book; the mechanic, a machine; the sailor, a rope of a ship.

Emerson, *The American Scholar* (1837)

The value of the universe contrives to throw itself into every point. If the good is there, so is the evil; if the affinity, so the repulsion; if the force, so the limitation.

Emerson, *Compensation* (1841)

An institution is the lengthened shadow of one man; as, Monachism, of the Hermit Antony; the Reformation, of Luther; Quakerism, of Fox; Methodism, of Wesley; Abolition, of Clarkson.

Emerson, *Self-Reliance* (1841)

Saying Things by Not Saying Them:
PRÆTERITIO

PRÆTERITIO (pry-te-*rit*-ee-oh; known less often by its Greek name, *paralipsis*) generally occurs when the speaker describes what he will not say, and so says it, or at least a bit of it, after all. Chesterton described some forms of the device this way:

Chesterton, *A Miscellany of Men* (1912)

The trick consists of first repudiating a certain view in unfavourable terms, and then repeating the same view in favourable terms. Perhaps the simplest form of it may be found in a landlord of my neighbourhood, who said to his tenants in an election speech, "Of course I'm not going to threaten you, but if this Budget passes the rents will go up." The thing can be done in many forms besides this. "I am the last man to mention party politics; but when I see the Empire rent in pieces by irresponsible Radicals," etc. "In this hall we welcome all creeds. We have no hostility against any honest belief; but only against that black priestcraft and superstition which can accept such a doctrine as," etc. "I would not say one word that could ruffle our relations with Germany. But this I will say; that when I see ceaseless and unscrupulous armament," etc.

Chesterton added that he did not like the device: "don't fancy that you have somehow softened the saying of a thing by having just promised not to say it." Præteritio nevertheless is an interesting and oft-used rhetorical figure, and it takes many forms besides the ones that Chesterton mentioned. The usual purposes that the device serves include these:

a. To gain credit – though not too much – for discretion or propriety while still setting loose an indiscre-
tion or impropriety. (The first few sections below contain
many examples, as do sections 6 and 9.)

b. To leave the substance of a sentiment, or a piece of
it, to the listener's imagination, and so enhance its force.
The fantasy of what the complete version of the thought
would have been may be more powerful than a plain
statement of it. (See, e.g., sections 5 and 8 below.)

c. To limit debate over a controversial utterance by
offering it as only half-said; when the speaker denies fully
saying it, he hopes to make a rebuttal seem uncalled for,
and to assign himself a relaxed burden of proof. (See, e.g.,
sections 5, 6, and 7 below.)

d. Amusement. The paradox inherent in a good use
of præteritio can be a source of humor and charm, at least
when it does not take itself too seriously.

1. *I will not speak of. . . .* We begin with some classic cases
in which the thing, or part of it, is said as the speaker
explains that it will not be.

> I shall make no address to your passions – I will not
> remind you of the long and rigorous imprison-
> ment he has suffered; – I will not speak to you of
> his great youth, of his illustrious birth, and of his
> uniformly animated and generous zeal in Parlia-
> ment for the constitution of his country. Such top-
> ics might be useful in the balance of a doubtful
> case; yet even then I should have trusted to the
> honest hearts of Englishmen to have felt them with-
> out excitation. At present, the plain and rigid rules
> of justice and truth are sufficient to entitle me to
> your verdict.

Erskine, argument in the
trial of Lord George Gordon
(1778)

> As one of the inducements to the projected mar-
> riage, he actually proposed the prospect of a £50
> annuity as an officer's widow's pension, to which
> she would be entitled in the event of his decease!

Phillips, argument in *Black
v. Wilkins* (1817)

I will not stop to remark on the delicacy of this inducement – I will not dwell on the ridicule of the anticipation – I will not advert to the glaring dotage on which he speculated, when he could seriously hold out to a woman of her years the prospect of such an improbable survivorship.

Trollope, *The Last Chronicle of Barset* (1867)

Am I to suppose that you intend to lower yourself by marrying a young woman who cannot possibly have enjoyed any of the advantages of a lady's education? I say nothing of the imprudence of the thing; nothing of her own want of fortune; nothing of your having to maintain a whole family steeped in poverty; nothing of the debts and character of the father, upon whom, as I understand, at this moment there rests a grave suspicion of – of – of – what I'm afraid I must call downright theft.

A case of our current theme combined with symploce:

Phillips, argument in *O'Mullan v. M'Korkill*

I seek not to impugn the verdict of that jury; I have no doubt they acted conscientiously. It weighs not with me that every member of my client's creed was carefully excluded from that jury – no doubt they acted conscientiously. It weighs not with me that every man impannelled on the trial of the priest, was exclusively Protestant, and that, too, in a city so prejudiced, that not long ago, by their Corporation law, no Catholic dare breathe the air of heaven within its walls – no doubt they acted conscientiously. It weighs not with me, that not three days previously, one of that jury was heard publicly to declare, he wished he could persecute the Papist to his death – no doubt they acted conscientiously.

Præteritio is Latin for *I pass over*. That particular language is a standard vehicle for the device in English.

Stevenson, letter to Edmund Gosse (1879)

Your statement about your initials, it will be seen, I pass over in contempt and silence.

Fain would I entertain the reader with the trium-
phant campaign of Peter Stuyvesant in the haunted
regions of those mountains, but that I hold all
Indian conflicts to be mere barbaric brawls, unworthy of the pen which has recorded the classic
war of Fort Christina; and as to these Helderberg
commotions, they are among the flatulencies which
from time to time afflict the bowels of this ancient
province, as with a wind-colic, and which I deem
it seemly and decent to pass over in silence.

Irving, *Knickerbocker's History of New York* (1809)

I wished to show, but I will pass it upon this occasion, that in the sentiment I have occasionally
advanced upon the Declaration of Independence
I am entirely borne out by the sentiments
advanced by our old Whig leader, Henry Clay, and
I have the book here to show it from but because
I have already occupied more time than I intended
to do on that topic, I pass over it.

Lincoln, debate with
Stephen Douglas at Quincy
(1858)

Sometimes præteritio is used with the subjunctive: the
review of what might be said or thought.

It is not for me to say by what means, or by what
degrees, some wives manage to keep down some
husbands as they do, although I may have my private opinion on the subject, and may think that
no Member of Parliament ought to be married,
inasmuch as three married members out of every
four, must vote according to their wives' con-
sciences (if there be such things), and not according to their own.

Dickens, *Nicholas Nickleby*
(1839)

Gentlemen, I observe an honest indignation rising
in all your countenances on the subject, which,
with the arts of an advocate, I might easily press in
the service of my friend: but as his defence does
not require the support of your resentments, or
even of those honest prejudices to which liberal
minds are but too open without excitation, I shall

Erskine, argument in the
trial of the Dean of St.
Asaph (1784)

draw a veil over all that may seduce you from the correctest and the severest judgment.

Macaulay, speech in the House of Commons (1831)

I might, perhaps, at a more convenient season, be tempted to inquire whether that defeat was more disgraceful to them or to their predecessors. I might, perhaps, be tempted to ask the right honourable gentleman whether, if he had not been treated, while in office, with more fairness than he has shown while in opposition, it would have been in his power to carry his best bill, the Beer Bill? He has accused the Ministers of bringing forward financial propositions, and then withdrawing those propositions. Did not he bring forward, during the Session of 1830, a plan respecting the sugar duties? And was not that plan withdrawn? But, Sir, this is mere trifling. I will not be seduced from the matter in hand by the right honourable gentleman's example.

Usually præteritio is used to communicate negative views about others, but on occasion it also is used to suggest positive things about oneself.

Paine, *The American Crisis* (1783)

In this state of political suspense the pamphlet *Common Sense* made its appearance, and the success it met with does not become me to mention.

Trollope, letter to a prospective publisher (1879)

It is an original novel, but it is not for me to say so.

Conan Doyle, *How the Brigadier Bore Himself at Waterloo* (1903)

At Waterloo, although, in a sense, I was present, I was unable to fight, and the enemy was victorious. It is not for me to say that there is a connection between these two things. You know me too well, my friends, to imagine that I would make such a claim. But it gives matter for thought, and some have drawn flattering conclusions from it.

2. *Never mind that....* One of the important points in a case of præteritio is the placement of the disclaimer. In many cases it comes at the end, when it is rather too late.

The disclaimer then may come across as an afterthought, or as a half-hearted effort to save the speaker from reproach.

> The first of the family which we have to do with, James, was a dirty, cowardly miscreant, of whom the less said the better.

Borrow, *The Romany Rye* (1857)

> The next book, in order of time, to influence me, was the New Testament, and in particular the Gospel according to St. Matthew. I believe it would startle and move any one if they could make a certain effort of imagination and read it freshly like a book, not droningly and dully like a portion of the Bible. Any one would then be able to see in it those truths which we are all courteously supposed to know and all modestly refrain from applying. But upon this subject it is perhaps better to be silent.

Stevenson, *Books Which Have Influenced Me* (1887)

> Your decision may affect more than the life of this defendant. If he be not convicted as principal, no one can be. Nor can any one be convicted of a participation in the crime as accessory. The Knapps and George Crowninshield will be again on the community. This shows the importance of the duty you have to perform, and serves to remind you of the care and wisdom necessary to be exercised in its performance. But certainly these considerations do not render the prisoner's guilt any clearer, nor enhance the weight of the evidence against him. No one desires you to regard consequences in that light.

Webster, argument for the prosecution in the murder trial of John Francis Knapp (1830)

3. *The short-lived promise.* The reverse order occurs as well: the claimed intention not to speak on a subject, which is contradicted immediately. In pure cases of this type, the initial promise is breached promptly and cleanly. The speaker thus can say that he disavowed any interest in a conversation on the subject, while still getting in a few shots about it.

Chesterton, *Manalive* (1912)	The proceedings opened with a speech from my colleague, of which I will say nothing. It was deplorable.
Webster, speech at Republican National Convention (1832)	Mr. President, I shall not discuss the doctrine of nullification. I am sure it can have no friends here. Gloss it and disguise it as we may, it is a pretence incompatible with the authority of the Constitution.
Dickens, *Bleak House* (1853)	"I have forgiven her" – but her face did not relent – "the wrong she did to me, and I say no more of it, though it was greater than you will ever know – than any one will ever know but I, the sufferer."
Wells, *An Englishman Looks at the World* (1914)	And so I will say no more of the idea that the novel is merely a harmless opiate for the vacant hours of prosperous men. As a matter of fact, it never has been, and by its nature I doubt if it ever can be.

In less pure cases, the initial promise is not entirely breached; but the claim made bears a disquieting resemblance to the claim disavowed. The examples Chesterton recounted at the start of this chapter would fit best under this heading.

Curran, argument for the defense in the trial of Archibald Rowan (1794)	Far am I from imputing any sinister design to the virtue or wisdom of our government; but who can avoid feeling the deplorable impression that must be made on the public mind when the demand for that reform is answered by a criminal information!
Lincoln, debate with Stephen Douglas at Peoria (1854)	I do not read this extract to involve Judge Douglas in an inconsistency. If he afterward thought he had been wrong, it was right for him to change.
Lincoln, speech at Edwardsville (1858)	I will not affirm that the Democratic party consider slavery morally, socially and politically right, though their tendency to that view has, in my opinion, been constant and unmistakable for the past five years.

The Miss Sharp, whom you mention as governess to Sir Pitt Crawley, Bart., M.P., was a pupil of mine, and I have nothing to say in her disfavour. Though her appearance is disagreeable, we cannot control the operations of nature: and though her parents were disreputable (her father being a painter, several times bankrupt, and her mother, as I have since learned, with horror, a dancer at the Opera); yet her talents are considerable, and I cannot regret that I received her *out of charity*.

Thackeray, *Vanity Fair* (1848)

4. *Withheld details.* In another type of præteritio the speaker truly does leave things unsaid but nevertheless makes their existence known. It is something like covering a child's eyes during the scandalous part of a movie: what he misses by not looking may be milder than what he is forced to imagine.

There are many other modes of retaliation, which, for several reasons, I choose not to mention. But be assured of this, that the instant you put your threat into execution, a counter-blow will follow it.

Paine, *The American Crisis* (1783)

It was followed, early in the next year, by that indescribable enormity, that appalling monument of barbarian cruelty, the destruction of Scio; a scene I shall not attempt to describe; a scene from which human nature shrinks shuddering away; a scene having hardly a parallel in the history of fallen man.

Webster, speech in the House of Representatives (1824)

Gentlemen, I will not disgust this audience; I will not debase myself by any description of the scene that followed; I will not detail the arts, the excitements, the promises, the pledges with which deliberate lust inflamed the passions, and finally over-powered the struggles of innocence and of youth.

Phillips, argument in *Creighton v. Townsend* (1816)

The weather I shall say nothing about, as I am incapable of explaining my sentiments upon that subject before a lady.

Stevenson, letter to his mother (1874)

| Twain, *A Tramp Abroad* (1880) | I have been strictly reared, but if it had not been so dark and solemn and awful there in that lonely, vast room, I do believe I should have said something then which could not be put into a Sunday-school book without injuring the sale of it. |

| Churchill, speech in the House of Commons (1938) | In all these matters I have a sincere and abiding confidence in them. But if you ask me whether I have confidence in their execution of Defence programmes, or even in their statements as to the degree to which those Defence programmes have at any moment advanced – there I must beg the House not to press me too far. |

5. *I will not call him fool.* The denial that a specific claim is being made sometimes communicates a bit of the claim's substance in any event, or more than a bit.

a. *The thing loudly not said*, and which is emphasized by the attention called to it and to its scandalous nature. Some commentators call this *apophasis* – affirming something while claiming to deny it.

| Grattan, *Invective Against Corry* (1800) | I will not call him villain, because it would be unparliamentary, and he is a privy counselor. I will not call him fool, because he happens to be chancellor of the exchequer. |

| O'Connell, speech on suppression of disturbances (1833) | It depends on the spirit of the patriarchs of Reform to prevent the people of Ireland from being fettered by ministers, on the ground of foolish, false, and I would say lying (if it were not too undignified a word) calumnies. |

| Sheil, speech in the House of Commons (1837) | Whether he deserves the appellation by which he has informed us that he is designated, his speech to-night affords some means of determining. I will not call him a bigot – I am not disposed to use an expression in any degree offensive to the right honourable baronet, but I will presume to call him a |

convert, who exhibits all the zeal for which conversion is proverbially conspicuous.

b. *The thing almost said.*

I almost venture to affirm that not one in a hundred amongst us participates in the "triumph" of the Revolution Society.

Burke, *Reflections on the Revolution in France* (1791)

I find in Lord John Russell, in the House of Commons, not simply great impatience but petulance, and I had almost said great insolence, in his dealings, particularly in the remarks he has made to our friend, Mr. Bright.

Cobden, speech in the House of Commons (1848)

All this, Sir, shows the inherent futility, I had almost used a stronger word, of conceding this power of interference to the State, and then attempting to secure it from abuse by imposing qualifications of which the States themselves are to judge.

Webster, Reply to Hayne (1830)

c. *I do not say* x, *but I say* y (*and probably suspect* x).

Sir, the eulogies are now written, the commendations are already elaborated. I do not say every thing fulsome, but every thing panegyrical, has already been written out, with *blanks* for names, to be filled when the convention shall adjourn.

Webster, speech in the Senate (1848)

To conclude, my Lords, if the ministers thus persevere in misadvising and misleading the King, I will not say that they can alienate the affections of his subjects from his crown, but I will affirm *that they will make the crown not worth his wearing.* I will not say that the King is betrayed, but I will pronounce *that the kingdom is undone.*

Pitt, speech in the House of Lords (1775)

Such a policy and principle, I will not call criminal; I will not call it repugnant to the doctrines of all the great authors that ever wrote on government; but it is that very policy, and that very principle,

Grattan, speech in the Irish Parliament (1790)

which all of them have pronounced to be the destruction of liberty, and one in particular, such a crime as to amount to a breach of trust, tending towards a dissolution of the state.

Sheil, argument in defense of Aeneas McDonnell (1827)

I will admit, for the sake of argument, that the charges preferred against him by Mr. McDonnell are unfounded, that he never presided over the torture of a miserable female – that he never applied to a sub-sheriff for liberty to play the part of an executioner, and inflict a frightful torment with his own hands – that he never prostrated houses, expelled their wretched occupiers, and filled the hearts of parents with despair and sorrow – but while, for a moment and no more, I admit all this, I appeal to the principle upon which this court regulates its decisions, and put this question – "Does not the man who sends a hostile message act against the laws of God, and the ordinances of society?"

d. *Disclaimed statements about the intentions of others.*

Lincoln, speech at Springfield (1858)

He then quotes, or attempts to quote, from my speech. I will not say that he wilfully misquotes, but he does fail to quote accurately.

Hamilton, Speech at New York Ratifying Convention (1788)

Sir, we hear constantly a great deal which is rather calculated to awake our passions, and create prejudices, than to conduct us to the truth, and teach us our real interests. I do not suppose this to be the design of the gentlemen. Why, then, are we told so often of an aristocracy?

Sheil, argument in defense of Aeneas McDonnell (1827)

I am indisposed to use any coarse or contumelious phrase in his regard – I will not accuse him of any directly sanguinary intent – I will not say that he went armed with the Riot Act, and attended by the police, in order to avail himself of the first opportunity of letting them loose upon a defenceless body of his fellow-citizens. But it is one question, whether a purpose so detestable entered distinctly into his contemplation, and another, whether he did not, while under the operation of those fanatical opinions, which obscure the understanding, while they indurate the heart, perpetrate a flatigious outrage. . . .

e. *Ostentatious or feigned agnosticism.*

I know not upon what complaisance this English seducer may calculate from a jury of this country; I know not, indeed, whether he may not think he does your wives and daughters some honour by their contamination.

Phillips, argument in *Creighton v. Townsend* (1816)

Whether there is any truth, or not, in the story of his attachment to, and favorable reception by, the daughter of the head of an extensive wholesale grocer's establishment, I will not venture an opinion; I may say, however, that I have met him repeatedly in company with a very well-nourished and high-colored young lady, who, I understand, is the daughter of the house in question.

Holmes, *The Professor at the Breakfast Table* (1859)

The doctrine which I imagine she stuffs into the pretty heads of your girl-guests is almost vengeful. A sort of moral fire-and-sword doctrine. How far the lesson is wise is not for me to say. I don't permit myself to judge. I seem to see her very delightful disciples singeing themselves with the torches, and cutting their fingers with the swords of Mrs. Fyne's furnishing.

Conrad, *Chance* (1913)

We have his own authority for stating, that, like the Apostle of the Gentiles, he received a special summons from the Lord. Whether what he takes for a ray from heaven may not be some stray moonbeam that has fallen upon his mind – whether his heart has been touched, or that pulp, of which the brain is compounded, has become diseased, I shall not stop to inquire.

Sheil, speech at Catholic Association (undated)

6. *Matters deferred to another time, place, or speaker.* The speaker may leave the substance of a claim for someone else to say – perhaps even the listener. The speaker thus makes a little show of humility.

Fielding, *Amelia* (1751)

How easy it is for a man who is at all tainted with the itch of gaming to leave off play in such a situation, especially when he is likewise heated with liquor, I leave to the gamester to determine.

Lincoln, debate with Stephen Douglas at Ottawa (1858)

I leave it to you to say whether, in the history of our government, this institution of slavery has not always failed to be a bond of union, and, on the contrary, been an apple of discord and an element of division in the house.

Twain, *Roughing It* (1872)

I submit that that unguarded remark of Philip Lynch convicts him of having been privy in advance to Mr. Winters' intentions whatever they may have been, or at least to his meaning to make an assault upon me, but I leave to others to determine how much censure an editor deserves for inveigling a weak, non-combatant man, also a publisher, to a pen of his own to be horsewhipped, if no worse, for the simple printing of what is verbally in the mouth of nine out of ten men, and women too, upon the street.

Or the speaker may make suggestive or inflammatory allusions to a matter but suggest that time and space constrain him from treating it fully.

de Quincey, *Confessions of an English Opium Eater* (1821)

It has no resemblance to the sufferings caused by renouncing wine. It is a state of unutterable irritation of stomach (which surely is not much like dejection), accompanied by intense perspirations, and feelings such as I shall not attempt to describe without more space at my command.

Stephen, *Liberty, Equality, Fraternity* (1873)

It is also a question which I cannot do more than glance at in two words in this place, whether the enormous development of equality in America, the rapid production of an immense multitude of commonplace, self-satisfied, and essentially slight people is an exploit which the whole world need fall down and worship.

7. *The thing already known.* This use of præteritio can create a clubby feeling between the speaker and the audience: the speaker assumes the reader is in the know, and the reader feels that he is – or perhaps that if he isn't, he should pretend to be. This pattern also can serve as a strategy of proof. If everyone is said to know something already, it must be very true.

In Virginia, armed men endeavored to stop the courts of justice. In South Carolina, creditors, by law, were obliged to receive barren and useless land for contracts made in silver and gold. I pass over the instance of Rhode Island: their conduct was notorious.

Thacher, speech at Massachusetts Ratifying Convention (1788)

With respect to the second object, namely, giving the Dutch an opportunity of shaking off the yoke of France, with what horror they received your proffered release from their bondage, and the execration with which they load your name, it is unnecessary to state.

Fox, Speech in the House of Commons (1801)

If it were necessary to exemplify the consequences of such an executive government as yours, in the management of great affairs, I should refer you to the late reports of M. de Montmorin to the National Assembly, and all the other proceedings relative to the differences between Great Britain and Spain. It would be treating your understanding with disrespect to point them out to you.

Burke, *Reflections on the Revolution in France* (1791)

8. *No offense.* The disclaimer of any offensive intentions on the speaker's own part, with questionable effectiveness.

Bright, speech in the House of Commons (1868)	Now, I must say – I hope the noble Lord will not think I am saying anything uncivil – but I must say that his proposition appears at once grotesque and imbecile, and I think at the same time – though I do not like to use unpleasant words – that to a certain extent it must be held to be – in fact, I think the hon. Gentleman the Member for North Warwickshire hinted as much – not only very wrong, but very dishonest.
Lincoln, debate with Stephen Douglas at Ottawa (1858)	But I cannot shake Judge Douglas's teeth loose from the Dred Scott decision. Like some obstinate animal (I mean no disrespect) that will hang on when he has once got his teeth fixed, you may cut off a leg, or you may tear away an arm, still he will not relax his hold.
Julius Caesar, 3, 2	Friends, Romans, countrymen, lend me your ears; I come to bury Caesar, not to praise him.

Antony's entire speech, in which he goes on to indirectly glorify Caesar until the audience is moved to riot, is the most celebrated case of præteritio in English literature.

9. *The speaker claims to have no choice.* Strictly speaking these are not cases of præteritio, but the pattern shown here is a kindred device for expressing something while avoiding complete responsibility for it.

Lincoln, letter to David Hunter (1861)	DEAR SIR: – Yours of the 23d is received, and I am constrained to say it is difficult to answer so ugly a letter in good temper.
Burke, *Reflections on the Revolution in France* (1791)	It is impossible not to observe, that, in the spirit of this geometrical distribution, and arithmetical arrangement, these pretended citizens treat France exactly like a country of conquest.
Huxley, *The Circulation of the Blood* (1858)	I believe, to speak frankly, though perhaps not quite so politely as I could wish – but I am getting

near the end of my lecture – that the whole theory is a speculation invented by cowards to excuse
knaves.

In one popular form of this construction, the speaker
claims he is compelled by requirements of honesty to
utter something distasteful.

I don't know any other way to meet it except this.
I don't want to quarrel with him – to call him a liar;
but when I come square up to him I don't know
what else to call him if I must tell the truth out.

Lincoln, debate with
Stephen Douglas at Jones-
boro (1858)

God forbid I should insinuate anything deroga-
tory to that profession which is another priest-
hood, administering the rights of sacred justice.
But whilst I revere men in the functions which
belong to them, and would do as much as one
man can do to prevent their exclusion from any, I
cannot, to flatter them, give the lie to nature.

Burke, *Reflections on the
Revolution in France* (1791)

You will as easily believe that this affection may possibly be lessened; nay, I do assure you, contempt
will wholly eradicate it. This contempt I now
began to entertain for my husband, whom I now
discovered to be – I must use the expression – an
arrant blockhead.

Fielding, *Tom Jones* (1743)

Breaking Off in Midstream:
APOSIOPESIS

A speaker commits an *APOSIOPESIS* (ap-o-sigh-o-*pee*-sis) by breaking off a sentence and leaving it unfinished.

Beerbohm, *Zuleika Dobson* (1911)

"If you are acquainted with Miss Dobson, a direct invitation should be sent to her," said the Duke. "If you are not –" The aposiopesis was icy.

Some general purposes of the device:

a. It creates suspense and interest. Starting to speak and then stopping may tantalize the listener.

b. It can serve as a natural instrument of præteritio: the speaker stops himself, and so leaves something half-said; but saying half may be enough to make the point.

c. It creates drama. The speaker is overcome by feeling or by the inadequacy of words to the occasion; silence is a more eloquent expression of this than a statement would be. (See, e.g., sections 3 and 4 below.)

d. It may be used to create a show of discretion. The speaker starts and then stops himself in a display of restraint. (See, e.g., section 5.)

e. The aposiopesis leaves things to the imagination. An utterance goes unmade; the space is filled in by the listener. (See, e.g., sections 6 and 7.)

f. An aposiopesis gives an utterance the texture of real speech – the sound of thinking happening rather than a record of thoughts already had. The speaker stops to grope for words, to start a digression, or to think better of what he had planned to say. (A general consequence of the device, but see especially section 8.)

1. *A loss for words.* A classic occasion for an aposiopesis arises when the speaker stops to struggle for the right thing to say, with or without success. This use of the

device can be highly expressive; instead of just saying that no words will do, the speaker tries to find words and fails.

> No, you unnatural hags,
> I will have such revenges on you both
> That all the world shall – I will do such things, –
> What they are, yet I know not; but they shall be
> The terrors of the earth.

King Lear, 2, 4

> "For which I must ask you to excuse me if it was a liberty, sir; but I remember that you had taken a sort of an interest in that person, and I thought it possible that you might – just – wish – to –" Mr. Tulkinghorn is not the man to help him to any conclusion or to admit anything as to any possibility concerning himself. So Mr. Snagsby trails off into saying, with an awkward cough, "I must ask you to excuse the liberty, sir, I am sure."

Dickens, *Bleak House* (1853)

> I have always been my own master; had at least always been so, till I met Dorian Gray. Then – but I don't know how to explain it to you.

Wilde, *The Picture of Dorian Gray* (1890)

> Little Jeanne was a case, an exquisite case of education; whereas the Countess, whom it so amused him to think of by that denomination, was a case, also exquisite, of – well, he didn't know what.

James, *The Ambassadors* (1903)

2. *Incapacity*. Similarly, the speaker may use an aposiopesis when drawing back or turning away from speech in horror, or to indicate some other incapacity to continue. Again the silence may demonstrate feeling better and more theatrically than words would.

> Bear with me,
> My heart is in the coffin there with Caesar,
> And I must pause till it come back to me.

Julius Caesar, 3, 2

> In such a night
> To shut me out! Pour on; I will endure.
> In such a night as this! O Regan, Goneril!

King Lear, 3, 4

Your old kind father, whose frank heart gave all, –
O! that way madness lies; let me shun that;
No more of that.

Hamlet, 1, 2

Must I remember? Why, she would hang on him
As if increase of appetite had grown
By what it fed on; and yet, within a month –
Let me not think on't; – Frailty, thy name is
    woman!

Burke, Speech on American
Taxation (1774)

Your scheme yields no revenue; it yields nothing
but discontent, disorder, disobedience: and such is
the state of America, that, after wading up to your
eyes in blood, you could only end just where you
begun, – that is, to tax where no revenue is to be
found, to – My voice fails me: my inclination,
indeed, carries me no further; all is confusion
beyond it.

James, *The Golden Bowl*
(1904)

"And she's not the least little bit," Mrs. Assingham
observed, "your mother-in-law. In such a matter a
shade of difference is enormous. She's no relation
to you whatever, and if she's known in high quar-
ters but as going about with you, then – then – !"
She failed, however, as from positive intensity of
vision.

3. *Thinking better of it.* The speaker may change his mind
about what he had planned to say. Many of these cases
might also be considered varieties of præteritio or of
metanoia (correcting oneself – a theme considered in the
next chapter). By stopping short of naming names, for
example, the speaker may surround himself with an air of
discretion, though he more likely surrounds himself with
an air of *seeking* such an air (the really discreet speaker
would not have brought up the matter at all).

Twain, *Municipal Corruption*
(1901)

Generally speaking it was a pretty good sort of
organization, and some of the very best boys in the
village, including – but I mustn't get personal on

an occasion like this – and the society would have got along pretty well had it not been for the fact that there were a certain number of the members who could be bought.

Never have I had so sweet a teacher as in Venice. Lucia was her first name, and her second – but a gentleman forgets second names.

Conan Doyle, *How Brigadier Gerard Lost His Ear* (1903)

"Look at this!" He held up a little note with a coat-of-arms upon the envelope. "That belongs to – well, perhaps it is hardly fair to tell the name until to-morrow morning. But at that time it will be in the hands of the lady's husband."

Conan Doyle, *The Adventure of Charles Augustus Milverton* (1904)

Or the speaker may conclude that he was about to say something that would have been ill-advised or indiscreet in some other way.

But one amongst them, the one on whose account I have at all introduced this subject – yet no! let me not class the, oh! noble-minded Ann – with that order of women.

de Quincey, *Confessions of an English Opium Eater* (1821)

The present condition of England is briefly this: That no Englishman can say in public a twentieth part of what he says in private. One cannot say, for instance, that – But I am afraid I must leave out that instance, because one cannot say it. I cannot prove my case – because it is so true.

Chesterton, *A Miscellany of Men* (1912)

Nay, Veblen is not the worst. Veblen is almost the best. The worst is – but I begin to grow indignant, and indignation, as old Friedrich used to say, is foreign to my nature.

Mencken, *The Free Man* (1919)

This spirit of this last example can be extended to a more explicit avoidance of foul language. The speaker's delicacy is kept conspicuously intact, and the listener is usually capable of filling in the void.

Sheil, Speech in Seconding a Vote of Thanks to Mr. Conway (undated)	Protestants of Ireland, cease, in mercy to your priesthood, to provoke us. We are your equals in invective, and we have a vantage ground in the materials of vituperations. You know – But I will not breathe so detestable a sound. Human nature shrinks from its utterance. It would taint and pollute the moral atmosphere.
Dickens, *Nicholas Nickleby* (1839)	He called for the lady's maid, and roared for the doctor; and then, rushing into the yard, kicked the two Lincoln greens who were the most used to it, and cursing the others all round, bade them go – but never mind where. I don't know the German for it, or I would put it delicately that way.
Brontë, *Wuthering Heights* (1847)	He swore it was not, nor ever should be, mine; and he'd – but I'll not repeat his language, nor describe his habitual conduct: he is ingenious and unresting in seeking to gain my abhorrence!
Twain, letter to Hartford Gas and Electric Co. (c. 1886)	Please take your electric light and go to – but never mind, it is not for me to suggest; you will probably find the way; and any way you can reasonably count on divine assistance if you lose your bearings.

4. *Why proceed?* The speaker may stop out of courtesy, real or feigned, because more words are needless or counterproductive. The breaking off makes the listener a partner in the discourse and invites him to fill in the details, as with some cases of præteritio seen in the last chapter. The speaker may claim, for example, that the matter is already known.

DuBois, *Darkwater* (1896)	[S]he was white and the niece of an Oxford professor. *Fourthly*, the children of such a union – but why proceed? You know it all by heart.
Conan Doyle, *How the Brigadier Slew the Brothers of Ajaccio* (1896)	You may judge how far I was a favourite in those days when I say that even now, in my sixtieth year – but why should I dwell upon that which is already sufficiently well known?

Nay, though I hate to say it, there is in the portrayal
of the Duke's attitude and expression a hint of
something like mockery – unintentional, I am
sure, but to a sensitive eye discernible. And – but it
is clumsy of me to be reminding you of the very
picture I would have you forget.

Beerbohm, *Zuleika Dobson*
(1911)

Or it may be said that the matter is not worth recounting.
Such a claim leaves the details to the reader's imagination,
and often throws a gently unflattering light on them.

[A]n honourable gentleman, this moment, reminds
me of a murder committed lately in his neighbourhood; another right honourable gentleman
reminds me of a robbery in his neighbourhood,
and another of – but it were wasting your time to
go into all of them.

Grattan, speech in the Irish
Parliament (1791)

But at times some lingering sense of outraged dignity, some fitful gleams of old sympathies, "the
hectic of a moment," came back upon her, and prevailed over the deadening stupor of her grief. Then
she shone for a moment into a starry light – sweet
and woeful to remember. Then – but why linger?
I hurry to the close: she was pronounced guilty....

de Quincey, *The Household
Wreck* (1838)

The mayor, not committing himself to any opinion of the validity of the document, said that he –
but there, it is tedious to report the speeches of
mayors.

Beerbohm, *Mobled King*
(1911)

5. *Goading the audience.* A speaker may use an aposiopesis to stop half-falsely. The interruption invites the audience to plead that the concealed thing be said after all,
which it typically is. Antony's reading of Caesar's will is
in this spirit (he tells the audience that he must not read
it to them, so of course they clamor to hear it), but that
example does not involve the kind of breaking off that for-
mally marks an utterance as an aposiopesis. Here are some
cases that make more precise use of the device.

Othello, 4, 1

> OTHELLO.   What hath he said?
> IAGO. Faith, that he did – I know not what he did.
> OTHELLO. What? What?
> IAGO. Lie –
> OTHELLO. With her?
> IAGO.   With her, on her; what you will.

Trollope, *The Last Chronicle of Barset* (1867)

> "He said one thing more."
>   "And what was that?"
>   "He said – but he had no right to say it."
>   "What was it, dear?"
>   "That he knew that I loved him, and that therefore – But, mamma, do not think of that. I will never be his wife – never, in opposition to his family."

Forster, *Howards End* (1910)

> "It cannot stand without them, and I sometimes think – But I cannot expect your generation to agree, for even my daughter disagrees with me here."
>   "Never mind us or her. Do say!"
>   "I sometimes think that it is wiser to leave action and discussion to men."

6. *To punctuate an utterance.* Sometimes the aposiopesis does not signal a change of mind or direction, or a retreat from something almost said. It is simply the deliberate end of a statement, with any further words left to the listener's imagination.

Trollope, *The Eustace Diamonds* (1873)

> "Poor Lord Fawn!" continued Lady Glencora. "I suppose he is terribly in want of money."
>   "But surely Lady Eustace is very pretty."
>   "Yes; she is very pretty; nay more, she is quite lovely to look at. And she is clever, very. And she is rich, very. But – "
>   "Well, Lady Glencora. What does your 'but' mean?"
>   "Who ever explains a 'but'? You're a great deal too clever, Mme. Goesler, to want any explanation."

"If you help we may succeed. Otherwise – "

   "Otherwise – ?"

   "Otherwise," she repeated as if the word held finality.

Forster, A Room with a View (1908)

He had arrived in London this very afternoon. Depositing his luggage at an hotel, he had come straight to his club. "And now. . ." He filled up his aposiopesis with an uncouth gesture, signifying "I may as well get back to Australia."

Beerbohm, A Club in Ruins (1909)

 – My sister, I dare say, added he, does not care to let a man come so near her. . . . I will not say whether my uncle Toby had completed the sentence or not; – 'tis for his advantage to suppose he had, – as, I think, he could have added no one word which would have improved it.

   If, on the contrary, my uncle Toby had not fully arrived at the period's end – then the world stands indebted to the sudden snapping of my father's tobacco-pipe for one of the neatest examples of that ornamental figure in oratory, which rhetoricians style the aposiopesis.

Sterne, Tristram Shandy (1760)

7. *Or else*. A special case of this last usage is the aposiopesis meant to convey a threat or other ominous consequences left unsaid. It is better to leave them to the listener's imagination, where they probably will be magnified.

Does not this sound like a demand of the repeal of the Test, at the peril of those, who dare refuse it? Is it not an application with a hat in one hand, and a sword in the other, and that too, in the style of a King of Ulster, to a King of Connaught, – "Repeal the Test, or if you don't. . . ."

Swift, A Narrative of the Several Attempts, Which the Dissenters of Ireland Have Made, for the Repeal of a Sacramental Test (1731)

[S]he should tell them that she will be eventually as strong as she is miserable, and exclaim, Do me justice – rescue me from wretchedness, and from

Sheil, Speech in Vindication of the Violence of the Association (undated)

distraction – give me back my liberty – raise me to
the place I should maintain in the empire – give
me back my spoliated rights – restore me to my
violated franchises – give me back my liberty, or –
I pause upon the brink of the alternative to which
I had hurried, and, receding from it, leave it to you
to complete the sentence.

Trollope, *Barchester Towers*
(1857)

She could furnish his room for him, turn him out
as smart a bishop as any on the bench, give him
good dinners, warm fires, and an easy life; all this
she would do if he would but be quietly obedient.
But if not – ! To speak sooth, however, his sufferings on that dreadful night had been as poignant,
as to leave him little spirit for further rebellion.

Dickens made vivid use of these constructions.

Dickens, *Oliver Twist* (1838)

"He is deceiving you, my good friend."
    "I'll swear he is not," replied Mr. Brownlow,
warmly.
    "If he is not," said Mr. Grimwig, "I'll –" and
down went the stick.

Dickens, *A Tale of Two Cities*
(1859)

"Nothing that we do, is done in vain. I believe,
with all my soul, that we shall see the triumph. But
even if not, even if I knew certainly not, show me
the neck of an aristocrat and tyrant, and still I
would –"
    Then madame, with her teeth set, tied a very
terrible knot indeed.

Dickens, *Nicholas Nickleby*
(1839)

"I'll slit his nose and ears, flog him, maim him for
life. I'll do more than that; I'll drag that pattern of
chastity, that pink of prudery, the delicate sister,
through – " It might have been that even Ralph's
cold blood tingled in his cheeks at that moment.
It might have been that Sir Mulberry remembered,
that, knave and usurer as he was, he must, in some
early time of infancy, have twined his arm about

her father's neck. He stopped, and menacing with his hand, confirmed the unuttered threat with a tremendous oath.

8. *As narrative device.* The aposiopesis is a valuable tool for the storyteller. It can be used to play with the sequence of a narrative and create some suspense, as when a portion of an account is deferred to another time or teller and the listener is made to wonder what will be told and when. A typical use of this kind occurs when the speaker gets ahead of himself, and now must backtrack to tell the story properly.

> It is the most astonishing coincidence that ever – but wait. I will tell you the former instance, and then you will see it for yourself.

Twain, *Mistaken Identity* (1906)

> [T]hus treated, this Steelkilt had long been retained harmless and docile. At all events, he had proved so thus far; but Radney was doomed and made mad, and Steelkilt – but, gentlemen, you shall hear.

Melville, *Moby-Dick* (1851)

Or the teller may prefer to let others do the speaking.

> Molly had too much spirit to bear this treatment tamely. Having therefore – but hold, as we are diffident of our own abilities, let us here invite a superior power to our assistance.

Fielding, *Tom Jones* (1749)

> This daughter, Juana, was – But stop – let her open the door of the saloon in which the Senora and the cornet are conversing, and speak for herself.

de Quincey, *The Spanish Nun* (1847)

> They were mere holes, tunnels, driven into the perpendicular clay bank, then branched Y shape, within the hill. Life in Vicksburg, during the six weeks was perhaps – but wait; here are some materials out of which to reproduce it: – . . . .

Twain, *Life on the Mississippi* (1883)

9. *Confusion.* An aposiopesis may be used to depict various sorts of confusion. Interruptions are common in a

train of thought; using them in speech gives an utterance the sound of thought occurring as it spoken. (This side of aposiopesis thus again serves purposes similar to some applications of polysyndeton and metanoia.) In milder cases of this pattern, the speaker breaks off because he has strayed.

Twain, *What is Man?* (1906)

The thug is aware that loudness convinces sixty persons where reasoning convinces but one. I wouldn't be a thug, not even if – but never mind about that, it has nothing to do with the argument, and it is not noble in spirit besides.

Twain, letter to Mrs. Grover Cleveland (1887)

Just so with a funeral; if it is the man's funeral, he is most always there, of course – but that is no credit to him, he wouldn't be there if you depended on him to remember about it; whereas, if on the other hand – but I seem to have got off from my line of argument somehow; never mind about the funeral.

Using the device several times in succession suggests a more extreme confusion.

Austen, *Pride and Prejudice* (1813)

Well, that is very decided indeed – that does seem as if – but, however, it may all come to nothing, you know.

Hornung, *The Shadow of the Rope* (1906)

If Steel had been guilty – but he isn't, I tell you – no, but if he had been, just for argument, would she ever have looked – hush! – idiot and egotist! – No, but *would* she? And could you have made her happy if she had?

Fielding, *Amelia* (1751)

"Do you believe it, Mr. Booth?" replied she; "indeed you know the contrary – you must know – for you can't have forgot. No Amelia in the world can have quite obliterated – forgetfulness is not in our own power. If it was, indeed, I have reason to think – but I know not what I am saying. – Pray do proceed in that story.

I *did* remember all you said to me. It came to me always. It came to me at the very last – that was the reason why I – But now, if you cannot bear with me when I tell you everything – if you turn away from me and forsake me, what shall I do?

Eliot, *Daniel Deronda* (1876)

Correcting Oneself:
METANOIA

METANOIA (met-a-*noi*-a) means correcting oneself; the speaker is, to take the old Greek name of the device literally, changing his mind about whatever has just been said. Of course it might seem more efficient to just say the thing right the first time, but metanoia can have attractive rhetorical consequences.

a. To stop and correct oneself usually is unexpected; it slightly disrupts the flow of a piece of writing or speech. The disruption attracts attention and gives emphasis to the revised claim.

b. The device allows the speaker to say something and then take it back, thus avoiding some responsibility for the utterance while still leaving it to linger with the listener; retracting a statement does not entirely erase the experience of hearing it. In this way some cases of metanoia also amount to cases of præteritio.

c. Metanoia can have mild persuasive value. The speaker may utter a less controversial claim, then revise it to make it stronger. This brings the reader along more gently than announcing the stronger claim on its own. Or conversely the stronger claim may be offered first but then reduced to something less ambitious that seems easy to accept by comparison.

d. Metanoia, like an aposiopesis, often creates the impression that the speaker is working out his words – that he is thinking, not just repeating something already thought out and polished. Sometimes the device more specifically suggests a conflict within the speaker. Different views or impulses audibly struggle for the mastery.

e. Metanoia can create an impression of scrupulousness, as the speaker starts to say one thing but then feels obliged to take the initiative in correcting it. (It also can suggest overscrupulousness, as when the speaker fusses too much.)

1. *Metanoia to state a point more strongly.* A claim can be thrown into relief by setting it against a milder version that is repudiated.

> I believe – nay, I know – that in general our officers and soldiers are humane. But in some cases they have carried on your warfare with a mixture of American ingenuity and Castilian cruelty.

Hoar, speech in the Senate (1902)

> In spite of the ordinance of '87, a few negroes were brought into Illinois, and held in a state of quasi-slavery, not enough, however, to carry a vote of the people in favor of the institution when they came to form a constitution. But into the adjoining Missouri country, where there was no Ordinance of '87 – was no restriction – they were carried ten times, nay, a hundred times, as fast, and actually made a slave State.

Lincoln, debate with Stephen Douglas at Peoria (1854)

> I did this very gently, however, because, though the civilest, nay, the blandest and most reverential of men in the morning, yet in the afternoon he was disposed, upon provocation, to be slightly rash with his tongue, in fact, insolent.

Melville, *Bartleby the Scrivener* (1853)

The use of *nay* is a classic if archaic method for correcting a statement to make it stronger, but a variety of other constructions are available as well. The example just seen from Melville shows this; it is a double case of metanoia: *nay, the blandest* at the start and *in fact, insolent* at the end. Some other mechanisms for revising a statement to strengthen it:

> You might have heard a pin fall – a pin! a feather – as he described the cruelties inflicted on muffin boys by their masters. . . .

Dickens, *Nicholas Nickleby* (1839)

Pitt, Speech in the House of Lords (1778)

I am old and infirm. I have one foot – more than one foot – in the grave.

Byron, letter to his mother (1799)

I recommend this to you because, if some plan of this kind is not adopted, I shall be called, or rather branded with the name of a dunce, which you know I could never bear.

This pattern sometimes can be combined with anadiplosis: the same words are offered at the end of one clause and then corrected, and made stronger, in the next.

Beerbohm, *Enoch Soames* (1919)

Dignified and doddering old men, who had never consented to sit to any one, could not withstand this dynamic little stranger. He did not sue: he invited; he did not invite: he commanded.

Phillips, argument in *Guthrie v. Sterne* (1816)

I do conjure you, not as fathers, but as husbands: – not as husbands but as citizens: – not as citizens, but as men: – not as men, but as Christians: – by all your obligations, public, private, moral, and religious; by the hearth profaned; by the home desolated; by the canons of the living God foully spurned; – save, oh! save your fire-sides from the contagion. . . .

2. *To state a point less strongly*. Metanoia can withdraw force from an overstatement. Sometimes the point of this construction is to gain part of the benefit of making the strong claim despite taking it back – the use of this device that resembles præteritio.

Lincoln, speech at Republican State Convention (1856)

But slavery will endure no test of reason or logic; and yet its advocates, like Douglas, use a sort of bastard logic, or noisy assumption it might better be termed, like the above, in order to prepare the mind for the gradual, but none the less certain, encroachments of the Moloch of slavery upon the fair domain of freedom.

On other occasions the withdrawal of the strong statement is complete, but offering the strong version first makes the weaker claim sharper or more precise by contrast.

> So I went down to Quincey and took him into the breakfast room, where the blinds were not drawn down, and which was a little more cheerful, or rather less cheerless, than the other rooms.

Stoker, *Dracula* (1897)

That also is a case of *litotes*, or the double negative, which we examine in the next chapter.

> [M]y illness proved at length to be only an ague, but my apprehensions were really that I should miscarry. I should not say apprehensions, for indeed I would have been glad to miscarry, but I could never be brought to entertain so much as a thought of endeavouring to miscarry. . . .

Defoe, *Moll Flanders* (1722)

3. *To emphasize an unfavorable interpretation.* The speaker starts by using a relatively neutral word, then discards it in favor of one less flattering; the revision throws emphasis onto the new, harsher version. Setting the new statement against a milder one also may create a small sense of surprise that the new statement could not have produced on its own.

> No, we trusted to others – to one who by accepting, or rather by seizing that post, obtained the greatest place in the country, and at this moment governs England.

Disraeli, speech on the Corn Laws (1841)

> When I married Ana's mother – or perhaps, to be strictly correct, I should rather say when I at last gave in and allowed Ana's mother to marry me – I knew that I was planting thorns in my pillow, and that marriage for me, a swaggering young officer thitherto unvanquished, meant defeat and capture.

Shaw, *Man and Superman* (1903)

Beerbohm, *Enoch Soames* (1912)

And how can I write about Enoch Soames without making him ridiculous? Or rather, how am I to hush up the horrid fact that he *was* ridiculous?

4. *To state an opposite*. The speaker refers to something, but then uses metanoia to state that in fact the opposite is closer to the truth. The device attracts attention in part because it has the ring of contradiction about it; the reversal is a bit startling, and invites the reader to reflect on the difference between the first and second ways of expressing the point.

Webster, Reply to Hayne (1830)

Would any thing, with such a principle in it, or rather with such a destitution of all principle, be fit to be called a government? No, Sir.

Smith, *The Wealth of Nations* (1776)

This plan of ecclesiastical government, or, more properly, of no ecclesiastical government, was what the sect called Independents (a sect, no doubt, of very wild enthusiasts), proposed to establish in England towards the end of the civil war.

Douglass, *My Bondage and My Freedom* (1855)

I felt glad that they were released from prison, and from the dread prospect of a life (or death I should rather say) in the rice swamps.

Conan Doyle, *The Engineer's Thumb* (1892)

"And now, Doctor, perhaps you would kindly attend to my thumb, or rather to the place where my thumb used to be."

He unwound the handkerchief and held out his hand.

Reversals of good and bad are common occasions for this pattern.

Lincoln, speech at Springfield (1858)

He says this Dred Scott case is a very small matter at most – that it has no practical effect; that at best, or rather, I suppose, at worst, it is but an abstraction.

Dickens, *Capital Punishment* (1846)

Those on record are so very numerous that selection is extremely difficult; but in reference to the possibility of mistake, and the impossibility of reparation, one case is as good (I should rather say as bad) as a hundred; and if there were none but Eliza Fenning's, that would be sufficient.

Sometimes this use of metanoia can include a little play on words between the original claim and the revised one.

> [I]t had been the system of government by the sale of peerages, to raise a purse to purchase the representation, or rather the misrepresentation of the people of Ireland.

Fox, speech in the House of Commons (1797)

> The first and grand leading, or rather misleading, principle in this debate, and on which the advocates for this system of unrestricted powers must chiefly depend for its support, is that, in forming a constitution, whatever powers are not expressly granted or given the government, are reserved to the people. . . .

Tredwell, speech at New York Ratifying Convention (1788)

> As this fort will be found to give rise to important events, it may be worth while to notice that it was afterwards called Nieuw-Amstel, and was the germ of the present flourishing town of Newcastle, or, more properly speaking, No Castle, there being nothing of the kind on the premises.

Irving, *Knickerbocker's History of New York* (1809)

5. *Pointed clarification or redefinition*. The speaker stops not to make the claim more or less extreme or to reverse it, but to make it more precise or perhaps change it substantially. By mentioning each of the claims – first the superficially accurate one, then the improvement – the speaker gets the rhetorical benefits of saying both.

> Don't be offended, Ursula, but twenty-two is twenty-two, or, I should rather say, that twenty-two in a woman is more than twenty-six in a man. You are still very beautiful, but I advise you to accept the first offer that's made to you.

Borrow, *The Romany Rye* (1857)

Orwell, *Arthur Koestler* (1944)

To take a rational political decision one must have a picture of the future. At present Koestler seems to have none, or rather to have two which cancel out.

Chesterton, *The Crimes of England* (1915)

Within the iron framework of the fixed State, the German has not only liberty but anarchy. Anything can be said although, or rather because, nothing can be done.

6. *To suggest a shift in perspective.* Metanoia may be used to reverse the relationship between words or events. Such reversals can be the makings of a chiasmus, and that device is easily paired with metanoia in cases like these.

Richardson, *Clarissa* (1748)

For although I am likely to be a considerable gainer by the poor man's death, yet I cannot say that I at all love these scenes of death and the doctor so near me. The doctor and death I should have said; for that is the natural order, and generally speaking, the one is but the harbinger to the other.

Adams, *Democracy* (1880)

After these hospitalities the Grand-ducal pair came on to Washington, where they became guests of Lord Skye, or, more properly, Lord Skye became their guest, for he seemed to consider that he handed the Legation over to them. . . .

With isocolon rather than chiasmus:

Fielding, *Tom Jones* (1749)

The reader will be pleased to remember, that we left Mr. Jones, in the beginning of this book, on his road to Bristol; being determined to seek his fortune at sea, or rather, indeed, to fly away from his fortune on shore.

7. *Correction in advance of a statement.* Usually metanoia corrects a statement just made, but the correction also can come first, as when the speaker catches the mistake before it is made. Sometimes this amounts just to a way of saying a thing while saying one is not saying it – yet another variety of præteritio.

And yet every one of these, the Christian ministers
of the United States, is by this devise denied the
privileges which are at the same time open to the
vilest of our race; every one is shut out from this,
I had almost said sanctum, but I will not profane
that word by such a use of it.

Webster, argument to the
Supreme Court in the
Girard Will case (1844)

So saying, she led the way to the library, and I followed – like a criminal, I was going to say, to execution; but, as I bethink me, I have used the simile
once, if not twice before. Without any simile at all,
then, I followed, with a sense of awkward and conscious embarrassment, which I would have given a
great deal to shake off.

Scott, *Rob Roy* (1817)

In other cases the speaker really does disclaim the thing
almost said, making clear that it would go a little too far.
Suggesting that it nearly was right gains some of the benefit of saying it outright without the need to defend it in
full or accept its implications.

But if this country cannot be saved without giving
up that principle – I was about to say I would rather
be assassinated on this spot than surrender it.

Lincoln, address at Philadelphia (1861)

[A]nd if we take naturally to one another I will
know more of her and she of me at the end of
forty days (I had almost said of forty minutes) than
I knew of my mother at the end of forty years.

Shaw, *A Treatise on Parents
and Children* (1910)

Thurlow is a man of such vigour of mind that I
never knew I was to meet him, but – I was going
to tell a falsehood; I was going to say I was afraid
of him, and that would not be true, for I was never
afraid of any man – but I never knew that I was
to meet Thurlow, but I knew I had something to
encounter.

Johnson, in Boswell's *Life*
(1791)

Finally, the correction in advance can be used to vigor-
ously disavow what almost was said, and thus give the
speaker an occasion to stress the negative.

Dickens, *Nicholas Nickleby* (1839)	It was with a heavy heart that Nicholas soon afterwards – no, not retired; there was no retirement there – followed – to his dirty and crowded dormitory.
Gladstone, *The Aggrandizement of Russia* (1880)	You are – deluded I was going to say, but I could not make a greater blunder, for deluded you are not; and deluded the people of England are not, and the people of Scotland will not be, but you are flattered and inveigled by compliments paid to the existing Administration in various newspapers abroad.
Chesterton, *The Elf of Japan* (1912)	The moment in which one really loves cats is the same as that in which one (moderately and within reason) loves crocodiles. It is that divine instant when a man feels himself – no, not absorbed into the unity of all things (a loathsome fancy) – but delighting in the difference of all things.

8. *Questioning oneself.* The correction in a case of metanoia may be made less directly: the speaker can put questions to himself in soliloquy, giving the result the sound of introspection and thinking aloud.

Othello, 5, 2	If she come in, she'll sure speak to my wife. My wife, my wife! What wife? I have no wife.
Fielding, *Joseph Andrews* (1742)	No; though I despise him myself, though I would spurn him from my feet, was he to languish at them, no other should taste the happiness I scorn. Why do I say happiness? To me it would be misery.
Shelley, *Frankenstein* (1818)	Farewell, Walton! Seek happiness in tranquillity and avoid ambition, even if it be only the apparently innocent one of distinguishing yourself in science and discoveries. Yet why do I say this? I have myself been blasted in these hopes, yet another may succeed.

I should, too, call it a signal instance of democratic humanity's luck that it has such enemies to contend with – so candid, so fervid, so heroic. But why do I say enemies? Upon the whole is not Tennyson – and was not Carlyle (like an honest and stern physician) – the true friend of our age?

Whitman, *A Word About Tennyson* (1892)

During the War one felt it a duty to know the worst before breakfast; now that the English polity is threatened merely from within, one is apt to dally. . . . Merely from within? Is that a right phrase when the nerves of unrestful Labour in any one land are interplicated with its nerves in any other, so vibrantly?

Beerbohm, *Something Defeasible* (1919)

Rhetorical Uses of the Negative:
LITOTES

Litotes (*lye*-tuh-teez) occurs when a speaker avoids making an affirmative claim directly and instead denies its opposite. Often this amounts to a double negative.

Churchill, London radio broadcast (1939)

But the Royal Navy has immediately attacked the U-boats, and is hunting them night and day – I will not say without mercy, because God forbid we should ever part company with that – but at any rate with zeal and not altogether without relish.

The effect of the device depends on how it is used. It may create a sense of modesty or understatement on the one hand or of emphasis on the other, as we shall see; or it may be an aid to precision or discretion.

While all rhetorical figures may be overused, litotes is among those that pose the greatest risk of this kind. Gowers said that "There are occasions when a writer's meaning may be conveyed more exactly by (say) *not unkindly*, *not unnaturally* or *not unjustifiably*. But the 'not un-' habit is liable to take charge, with disastrous effects, making the victim forget all straightforward adjectives and adverbs." (*The Complete Plain Words*, 1948). In the event that the device does take over, Orwell advised that "One can cure oneself of the not un- formation by memorizing this sentence: *A not unblack dog was chasing a not unsmall rabbit across a not ungreen field.*" (*Politics and the English Language*, 1946). In this chapter we will try to focus on the reputable uses of the device. We also will look briefly at two other rhetorically interesting uses of the negative: as an aid to definition and as a source of paradox.

1. *Literal accuracy.* A primitive complaint about the double negative holds it, like metanoia, to be inefficient: whatever one is trying to say, why not say it in the shorter

and more direct affirmative form? But of course two negatives do not necessarily amount to an affirmative claim, even literally. Intermediate possibilities can lie between them, in which case the double negative may be more precisely accurate.

> Thus I consent, sir, to this Constitution, because I expect no better, and because I am not sure that it is not the best.

Franklin, speech at Federal Ratifying Convention (1787)

> Men whom one met in Washington were not unhappy about the state of things, as I had seen men unhappy in the North and in the West.

Trollope, *North America* (1862)

> She says the Prince of Denmark is not so tall as his bride, but far from a bad figure: he is thin, and not ugly, except having too wide a mouth.

Walpole, letter to Horace Mann (1743)

For Franklin to say he is sure that the Constitution *is* the best, or for Trollope to say that men in Washington were *happy* about the state of things, or for the Prince to be described as attractive, would have been too strong. *Not unhappy*, or a comparable double negative, is the most that the speaker can offer. Or again:

> She was not quite what you would call refined. She was not quite what you would call unrefined. She was the kind of person that keeps a parrot.

Twain, *Following the Equator* (1897)

2. *Contrast.* Even where the literal meaning of a claim can be duplicated, or nearly so, with affirmative words, the speaker may use litotes to pointedly disavow a negative possibility.

> A physician being mentioned who had lost his practice, because his whimsically changing his religion had made people distrustful of him, I maintained that this was unreasonable, as religion is unconnected with medical skill. Johnson. "Sir, it is not unreasonable; for when people see a man absurd in what they understand, they may conclude the same of him in what they do not understand."

Boswell, *Life of Johnson* (1791)

Not unreasonable, rather than *reasonable,* is an apt way to speak here, because Johnson is refuting Boswell's claim.

Or negative claims may have been made about one thing, but now, by way of comparison, should be denied about another:

Burke, *Reflections on the Revolution in France* (1791)

All things in this his fulminating bull are not of so innoxious a tendency.

Macaulay, *The History of England* (1861)

In his youth, however, though too imbecile for study or for business, he was not incapable of being amused.

Schurz, speech in the Senate (1872)

Sir, such appeals as these, which we have heard so frequently, may be well apt to tickle the ear of an unthinking multitude. But unless I am grievously in error, the people of the United States are a multitude not unthinking.

The pattern also can be reversed: the double negative forms a contrast not with what has just been said, but with what is about to come.

Twain, *A Tramp Abroad* (1880)

These are not unpleasant subjects; they are not uninteresting subjects; they are even exciting subjects – until one of these massive scientists gets hold of them. He soon convinces you that even these matters can be handled in such a way as to make a person low-spirited.

3. *Against expectations.* The double negative likewise may be justified when set against the assumptions of the speaker or audience: one might have expected the negative under the circumstances shown, but it isn't so.

Trollope, *He Knew He Was Right* (1869)

There be men, and not bad men either, and men neither uneducated, or unintelligent, or irrational in ordinary matters, who seem to be absolutely unfitted by nature to have the custody or guardianship of others.

[M]ost of the wretches whose crimes have so shocked humanity in recent years were men not unlettered, who have gone from the common schools, through murder to the scaffold.

Hay, tribute to McKinley (1903)

[H]e still drew prison rations, the sole and not unwelcome reminder of his chains, and, I believe, looked forward to the date of his enfranchisement with mere alarm.

Stevenson, *In the South Seas* (1896)

What is best let alone, that accursed thing is not always what least allures.

Melville, *Moby-Dick* (1851)

4. *Understatement*. The double negative is a useful tool for indicating small amounts, for making a show of modesty, or for creating a tone of allowance. The first example here is familiar from an earlier chapter:

This pulpit style, revived after so long a discontinuance, had to me the air of novelty, and of a novelty not wholly without danger.

Burke, *Reflections on the Revolution in France* (1791)

It will then be answered, not without a sneer, And what would you prefer?

Chesterton, *What's Wrong with the World* (1910)

"You'll be quite safe now," the curate was saying in the adjoining room, not without a touch of complacent self-approval such as becomes the victor in a battle of wits.

Wodehouse, *A Damsel in Distress* (1919)

The same idea can be used to create a mood of fairness and partial concession in describing the claims of others.

Historic Christianity was accused, not entirely without reason, of carrying martyrdom and asceticism to a point, desolate and pessimistic.

Chesterton, *Orthodoxy* (1908)

[W]e find from all the eminent men of the time the clearest expression of their opinion that slavery is an evil. They ascribed its existence here, not without truth, and not without some acerbity of

Webster, speech in the Senate (1850)

temper and force of language, to the injurious policy of the mother country, who, to favor the navigator, had entailed these evils upon the Colonies.

Litotes as a means of understatement also is useful for administering faint or diffident praise.

Fielding, *Tom Jones* (1749)

He was not ungenteel, nor entirely devoid of wit, and in his youth had abounded in sprightliness, which, though he had lately put on a more serious character, he could, when he pleased, resume.

Gibbon, *Memoirs* (1796)

In the Automathes I cannot praise either the depth of thought or elegance of style; but the book is not devoid of entertainment or instruction. . . .

Gibbon, *History of the Decline and Fall of the Roman Empire* (1776)

By each of his concubines, the younger Gordian left three or four children. His literary productions, though less numerous, were by no means contemptible.

By no means contemptible is a mild case of our current pattern. It is a denial of a negative state rather than the assertion of a positive one.

5. *As an aid to discretion*. A double negative may be a helpful substitute for a direct admission when directness would be indiscreet. The substance of the admission is put across anyway; the negatives just acknowledge that the facts may be an occasion for apology, embarrassment, or at least modesty.

Holmes, *The Poet at the Breakfast Table* (1872)

We had gone, not to scoff, but very probably to smile, and I will not say we did not.

Beerbohm, *James Pethel* (1919)

I was shocked this morning when I saw in my newspaper a paragraph announcing his sudden death. I do not say that the shock was very disagreeable.

Stevenson, *New Arabian Nights* (1882)

It was not without satisfaction that I recognised my own handiwork in a great cut under his right eye, and a considerable discolouration round the socket.

At this time she was very close to him, and though her words were severe, the glance from her eyes was soft. And the scent from her hair was not objectionable to him as it would have been to Miss Stanbury. And the mode of her head-dress was not displeasing to him.

Trollope, *He Knew He Was Right* (1869)

6. *The double negative to emphasize the affirmative*, as when the speaker means to dispel any suspicion that the size of the thing under discussion has a negative quality.

And out of them shall proceed thanksgiving and the voice of them that make merry: and I will multiply them, and they shall not be few; I will also glorify them, and they shall not be small.

Jeremiah 30:19

Many other observations might be made on this subject, but I cannot now pursue them; for I feel myself not a little exhausted.

Hamilton, speech at New York Ratifying Convention (1788)

I have already been bored more than enough about it; not the least of which annoyance is his cursed, unreadable, and ungodly handwriting.

Lincoln, letter to William Herndon (1848)

It is no inconsiderable part of wisdom, to know how much of an evil ought to be tolerated. . . .

Burke, *Thoughts on the Cause of the Present Discontents* (1770)

7. *Definition by negatives*. We now turn briefly to two other rhetorical uses of the negative, starting with its use as an aid to definition or as a basis for comparison. The force of a claim may be made more vivid by denying that it can be exceeded in various picturesque ways.

What wouldst thou beg, Laertes,
That shall not be my offer, not thy asking?
The head is not more native to the heart,
The hand more instrumental to the mouth,
Than is the throne of Denmark to thy father.

Hamlet, 1, 2

Never did hermit or saint condemn himself to solitude more consciously than Congress and

Adams, *History of the United States* (1891)

the Executive in removing the government from Philadelphia to Washington. . . .

Fielding, *Tom Jones* (1749)

Vice hath not, I believe, a more abject slave; society produces not a more odious vermin; nor can the devil receive a guest more worthy of him, nor possibly more welcome to him, than a slanderer.

Or the claim may be that other extreme instances of a phenomenon are weaker than the present one.

Congreve, *The Mourning Bride*, 3, 8 (1697)

Heaven has no rage, like love to hatred turned
Nor hell a fury, like a woman scorned.

Dickens, *A Christmas Carol* (1843)

No change, no degradation, no perversion of humanity, in any grade, through all the mysteries of wonderful creation, has monsters half so horrible and dread.

Melville, *Moby-Dick* (1851)

Had these Leviathans been but a flock of simple sheep, pursued over the pasture by three fierce wolves, they could not possibly have evinced such excessive dismay.

8. *Paradoxical denials*, in which a thing is named and the name is then contradicted.

a. *The thing unworthy of its name.*

Burke, Speech on a Bill for Shortening the Duration of Parliaments (1780)

But an House of Commons without power and without dignity, either in itself or its members, is no House of Commons for the purposes of this Constitution.

Melville, *Moby-Dick* (1851)

In a word, Frederick Cuvier's Sperm Whale is not a Sperm Whale, but a squash.

Chesterton, *The Sentimental Scot* (1912)

Our scientific civilisation is not a civilisation; it is a smoke nuisance.

This construction can be used to create lively comparisons. One thing deserves its name and the other does not – a favorite pattern of Chesterton's.

The real difference between the test of happiness and the test of will is simply that the test of happiness is a test and the other isn't.

Chesterton, *Orthodoxy* (1908)

But Grimm's Law is far less intellectual than Grimm's Fairy Tales. The tales are, at any rate, certainly tales; while the law is not a law.

Chesterton, *Orthodoxy* (1908)

[W]hen you find (as you often do) three young cads and idiots going about together and getting drunk together every day you generally find that one of the three cads and idiots is (for some extraordinary reason) not a cad and not an idiot.

Chesterton, *The Diabolist* (1909)

b. *The exception that swallows the rule.*

As a writer he has mastered everything except language: as a novelist he can do everything, except tell a story: as an artist he is everything except articulate.

Wilde, *The Decay of Lying* (1889)

Everything is ugly and discreditable, except the facts; everything is wrong about him, except that he has done no wrong.

Chesterton, *Manalive* (1912)

Carlyle understood everything about the French Revolution, except that it was a French revolution.

Chesterton, *The Crimes of England* (1915)

c. *The simple paradox.*

Lord Henry Somerset has too much heart and too little art to make a good poet, and such art as he does possess is devoid of almost every intellectual quality and entirely lacking in any intellectual strength. He has nothing to say and says it.

Wilde, *The Poet's Corner* (1889)

The golden rule is that there are no golden rules.

Shaw, *Maxims for Revolutionists* (1903)

Rhetorical Questions:

EROTEMA

A rhetorical question – known anciently as a case of EROTEMA (e-ro-*tem*-a), or sometimes as EROTESIS – is a question that does not call for a reply.

Sterne, *Tristram Shandy* (1760)

[I]n the midst of a dispute on the subject, in which, by the bye, he was frequently involved, – he would sometimes break off in a sudden and spirited Epiphonema, or rather Erotesis, raised a third, and sometimes a full fifth above the key of the discourse, – and demand it categorically of his antagonist, Whether he would take upon him to say, he had ever remembered, – whether he had ever read, – or even whether he had ever heard tell of a man, called Tristram, performing any thing great or worth recording?

Usually a rhetorical question implies its own answer. In other cases the speaker expects that no good answer is possible, or wants to make a statement indirectly by burying it in the question's premise. A famous rhetorical question of the last variety was put to Sen. Joseph McCarthy by Joseph Welch in the Senate hearings of 1954: *Have you no sense of decency, sir, at long last? Have you left no sense of decency?* In a moment we will consider specific types of rhetorical questions and occasions for them in more detail, but here, first, are some general purposes served by the device.

a. Although the rhetorical question does not invite a reply, the direct appeal it makes to the listener does create a kind of involvement between speaker and audience, with resulting gains in presence and liveliness.

b. The rhetorical question may be used to express a

high pitch of incredulity or passion. If the question is a departure from the declarative tone of what has come before, it may serve as an outburst similar in effect to an exclamation.

c. By asking a rhetorical question the speaker may call on the listener to help complete a point and to share responsibility for it.

d. The open assertion of a point typically carries with it an implied burden of proof; the reader wonders what basis the speaker has for it. Stating the point as a rhetorical question can shift the burden. Now the speaker does not directly insist on a claim, but impliedly dares the listener to say it is false (and, if this cannot be said, to accept that it is true). Or the question may be a gentler appeal to shared understandings, which again reduces the pressure to support the point with conventional evidence or argument.

1. *To convey incredulity.* The rhetorical question may be used to heap derision on its subject or challenge the listener by asking whether something so dreadful or ridiculous can possibly be the case.

> Alas! are those people who call themselves Englishmen, of so little internal consequence, that when America is gone, or shuts her eyes upon them, their sun is set, they can shine no more, but grope about in obscurity, and contract into insignificant animals?

Paine, *The American Crisis* (1783)

> Did we brave all then to falter now – now, when that same enemy is wavering, dissevered, and belligerent?

Lincoln, debate with Stephen Douglas at Springfield (1858)

> Is this, sir, a government for freemen? Are we thus to be duped out of our liberties?

Tredwell, speech at New York Ratifying Convention (1788)

A question of this kind may be used to challenge a doubtful version of events.

Melville, *The Confidence-Man*
(1857)

For I put it to you, is it reasonable to suppose that a man with brains, sufficient to act such a part as you say, would take all that trouble, and run all that hazard, for the mere sake of those few paltry coppers, which, I hear, was all he got for his pains, if pains they were?

This sort of rhetorical question also may be usefully set up with a preamble. The facts are arranged in advance to make the question an easy one.

Harrison, speech at New
York Ratifying Convention
(1788)

We may suppose two of the most enlightened and eminent men in the state, in whom the confidence of the legislature and the love of the people are united, engaged, at the expiration of their office, in the most important negotiations, in which their presence and agency may be indispensable. In this emergency, shall we incapacitate them?

2. *Who will say otherwise?* A rhetorical question may be used to suggest that everyone knows the truth of what the speaker means to assert, or that no one would say otherwise. As noted at the start of this chapter, this type of question partly amounts to a strategy of proof. Instead of offering argument or facts, the speaker relies on the actual or posited unanimity of the audience; a debate over the merits of the claim is turned into a debate about whether anyone can be found to gainsay it. The appeal to what everybody knows also may enlist the listener as an ally who has had the same experience as the speaker.

Hamilton, speech at New
York Ratifying Convention
(1788)

We contend that the radical vice in the old Confederation is, that the laws of the Union apply only to states in their corporate capacity. Has not every man who has been in our legislature experienced the truth of this position?

Lincoln, speech at Columbus
(1859)

Take these two things and consider them together, present the question of planting a State with the institution of slavery by the side of a question who shall be Governor of Kansas for a year or two, and is there a man here, is there a man on earth, who would not say the governor question is the little one, and the slavery question is the great one?

Of ten thousand people who get drunk, is there one who could say with truth that he did so because he had been brought to think on full deliberation and after free discussion that it was wise to get drunk?

Stephen, *Liberty, Equality, Fraternity* (1873)

It may bring other gifts, but is there a single Londoner to whom Christmas is peaceful? The craving for excitement and for elaboration has ruined that blessing.

Forster, *Howards End* (1910)

Who would not have jumped for joy, in 1940, at the thought of seeing S.S. officers kicked and humiliated? But when the thing becomes possible, it is merely pathetic and disgusting.

Orwell, *Revenge Is Sour* (1945)

A dash of pressure can be added – or perhaps a bit of intimidation – by asking if anyone dares to say or try that which the speaker claims cannot be said or tried, or to unfavorably characterize in advance anyone who might rise to the challenge.

We have tried anodynes. We have tried cruel operations. What are we to try now? Who flatters himself that he can turn this feeling back?

Macaulay, speech in the House of Commons (1831)

The articles here are anonymous. Who writes? – who causes to be written? Who but an ass will put faith in tirades which may be the result of personal hostility, or in panegyrics which nine times out of ten may be laid, directly or indirectly, to the charge of the author himself?

Poe, *The Quacks of Helicon* (1850)

But, sir, who will presume to say to what precise point the representation ought to be increased?

Hamilton, speech at New York Ratifying Convention (1788)

3. *Mental challenges.* The examples in the last entry amounted to challenges of a certain kind: anyone who disagreed was defied to come forward. The rhetorical question also can issue a challenge to the *mind* of the listener.

a. *Is there anything worse?* Thus the question may defy the listener to think of anything worse than what the speaker describes. It is much like asking if anyone present will disagree, but here the challenge is more formidable because it cannot be met just by speaking up; it can be met only with an example. If the question is taken seriously it causes the listener to pause and search for an answer among terrible things, and then the game is largely won; for even if the answer is found, the speaker has succeeded in putting the subject into bad company.

Webster, argument in the murder trial of John Francis Knapp (1830)	Have you ever read or known of folly equal to this? Can you conceive of crime more odious and abominable?
Webster, speech in the House of Representatives (1824)	Look at Spain, and at Greece. If men may not resist the Spanish Inquisition, and the Turkish cimeter, what is there to which humanity must not submit? Stronger cases can never arise.
Sheil, speech in the House of Commons (1837)	He will, however, pardon me for suggesting to him, that, if I did assail him with far more acrimony than I am disposed to do, he is the last man in this house who ought to complain. Who is there that shows less mercy to a political adversary? Who is so relentless in the infliction of his sarcasms, even on his old friends and associates?

b. *Can one example be named?* Or instead of calling for a comparison, the speaker may suggest that a set is empty and defy the listener to fill it.

Fielding, *Joseph Andrews* (1742)	Thou odious, deformed monster! whom priests have railed at, philosophers despised, and poets ridiculed; is there a wretch so abandoned as to own thee for an acquaintance in public?

Sir, is there a people under heaven, who, countenanced and imboldened by the voice of their state legislatures, will ever pay a farthing of such a tax? They will resist it as they would a foreign tribute, or the invasion of an enemy.

Livingston, speech at New York Ratifying Convention (1788)

It is ascertained, by history, that there never was a government over a very extensive country without destroying the liberties of the people: history also, supported by the opinions of the best writers, shows us that monarchy may suit a large territory, and despotic governments ever so extensive a country, but that popular governments can only exist in small territories. Is there a single example, on the face of the earth, to support a contrary opinion?

Mason, speech at Virginia Ratifying Convention (1788)

4. *Who but, etc.* The *who but* and *what but* forms allow the speaker to issue a challenge of another kind: instead of being stated directly, claim *x* is offered as the only plausible answer to a question; the listener is free to try to think up some other answer, but the prospect sounds daunting.

Who but an atheist could think of leaving the world without having first made up his account?

Fielding, *Tom Jones* (1749)

Such are the Cornishmen; but who are you? who, but the unauthorised and lawless children of intruders, invaders, and oppressors? who, but the transmitters of wrong, the inheritors of robbery?

Johnson, *Taxation No Tyranny* (1775)

Is not the state of Rhode Island, at this moment, struggling under difficulties and distresses, for having been led blindly by the spirit of the multitude? What is her legislature but the picture of a mob?

Hamilton, speech at New York Ratifying Convention (1788)

[T]o introduce a system of representation which must inevitably render all discipline impossible, what is it but madness – the madness of ignorant vanity, and reckless obstinacy?

Coleridge, *Table Talk* (1831)

Here is a case where the constructions just shown are mixed and serve as a little motif:

Curran, argument in suit of Charles Massy against the Marquis of Headfort (1804)

From whom, but a man hackneyed in the paths of shame and vice – from whom, but from a man having no compunctions in his own breast to restrain him, could you expect such a brutal disregard for the feelings of others – from whom, but the cold-blooded veteran seducer – from what but from the exhausted mind – the habitual community with shame – from what, but the habitual contempt of virtue and of man, could you have expected the arrogance, the barbarity, and folly of so foul – because so false an imputation?

5. *Is it not, etc.* The *is it not* construction softens a point by inviting the listener to agree with it. This sort of rhetorical question proposes an alliance with the listener rather than confronting or challenging him.

Hamilton, speech at New York Ratifying Convention (1788)

Thus, on the gentleman's scheme, they will be almost free from burdens, while we shall be loaded with them. Does not the partiality of this strike every one? Can gentlemen, who are laboring for the interest of their state, seriously bring forward such propositions?

Cobden, speech at London (1850)

I really pity the mendicant Czar who is obliged to come to us with such a story. Is it not humiliating?

Melville, *Moby-Dick* (1851)

Consider all this; and then turn to this green, gentle, and most docile earth; consider them both, the sea and the land; and do you not find a strange analogy to something in yourself?

Stevenson, letter to Maud Babington (1871)

I have possessed myself of Mrs. Hutchinson, which, of course, I admire, etc. But is there not an irritating deliberation and correctness about her and everybody connected with her?

Constructions of this kind may be used in serial.

We live the time that a match flickers; we pop the cork of a ginger-beer bottle, and the earthquake swallows us on the instant. Is it not odd, is it not incongruous, is it not, in the highest sense of human speech, incredible, that we should think so highly of the ginger-beer, and regard so little the devouring earthquake?

Stevenson, *Aes Triplex* (1878)

Do not the pride, superciliousness, and selfishness of a certain aristocracy make it all the more regarded by its worshippers? and do not the clownish and gutter-blood admirers of Mr. Flamson like him all the more because they are conscious that he is a knave? If such is the case – and, alas! is it not the case? – they cannot be too frequently told that fine clothes, wealth, and titles adorn a person in proportion as he adorns them. . . .

Borrow, *The Romany Rye* (1857)

6. *If . . . why?* Rhetorical questions can be used to probe the logic and implications of a claim. If x is true, then why isn't y true? (And z, and. . .) Usually the point is to show the logical failure of x.

If I desired to kill the senator why did I not do it? You all admit that I had him in my power. It was expressly to avoid taking life that I used an ordinary cane. . . .

Brooks, speech in the House of Representatives in defense of his attack on Charles Sumner (1856)

This is mere desperation. If they had no connection, why are they always spoken of in connection? Why has he so spoken of them a thousand times? Why has he constantly called them a series of measures? Why does everybody call them a compromise? Why was California kept out of the Union six or seven months, if it was not because of its connection with the other measures?

Lincoln, debate with Stephen Douglas at Peoria (1854)

The *if . . . why* construction also can be used to make conceptual or forward-looking arguments: if we are to do x, why not y? The pattern is useful for arguments by *reductio ad absurdum*.

Plunket, speech in the
House of Commons (1821)

Again, if religion is to be an affair of state, why not require some positive profession of faith as a qualification? Such as that he is a Christian, or that he believes in God, or in a future state, or that he has an immortal soul? Why does the declaration sound only in horror, and antipathy, and denunciation of another religion? If the law is to be put into a state of electricity by the Church, why not of positive electricity? Again; if we are to denounce, why denounce only one particular sect of Christians? Why not Socinians? Why not those who deny the divine nature of our Lord? Why select those who believe all that we do, merely because they believe something more? Why not Jews, Mohammedans, Pagans?

7. *Begging the question*. Sometimes the premise of a rhetorical question contains more controversial matter than the question itself. Embedding the incendiary claim in the premise makes it sound secure, since it serves as a basis for the question and seems to be taken for granted. This construction also calls the direct attention of the audience away from the underlying claim and toward the question about it, which typically is unanswerable. The line from the Army-McCarthy hearings mentioned at the start of this chapter probably fits best under this heading. Here are a few others in the same genre.

Henry, speech at the Second
Revolutionary Congress of
Virginia (1775)

Why stand we here idle? What is it that gentlemen wish? What would they have? Is life so dear, or peace so sweet, as to be purchased at the price of chains and slavery? Forbid it, Almighty God! I know not what course others may take; but as for me, give me liberty or give me death!

Paine, *The American Crisis*
(1783)

Has not the name of Englishman blots enough upon it, without inventing more?

Burke, argument in the
impeachment of Warren
Hastings (1788)

Will your lordships submit to hear the corrupt practices of mankind made the principles of government?

Where slumbers the public morality of England?

Sullivan, speech in the House of Commons (1879)

With irony:

> I cannot help asking, Why all these pains to clear the British nation of ambition, perfidy, and the insatiate thirst of war? At what period of time was it that our country has deserved that load of infamy of which nothing but preternatural humiliation in language and conduct can serve to clear us?

Burke, *Letter on the Proposals for Peace with the Regicide Directory of France* (1797)

8. *The onslaught.*

a. *Generally.* A string of rhetorical questions is a fine vehicle for suggesting a fever of indignation or a high pitch of forensic energy.

> PANDULPH. Courage and comfort! All shall yet go
>   well.
> KING PHILIP. What can go well, when we have
>   run so ill?
> Are we not beaten? Is not Angiers lost?
> Arthur ta'en prisoner? Divers dear friends slain?
> And bloody England into England gone,
> O'erbearing interruption, spite of France?

King John, 3, 4

> Can there be a more mortifying insult? Can even our ministers sustain a more humiliating disgrace? Do they dare to resent it? Do they presume even to hint a vindication of their honor, and the dignity of the State, by requiring the dismission of the plenipotentiaries of America?

Pitt, speech in the House of Commons (1777)

For the fullest effect of this kind, a half dozen questions or more may be indicated.

> He says, Let requisitions precede coercion. Sir, what are these requisitions? What are these pompous petitions for public charity, which have made so much noise, and brought so little cash into the treasury? Have we not sported with the bubble long enough to discover its emptiness? What have

Livingston, speech at New York Ratifying Convention (1788)

requisitions done? Have they paid off our foreign and domestic debts? Have they supported our civil and small military establishments?

Dickens, *Nicholas Nickleby* (1839)

"Wasn't it so!" repeated Sir Mulberry. "How would you have had it? How could we have got a general invitation at first sight – come when you like, go when you like, stop as long as you like, do what you like – if you, the lord, had not made yourself agreeable to the foolish mistress of the house? Do I care for this girl, except as your friend? Haven't I been sounding your praises in her ears, and bearing her pretty sulks and peevishness all night for you? What sort of stuff do you think I'm made of? Would I do this for every man? Don't I deserve even gratitude in return?"

Lincoln, speech at Peoria (1858)

I go against the repeal of the Missouri Compromise; did they ever go for it? They went for the Compromise of 1850; did I ever go against them? They were greatly devoted to the Union; to the small measure of my ability was I ever less so? Clay and Webster were dead before this question arose; by what authority shall our Senator say they would espouse his side of it if alive? Mr. Clay was the leading spirit in making the Missouri Compromise; is it very credible that if now alive he would take the lead in the breaking of it?

There can be something airy about rhetorical questions, especially when strung together in a series. That tendency is relieved, and some pleasures of variety are gained, when the questions dip into particulars that are concrete and easy to picture.

Livingston, speech at New York Ratifying Convention (1788)

I am not interested in defending rich men: but what does he mean by telling us that the rich are vicious and intemperate? Will he presume to point out to us the class of men in which intemperance is not to be found? Is there less intemperance in feeding on beef than on turtle? or in drinking rum than wine?

This is fine reasoning. To what shall I compare it? Shall I liken it to children in the market-place, or shall I liken it to children making bubbles with a pipe? Shall I not rather compare it to two boys upon a balanced board? One goes up, the other down; and so they go up and down, down and up, till the sport is over, and the board is left exactly on the balance in which they found it.

Livingston, speech at New York Ratifying Convention (1788)

And I am sorry to say that this pamphlet of progressive religious views is full of baffling observations of that kind. What can people mean when they say that science has disturbed their view of sin? What sort of view of sin can they have had before science disturbed it? Did they think that it was something to eat? When people say that science has shaken their faith in immortality, what do they mean? Did they think that immortality was a gas?

Chesterton, *Science and Religion* (1915)

Why do we choose one word more than another if there isn't any difference between them? If you called a woman a chimpanzee instead of an angel, wouldn't there be a quarrel about a word? If you're not going to argue about words, what are you going to argue about?

Chesterton, *The Ball and the Cross* (1910)

9. *Sarcasm*. A succession of questions is useful for a sarcastic or otherwise ironic review of an adversary's position and its implications.

They tell us, sir, that we are weak – unable to cope with so formidable an adversary. But when shall we be stronger? Will it be the next week, or the next year? Will it be when we are totally disarmed, and when a British guard shall be stationed in every house?

Henry, speech at Second Revolutionary Congress of Virginia (1775)

Henry, speech at Virginia
Ratifying Convention
(1788)

A bill of rights may be summed up in a few words. What do they tell us? – That our rights are reserved. Why not say so? Is it because it will consume too much paper?

Macaulay, *Southey's Colloquies*
(1830)

Can Mr. Southey select any family, any profession, any class, in short, distinguished by any plain badge from the rest of the community, whose opinion is more likely to be just than this much abused public opinion? Would he choose the peers, for example? Or the two hundred tallest men in the country? Or the poor Knights of Windsor? Or children who are born with cauls? Or the seventh sons of seventh sons? We cannot suppose that he would recommend popular election; for that is merely an appeal to public opinion.

Dickens, *Nicholas Nickleby*
(1839)

"No," replied Squeers. "We call it a Hall up in London, because it sounds better, but they don't know it by that name in these parts. A man may call his house an island if he likes; there's no act of Parliament against that, I believe?"

10. *With repetition of words.* A string of rhetorical questions can be combined to good effect with some devices treated earlier in this book. A series of questions may, for example, lend themselves to anaphora, or repetition of words at the start of consecutive sentences.

Wilberforce, speech in the
House of Commons (1789)

What if I should be able to show this House that in a civilized part of Europe, in the time of our Henry VII, there were people who actually sold their own children? What if I should tell them that England itself was that country? What if I should point out to them that the very place where this inhuman traffic was carried on was the city of Bristol?

Emerson, *Self-Reliance*
(1841)

If I know your sect, I anticipate your argument. I hear a preacher announce for his text and topic the expediency of one of the institutions of his

church. Do I not know beforehand that not possibly can he say a new and spontaneous word? Do
I not know that with all this ostentation of exam-
ining the grounds of the institution he will do no
such thing? Do I not know that he is pledged to
himself not to look but at one side, the permitted
side, not as a man, but as a parish minister?

These speeches of his, sown broadcast over the
land, what clear distinct meaning have they? Are
they not intended for disorganization in our very
midst? Are they not intended to dull our weapons?
Are they not intended to destroy our zeal? Are they
not intended to animate our enemies? Sir, are they
not words of brilliant polished treason?

Baker, speech in the Senate
(1861)

With epistrophe (repetition at the end), as well as a bit of
symploce:

What! no capital! Is my mastery of Greek no capital?
Is my access to the subtlest thought, the loftiest
poetry yet attained by humanity, no capital? my
character! my intellect! my life! my career! what
Barbara calls my soul! are these no capital?

Shaw, *Major Barbara* (1907)

This example also makes use of isocolon and the oscillation discussed at the end of the chapter on that subject.

Asking Questions and Answering Them:
HYPOPHORA

Anticipating Objections and Meeting Them:
PROLEPSIS

HYPOPHORA – accent on the second syllable; it sounds like *hypothesis*, not like *hypodermic* – occurs when the speaker asks a question and answers it. PROLEPSIS occurs when the speaker anticipates an objection (not necessarily a question) and comments on it. We treat the two devices in the same chapter because they sometimes sound alike and serve similar purposes. Here is a distinguished example of hypophora from Churchill:

Churchill, speech in the House of Commons (1940)

You ask, what is our policy? I can say: It is to wage war, by sea, land, and air, with all our might and with all the strength that God can give us; to wage war against a monstrous tyranny, never surpassed in the dark and lamentable catalogue of human crime. That is our policy. You ask, what is our aim? I can answer in one word: It is victory. Victory at all costs, victory in spite of all terrors, victory, however long and hard the road may be; for without victory there is no survival.

Some purposes of hypophora (and, often, prolepsis):

a. Hypophora may heighten interest by creating a moment of suspense. The speaker offers a little mystery, asking a question that the listener cannot answer, at least not readily; then it is solved.

b. The speaker's question may supply a motive for offering the answer, and so provide an excuse for what is said next; the speaker does not make a statement gratuitously, but merely answers a question, whether actually asked or anticipated from the audience.

c. Like the rhetorical question, hypophora creates a bit of involvement with the listener. It may not be quite clear where the question comes from, but it often seems asked partly on the listener's behalf, and in any event it invites the listener to spend a bit of thought in trying to answer it. But the speaker retains control of the discourse by supplying the answer.

d. Hypophora also can create a sense of empathy and alliance between speaker and listener if the speaker accurately describes the questions on the listener's mind, or raises questions the listener recognizes as important.

e. Hypophora may create a disarming impression that the speaker is dealing with objections openly.

f. The impressions described above – of moderation, of open-handedness, etc. – may or may not be accurate; an advantage of hypophora is that the speaker picks the questions to be answered, and in fact they may not be the ones the listener would most like to have addressed. The same is true when the speaker addresses an objection he has described without stating it as a question – where, in other words, he employs prolepsis rather than hypophora. The speaker gets to decide how the objection ought to be described in order to make the reply fully effective.

g. Asking questions and answering them may pre-empt a more forceful statement of objections from an adversary.

1. *Why? Because* –. We begin at the top of the list just shown: with hypophora to create a brief worry or mystery that is speedily dispelled. The question need not be on anyone else's mind; it just sets up the statement to come by furnishing a motive for uttering it. In effect the question raises the hammer so that it may be brought down hard, with the answer often stated as an exclamation.

> There was scarce a word he uttered that was not a violation of the privileges of the House; but I did not call him to order – why? because the limited talents of some men render it impossible for them to be severe without being unparliamentary. But

Grattan, *Invective Against Corry* (1800)

before I sit down I shall show him how to be severe and parliamentary at the same time.

Hazlitt, *On People with One Idea* (1821)

He put his metaphysics, his bamboo manuscript, into the boat with him, and as he floated down the Ganges, said to himself, "If I live, this will live; if I die, it will not be heard of." What is fame to this feeling? The babbling of an idiot!

Borrow, *The Bible in Spain* (1842)

[B]ut I could not command myself when I heard my own glorious land traduced in this unmerited manner. By whom? A Portuguese! A native of a country which has been twice liberated from horrid and detestable thraldom by the hands of Englishmen.

Dickens, *Hard Times* (1854)

[A]nd now, I say, my friends, what appellation has that dastard craven taken to himself, when, with the mask torn from his features, he stands before us in all his native deformity, a What? A thief! A plunderer! A proscribed fugitive, with a price upon his head; a fester and a wound upon the noble character of the Coketown operative!

The doublet:

Grattan, speech in the Irish Parliament (1797)

[A]nd yet with all this superiority of force, and such publicity of the destination of the French fleet, our coasts had been left for sixteen days at the mercy of its enemy! Where was the British navy during this period? Absent. To what had our defence been committed? To the wind.

Shaw, *Man and Superman* (1903)

Oh, I protest against this vile abjection of youth to age! Look at fashionable society as you know it. What does it pretend to be? An exquisite dance of nymphs. What is it? A horrible procession of wretched girls, each in the claws of a cynical, cunning, avaricious, disillusioned, ignorantly experi-

enced, foul-minded old woman whom she calls
mother, and whose duty it is to corrupt her mind
and sell her to the highest bidder.

Questions of this kind can also be put to the audience
more expressly, which creates a greater sense of involvement.

> If you withhold that necessary legislation for the
> support of the Constitution and constitutional
> rights, do you not commit perjury? I ask every sen-
> sible man if that is not so? That is undoubtedly just
> so, say what you please. Now, that is precisely what
> Judge Douglas says, that this is a constitutional
> right.

Lincoln, debate with
Stephen Douglas at Quincy
(1858)

> But when I came to reckon up what remained to
> me of my capital, I found it amounted to some-
> thing less than four hundred pounds! I ask you
> fairly – can a man who respects himself fall in love
> on four hundred pounds? I concluded, certainly
> not; left the presence of my charmer, and slightly
> accelerating my usual rate of expenditure, came
> this morning to my last eighty pounds.

Stevenson, *New Arabian
Nights* (1882)

2. *If I am asked…* A classic use of hypophora is to suggest questions that the audience might like to ask, and
then to answer them.

a. *Explicitly raising the question.* The speaker can make a
show of anticipating the question. A famous example of
this application comes in a passage we viewed for another
purpose in the chapter on isocolon:

> If there be any in this assembly, any dear friend of
> Caesar's, to him I say, that Brutus' love to Caesar
> was no less than his. If then that friend demand
> why Brutus rose against Caesar, this is my answer:
> Not that I loved Caesar less, but that I loved Rome
> more.

Julius Caesar, 3, 2

Stephen, *Liberty, Equality, Fraternity* (1873)	If I am asked, What do you propose to substitute for universal suffrage? Practically, What have you to recommend? I answer at once, Nothing.
Chesterton, *The Club of Queer Trades* (1905)	If you ask me why I think so I can only answer that I am a Zulu; and if you ask me (as you most certainly will) what is my definition of a Zulu, I can answer that also.

The question also can be attributed more definitely – not *if I am asked*, but *there are those who ask*, etc.

Churchill, London radio broadcast (1940)	Although the fate of Poland stares them in the face, there are thoughtless dilettanti or purblind worldlings who sometimes ask us: "What is it that Britain and France are fighting for?" To this I answer: "If we left off fighting you would soon find out."

b. *Implied attribution to the listener*. A similar construction likewise puts questions that might come to the listener's mind, but without bothering to set them up with any sort of preamble. The question is asked in a reactive tone as if speaking the listener's mind. The effect is to create a sense of dialogue with the audience.

Burke, *Reflections on the Revolution in France* (1791)	What! a qualification on the indefeasible rights of men? Yes; but it shall be a very small qualification.
Dickens, *A Christmas Carol* (1843)	The Spirit did not tarry here, but bade Scrooge hold his robe, and passing on above the moor, sped – whither? Not to sea? To sea.
Melville, *Moby-Dick* (1851)	But how now? in this zoned quest, does Ahab touch no land? does his crew drink air? Surely, he will stop for water. Nay. For a long time, now, the circus-running sun had raced within his fiery ring, and needs no sustenance but what's in himself. So Ahab.
Twain, *Roughing It* (1872)	Not one of those escaped tarantulas was ever seen again. There were ten or twelve of them. We took

candles and hunted the place high and low for them, but with no success. Did we go back to bed then? We did nothing of the kind. Money could not have persuaded us to do it.

He looked older, it is true, in the strong light. But these added years made only more notable his youngness of heart. An illustrious bibliophile among his books? A birthday child, rather, among his toys.

Beerbohm, *No. 2. The Pines* (1920)

A series of comments or objections may be surveyed in this fashion.

Rare and reprehensible was the maid who, having found one roof, hankered after another. Improvident, too; for only by long and exclusive service could she hope that in her old age she would not be cast out on the parish. She might marry meanwhile? The chances were very much against that. That was an idea misbeseeming her station in life. By the rules of all households, "followers" were fended ruthlessly away. Her state was sheer slavery? Well, she was not technically a chattel. The Law allowed her to escape at any time, after giving a month's notice; and she did not work for no wages at all, remember. This was hard on her owners? Well, in ancient Rome and elsewhere, her employers would have had to pay a large-ish sum of money for her, down, to a merchant. Economically, her employers had no genuine grievance. Her parents had handed her over to them, at a tender age, for nothing.

Beerbohm, *Servants* (1918)

3. *Hypophora in soliloquy.* The sense of dialogue just seen also can be had when the speaker interrogates himself, perhaps on behalf of the audience.

HAMLET. Was't Hamlet wrong'd Laertes?
  Never Hamlet:

Hamlet, 5, 2

If Hamlet from himself be ta'en away,
And when he's not himself does wrong Laertes,
Then Hamlet does it not, Hamlet denies it.
Who does it, then? His madness: if't be so,
Hamlet is of the faction that is wrong'd;
His madness is poor Hamlet's enemy.

1 Henry IV, 5, 1

PRINCE. Why, thou owest God a death. [*Exit.*]
FALSTAFF. 'Tis not due yet; I would be loth to pay
Him before His day. What need I be so forward
with him that calls not on me? Well, 'tis no matter;
honour pricks me on. Yea, but how if honour prick
me off when I come on? how then? Can honor set-
to a leg? No. or an arm? No. Or take away the grief
of a wound? No. Honour hath no skill in surgery
then? No. What is honour? A word. What is that
word, honour? Air. A trim reckoning! – Who hath
it? He that died o'Wednesday. Doth he feel it? No.
Doth be hear it? No. Is it insensible, then? yea, to
the dead. But will it not live with the living? no.
Why? detraction will not suffer it. Therefore I'll
none of it: honour is a mere scutcheon: – and so
ends my catechism.

Thus Ishmael's soliloquy in *Moby-Dick*, and the soliloquy
of the eponymous narrator in *White-Jacket*:

Melville, *Moby-Dick* (1851)

But how now, Ishmael? How is it, that you, a mere
oarsman in the fishery, pretend to know aught
about the subterranean parts of the whale? Did
erudite Stubb, mounted upon your capstan, deliver
lectures on the anatomy of the Cetacea; and by
help of the windlass, hold up a specimen rib for
exhibition? Explain thyself, Ishmael. Can you land
a full-grown whale on your deck for examination,
as a cook dishes a roast-pig? Surely not. A veritable
witness have you hitherto been, Ishmael; but have
a care how you seize the privilege of Jonah alone;
the privilege of discoursing upon the joists and

beams; the rafters, ridge-pole, sleepers, and under-
pinnings, making up the frame-work of leviathan;
and belike of the tallow-vats, dairy-rooms, butter-
ies, and cheeseries in his bowels.

What happened to those three sailors on board an
American armed vessel a few years ago, quite within your memory, White-Jacket; yea, while you yourself were yet serving on board this very frigate, the
Neversink? What happened to those three Ameri-
cans, White-Jacket – those three sailors, even as
you, who once were alive, but now are dead? "*Shall
suffer death!*" those were the three words that hung
those three sailors.

Melville, *White-Jacket* (1850)

Compare the similar device used here, where the speaker
instructs himself about which box to open:

PRINCE OF MOROCCO. ... I'll then nor
    give nor hazard aught for lead.
What says the silver with her virgin hue?
"Who chooseth me shall get as much as he
    deserves."
As much as he deserves! Pause there, Morocco,
And weigh thy value with an even hand.

The Merchant of Venice, 2, 7

4. *Answering a question with a question.*

"But is not a real Miracle simply a violation of the
Laws of Nature?" ask several. Whom I answer by
this new question: What are the Laws of Nature?

Carlyle, *Sartor Resartus*
(1831)

But Stubb, he eats the whale by its own light, does
he? and that is adding insult to injury, is it? Look at
your knife-handle, there, my civilized and enlightened gourmand, dining off that roast beef, what is
that handle made of? – what but the bones of the
brother of the very ox you are eating? And what
do you pick your teeth with, after devouring that
fat goose? With a feather of the same fowl.

Melville, *Moby-Dick* (1851)

The ring of the rejoinder can be intensified by repeating some of the wording or structure of the question.

Pitt, speech in the House of Commons (1766)	The gentleman asks, When were the colonies emancipated? I desire to know, when were they made slaves?
Shaw, *The Apple Cart* (1929)	If you ask me "Why should not the people make their own laws?" I need only ask you, "Why should not the people write their own plays?" They cannot.
Churchill, speech at Waltham Abbey (1939)	And who are these people who go about saying that even if it were true, why state the facts? I reply, why mislead the nation?

5. *The same answer to different questions.* We turn to an important and more involved branch of hypophora: the use of multiple questions and answers, starting with cases where the answer is always the same. These patterns resemble some cases in the chapter on epistrophe where different conditions all produced identical outcomes. The repeated verbal pattern underscores the substantive claim that different paths lead to the same place. The simplest use of this pattern is the repeated negative.

Henry, speech at Virginia Ratifying Convention (1788)	The Parliament gave you the most solemn assurances that they would not exercise this power. Were you satisfied with their promises? No. Did you trust any man on earth? No. You answered that you disdained to hold your innate, indefeasible rights of any one.
Grattan, speech in the Irish Parliament (1786)	Sir, when gentlemen say, that the new charge for pensions is small, let me assure them they need not be alarmed; the charge will be much greater; for, unless your interposition should deter, what else is there to check it? – will public poverty? No. New taxes? No. – Gratitude for those taxes? No. – Principle? No. – Profession? No. – The love of fame, or sense of infamy? No.

With elaboration:

> Should not such a case as this require some palli-
> ation? Is there any? Perhaps the defendant might
> have been misled as to circumstances? No, he lived
> upon the spot, and had the best possible informa-
> tion. Do you think he believed in the truth of the
> publication? No; he knew that in every syllable it
> was as false as perjury. Do you think that an anxi-
> ety for the Catholic community might have
> inflamed him against the imaginary dereliction of
> its advocate? No; the very essence of his Journal is
> prejudice. Do you think that in the ardour of lib-
> erty he might have venially transgressed its bound-
> aries? No! in every line he licks the sores, and
> pampers the pestilence of authority.

Phillips, argument in
O'Mullan v. M'Korkill
(1816).

The same device – identical replies to a series of questions
– naturally may be used with answers that are more interesting than *no*, and for a range of purposes: to persuade,
to rouse fury, etc.

> I speak as concerning reproach, as though we had
> been weak. Howbeit whereinsoever any is bold, (I
> speak foolishly,) I am bold also.
>   Are they Hebrews? so am I. Are they Israelites?
> so am I. Are they the seed of Abraham? so am I.

2 Corinthians 11:21-22

> O, how hast thou with jealousy infected
> The sweetness of affiance! Show men dutiful?
> Why, so didst thou. Seem they grave and learned?
> Why, so didst thou. Come they of noble family?
> Why, so didst thou. Seem they religious?
> Why, so didst thou.

Henry V, 2, 2

> No foresight can anticipate, nor any document of
> reasonable length contain express provisions for
> all possible questions. Shall fugitives from labor
> be surrendered by national or State authority? The
> Constitution does not expressly say. May Congress

Lincoln, First Inaugural
Address (1861)

prohibit slavery in the Territories? The Constitution does not expressly say. Must Congress protect slavery in the Territories? The Constitution does not expressly say.

Letter to the public from "A Whig," *Pennsylvania Packet* (1779)

Who dissuade men from entering the army? the Tories. Who persuade those who have enlisted to desert? the Tories. Who harbour those who do desert? the Tories. In short, who wish to see us conquered, to see us slaves, to see us hewers of wood and drawers of water? the Tories.

In mercy to the reader, that last example omits, at its start, sixteen more questions to which the answer is the same.

Grattan, speech in the Irish Parliament (1791)

These gentlemen subject all packages of tea, except from England, to forfeiture. Why? Because they know the fact to be contrary to their argument, and that the tea of England is dearer. Those gentlemen strengthen that penal clause by another, which subjects the vessel to forfeiture. Why? Because the tea of England is much dearer. Those gentlemen strengthen this clause by another, which subjects the vessel from whence the tea is subducted to forfeiture. Why? Because the tea from England is much dearer. Thus their law falsifies their argument, and their argument disgraceful secretly falsifies their law. . . .

It often is conventional, after repeating an answer, to extend it a little when it is said for the last time; as is typical of constructions of this kind, the extension at the end gives the arrival of the words an extra blast of emphasis and alerts the reader that the repetition is ending and the climax is here.

Fox, speech in the House of Commons (1780)

What was it that produced the French rescript and a French war? The American war! What was it that produced the Spanish manifesto and Spanish war? The American war! What was it that armed forty-

two thousand men in Ireland with the arguments
carried on the points of forty thousand bayonets?
The American war! For what are we about to incur
an additional debt of twelve or fourteen millions?
This accursed, cruel, diabolical American war!

What are his tastes? Shares. Has he any principles?   Dickens, *Our Mutual Friend*
Shares. What squeezes him into Parliament? Shares.   (1865)
Perhaps he never of himself achieved success in
anything, never originated anything, never pro-
duced anything? Sufficient answer to all; Shares.
O mighty Shares!

The same general answer to several questions also may
be repeated in different words. The speaker gets some of
the benefits of repetition as well as variety.

What must the king do now? must he submit?   *Richard II*, 3, 3
The king shall do it: must he be deposed?
The king shall be contented: must he lose
The name of king? o' God's name, let it go:
I'll give my jewels for a set of beads,
My gorgeous palace for a hermitage....

Who, in Scotland, lowered the condition of her   O'Connell, speech in the
people by working almost for nothing? The wretch   House of Commons (1833)
flung from Ireland. Who filled the factories all over
England, and reduced the already too low rate of
wages? The outcast of Ireland. Who made the poor-
rate so burdensome? The Irish, not casually, but, he
confessed it, designedly.

Oh, gentlemen, only imagine him on the lakes of   Phillips, argument in *Blake*
North America! Alike to him the varieties of season   *v. Wilkins* (1817)
or the vicissitudes of warfare. One sovereign image
monopolizes his sensibilities. Does the storm rage?
The Widow Wilkins outsighs the whirlwind. Is the
ocean calm? Its mirror shows him the lovely Widow
Wilkins. Is the battle won? he thins his laurel that
the Widow Wilkins may interweave her myrtles.

Does the broadside thunder? he invokes the Widow Wilkins!

A further use of variety can be made by repeating similar answers to a series of questions, then introducing a different answer at the finish.

Madison, Federalist 38 (1788)

Do the monitors deny the reality of her danger? No. Do they deny the necessity of some speedy and powerful remedy? No. Are they agreed, are any two of them agreed, in their objections to the remedy proposed, or in the proper one to be substituted? Let them speak for themselves.

Grattan, speech in the Irish Parliament (1795)

Let the honourable gentleman deduct these from his calculations, and what remains? He does not know! Let him deduct the generosity of the country to the widow and her orphans, and what will he then draw from his pension list? He does not know! What then is his calculation? A fallacy!

Dickens, *Hard Times* (1854)

"Very well," said Bounderby. "I was born in a ditch, and my mother ran away from me. Do I excuse her for it? No. Have I ever excused her for it? Not I. What do I call her for it? I call her probably the very worst woman that ever lived in the world, except my drunken grandmother."

6. *The same question with different answers*. The opposite pattern is less common but also compelling: repetition of the identical question followed by different answers.

Hamlet, I, 5

Remember thee?
Ay, thou poor ghost, while memory holds a seat
In this distracted globe. Remember thee?
Yea, from the table of my memory
I'll wipe away all trivial fond records. . . .

Meagher, speech at Dublin (1846)

Abhor the sword – stigmatize the sword? No, my lord, for, in the passes of the Tyrol, it cut to pieces the banner of the Bavarian, and, through those

cragged passes, struck a path to fame for the peasant insurrectionist of Insprück! Abhor the sword –
stigmatize the sword? No, my lord, for at its blow,
a giant nation started from the waters of the
Atlantic, and by its redeeming magic, and in the
quivering of its crimson light, the crippled colony
sprang into the attitude of a proud Republic –
prosperous, limitless, and invincible! Abhor the
sword – stigmatize the sword? No, my lord, for it
swept the Dutch marauders out of the fine old
towns of Belgium, scourged them back to their
own phlegmatic swamps, and knocked their flag
and scepter, their laws and bayonets, into the slug-
gish waters of the Scheldt.

7. *Different questions and answers.* Hypophora also can be
used with a series of different questions that all receive
different answers. Since the substance does not repeat in
either part, something else usually is needed to give the
questions and answers a sense of unity. Typically the need
is supplied by repetition of words (anaphora) or structure
(isocolon) or both. Thus the argument of Shaw's devil:

> Man measures his strength by his destructiveness.
> What is his religion? An excuse for hating me. What
> is his law? An excuse for hanging you.

Shaw, *Man and Superman*
(1903)

The substance of the questions changes, but they are
asked in parallel structure with the same words at the
start of each of them. The same is true of the answers. The
effect is to give the sequence a more convincing sound;
the fact that everything matches up verbally tempts the
listener to feel that everything also matches up conceptually and that the concepts match the truth. An utterance so verbally seamless and finely wrought shouldn't
be false – though then again it might be. Here are some
further examples of verbal and structural parallelism in
sets of questions and answers that change.

Sumner, speech in the Senate (1865)	Are you against sacrilege? I present it for your execration. Are you against robbery? I hold it up to your scorn. Are you for the protection of American citizens? I show you how their dearest rights have been cloven down, while a tyrannical usurpation has sought to install itself on their very necks!
Lloyd George, *International Honour* (1914)	Treaties? They tangled the feet of Germany in her advance. Cut them with the sword. Little nations? They hinder the advance of Germany. Trample them in the mire under the German heel. The Russian Slav? He challenges the supremacy of Germany and Europe. Hurl your legions at him and massacre him. Britain? She is a constant menace to the predominancy of Germany in the world. Wrest the trident out of her hands.

More modest and informal effects can be gained by just using half of these methods – a bit of anaphora or isocolon or both in the questions to give them rhythm and consistency, but then answers that are more colloquial and that each have their own wording and structure.

Livingston, speech at New York Ratifying Convention (1788)	America had then a sufficiency of this virtue to resolve to resist perhaps the first nation in the universe, even unto bloodshed. What was her aim? Equal liberty and safety. What ideas had she of this equal liberty? Read them in her Articles of Confederation.
Burke, argument in the impeachment trial of Warren Hastings (1788)	Will he fly to the Mahomedan law? That condemns him. Will he fly to the high magistracy of Asia to defend taking of presents? Padishah and the Sultan would condemn him to a cruel death. Will he fly to the Sophis, to the laws of Persia, or to the practice of those monarchs? I cannot utter the pains, the tortures, that would be inflicted on him, if he were to govern there as he has done in a British province.

I know not by what palliation the defendant means to mitigate this enormity; – will he plead her youth? It should have been her protection. – Will he plead her levity? I deny the fact; but even were it true, what is it to him? What right has any man to speculate on the temperature of your wives and your daughters that he may defile your bed, or desolate your habitation? Will he plead poverty? I never knew a seducer or an adulterer that did not. He should have considered that before.

Phillips, argument in *Creighton v. Townsend* (1816)

8. *Questions that lead to a single answer.* Multiple questions can lead to one answer, either to the last of the questions or to all of them. Tension accumulates with each question and is released at the end. Again, the simplest examples involve questions that lead up to a single negative.

> Is the emperor a gentleman, with spatters of blood on his clothes, scourged from the backs of noble Hungarian women? Are the aristocracy gentlefolks, who admire him? Is Mr. Flamson a gentleman, although he has a million pounds? No!

Borrow, *The Romany Rye* (1857)

> But, I would ask, in what tone, temper, and spirit does the president come to the Senate? As a great State culprit who has been arraigned at the bar of justice, or sentenced as guilty? Does he manifest any of those compunctious visitings of conscience which a guilty violator of the Constitution and laws of the land ought to feel? Does he address himself to a high court with the respect, to say nothing of humility, which a person accused or convicted would naturally feel? No, no. He comes as if the Senate were guilty, as if he were in the judgment-seat, and the Senate stood accused before him.

Clay, speech in the Senate (1834)

As these examples show, when the answer to a series of questions is saved until the series ends, the questions tend to be rhetorical or nearly so. That is why waiting for the answer does not try the listener's patience too much.

The final answer may, of course, be something more elaborate than a "no."

Sheil, speech in the House of Commons (1834)	By whom was Ireland oppressed and degraded? By whom was the penal system (the parent of such a brood of evil) maintained? Englishmen, by you!
Smith, speech at New York Ratifying Convention (1788)	Can the liberties of three millions of people be securely trusted in the hands of twenty-four men? Is it prudent to commit to so small a number the decision of the great questions which will come before them? Reason revolts at the idea.
Dickens, *David Copperfield* (1850)	I wish Mr. Micawber to take his stand upon that vessel's prow, and firmly say, "This country I am come to conquer! Have you honours? Have you riches? Have you posts of profitable pecuniary emolument? Let them be brought forward. They are mine!"

9. *Anticipating the answer.* The speaker may supply the answers likely to be offered to questions by an adversary. This pattern is often put into the service of mockery.

Burke, *A Vindication of Civil Society* (1756)	But I demand of this politician, how such arts came to be necessary? He answers, that civil society could not well exist without them. So that these arts are necessary to civil society, and civil society necessary again to these arts. Thus running in a circle, without modesty, and without end....
Lincoln, speech at Columbus (1859)	If they were not driven out, but remained there as trespassers upon the public land in violation of the law, can they establish slavery there? No; the judge says popular sovereignty don't pertain to them then. Can they exclude it then? No; popular sovereignty don't pertain to them then. I would like to know, in the case covered by the essay, what con-

dition the people of the Territory are in before they reach the number of ten thousand?

You charge that we stir up insurrections among your slaves. We deny it; and what is your proof? Harper's Ferry! John Brown! John Brown was no Republican; and you have failed to implicate a single Republican in his Harper's Ferry enterprise.

Lincoln, speech at Spring-field (1859)

If by the visitation of God a person receives any injury which impairs the intellect or the moral perceptions, is it not monstrous to judge such a person by our common working standards of right and wrong? Certainly, everybody will answer, in cases where there is a palpable organic change brought about, as when a blow on the head produces insanity. Fools!

Holmes, Elsie Venner (1861)

10. *What the answer is not.* The climax in an extended case of hypophora can be made more forceful by first recounting some wrong answers.

We are told that we are bound to confer on our subjects every benefit – which they are capable of enjoying? – no; – which it is in our power to confer on them? – no; – but which we can confer on them without hazard to the perpetuity of our own domination.

Macaulay, speech in the House of Commons (1833)

Kentucky is entirely covered with slavery; Ohio is entirely free from it: What made that difference? Was it climate? No. A portion of Kentucky was farther north than this portion of Ohio. Was it soil? No. There is nothing in the soil of the one more favorable to slave labor than the other. It was not climate or soil that mused one side of the line to be entirely covered with slavery, and the other side free of it. What was it? Study over it. Tell us, if you can, in all the range of conjecture, if there be anything you can conceive of that made that difference,

Lincoln, speech at Cincin-nati (1859)

other than that there was no law of any sort keeping it out of Kentucky, while the Ordinance of '87 kept it out of Ohio.

With irony:

Livingston, speech at New York Ratifying Convention (1788)

But whom, in the name of common sense, will we have to represent us? Not the rich, for they are sheer aristocrats. Not the learned, the wise, the virtuous, for they are all aristocrats. Whom then? Why, those who are not virtuous; those who are not wise; those who are not learned: these are the men to whom alone we can trust our liberties.

Descending numbers provide a classic occasion for this device.

Sheil, speech in the House of Commons (1835)

And what was the course taken by indignant justice? – what, do you conjecture, was their sentence? Not two years' imprisonment – not one year – not six months. The learned judge tempers justice with mercy, and sentences those presumptuous delinquents to an imprisonment of three weeks.

Sheil, speech in the House of Commons (1835)

There are 1,100,000 Catholics; and, what will the house think? – 300,000 Protestants? – No; 200,000? – No; One? – No, no; only 45,000. Gracious God! £100,000 a-year for the "spiritual consolation" of 45,000 Protestants! This is in itself most gross; but contrast makes it monstrous.

Churchill, *The People's Rights* (1909)

We say that the State and the municipality should jointly levy a toll upon the future unearned increment of the land. The toll of what? Of the whole? No. Of a half? No. Of a quarter! No. Of a fifth – that is the proposal of the Budget, and that is robbery, that is Plunder, that is communism and spoliation, that is the social revolution at last, that is the overturn of civilized society, that is the end of the world foretold in the Apocalypse!

11. *To tour an argument.* Hypophora can be used to lead a listener through a chain of reasoning, or to bring a series of claims to life by making each of them the answer to a question. Question leads to answer; the answer leads to a new question.

> We have done with precedent. She then resorts to authority; to what authority? To her judges. To do what? To repeal acts of parliament by interpretation. What act? magna charta, – the act that forms the security of the realm.

Grattan, speech in the Irish Parliament (1782)

> [I]t is contended by some, as before mentioned, that, if both powers – the supreme, coexisting, coequal powers – should tax the same objects, the state taxes would be best paid. What, sir, would be the consequence? Why, the others would be badly paid, or not paid at all. What, then, is to become of your government? In this case, it must be annihilated indeed.

Livingston, speech at New York Ratifying Convention (1788)

> The receiver-general of the taxes of North Carolina must be one of the greatest men in the country. Will he come to me for his taxes? No. He will send his deputy, who will have special instructions to oppress me. How am I to be redressed? I shall be told that I must go to Congress, to get him impeached. This being the case, whom am I to impeach? A friend of the representatives of North Carolina.

Taylor, speech at North Carolina Ratifying Convention (1788)

Lincoln often used this branch of hypophora to present his arguments and those of others.

> He says he is unalterably opposed to the repeal of the laws against the African slave trade. And why? He then seeks to give a reason that would not apply to his popular sovereignty in the Territories. What is that reason? "The abolition of the African slave trade is a compromise of the Constitution!" I deny it.

Lincoln, speech at Columbus (1859)

Lincoln, speech at Cooper
Institute (1860)

You say we are sectional. We deny it. That makes an issue; and the burden of proof is upon you. You produce your proof; and what is it? Why, that our party has no existence in your section – gets no votes in your section. The fact is substantially true; but does it prove the issue? If it does, then in case we should, without change of principle, begin to get votes in your section, we should thereby cease to be sectional. You cannot escape this conclusion; and yet, are you willing to abide by it? If you are, you will probably soon find that we have ceased to be sectional, for we shall get votes in your section this very year.

Lincoln, speech at Hartford
(1860)

Now this strike is caused by a withdrawal of Southern trade, or it is not. If it is, what can you do to help it? Have you ever made war upon the South? No. Then how can you help yourselves? They withdraw their trade on a false accusation, because you never warred upon them, and consequently cannot stop the war they charge you with. You can, however, conform to their idea that slavery is right. This will satisfy them, but what is the effect on you? Why *slavery comes in upon you!* Public opinion against it gives way. The barriers which protected you from it are down; slavery comes in, and white free labor that *can* strike will give way to slave labor that *cannot!*

12. *Prolepsis.* Cases of prolepsis occur when the speaker anticipates a point and meets it. This differs from hypophora because no question need be asked, but the devices bear an obvious resemblance. In both of them a real or hypothetical objection may be suggested and then answered.

Tollope, *North America*
(1862)

It will be said that the American cars are good enough for all purposes. The seats are not very hard, and the room for sitting is sufficient. Nevertheless I deny that they are good enough for all purposes.

They are very long, and to enter them and find a place often requires a struggle and almost a fight.

If men loved Pimlico as mothers love children, arbitrarily, because it is *theirs*, Pimlico in a year or two might be fairer than Florence. Some readers will say that this is a mere fantasy. I answer that this is the actual history of mankind.

Chesterton, *Orthodoxy* (1908)

Cases of prolepsis may be stacked upon one another to vigorous effect.

It may be objected, that very wise men have been notoriously avaricious. I answer, Not wise in that instance. It may likewise be said, That the wisest men have been in their youth immoderately fond of pleasure. I answer, They were not wise then.

Fielding, *Tom Jones* (1749)

So we go on preparing more months and years – precious, perhaps vital to the greatness of Britain – for the locusts to eat. They will say to me, "A Minister of Supply is not necessary, for all is going well." I deny it. "The position is satisfactory." It is not true. "All is proceeding according to plan." We know what that means.

Churchill, speech in the House of Commons (1936)

The same construction can be turned directly on the listener, resulting in *you say*/*I say* constructions in which the speaker recapitulates the adversary's position and his own.

Will these few protect our rights? Will they be incorruptible? You say they will be better men than the English commoners. I say they will be infinitely worse men, because they are to be chosen blindfolded: their election (the term, as applied to their appointment, is inaccurate) will be an involuntary nomination, and not a choice.

Henry, speech at Virginia Ratifying Convention (1788)

You hope to place me in the dock. I tell you that I will never stand in the dock. You hope to beat me. I tell you that you will never beat me.

Conan Doyle, *The Final Problem* (1893)

Chesterton, *The Club of Queer Trades* (1905)

I am as right about that man as I am about your having a hat on your head. You say it cannot be tested. I say it can.

13. *Combinations*. Prolepsis, hypophora, and the rhetorical question – any two, or all three – may be combined in a short space to create a lively rhetorical mood. Thus observe the structural similarities in these two passages, where in both the speaker starts with prolepsis (repeating a charge and replying to it) then moves to various types of hypophora (asking a question and answering it).

Burke, *Letter on the Proposals for Peace with the Regicide Directory of France* (1797)

"Well," some will say, "in this case we have only submitted to the nature of things." The nature of things is, I admit, a sturdy adversary. This might be alleged as a plea for our attempt at a treaty. But what plea of that kind can be alleged, after the treaty was dead and gone, in favor of this posthumous Declaration? No necessity has driven us to that pledge.

Lincoln, speech at Galena (1856)

You further charge us with being disunionists. If you mean that it is our aim to dissolve the Union, I for myself answer that it is untrue; for those who act with me I answer that it is untrue. Have you heard us assert that as our aim? Do you really believe that such is our aim? Do you find it in our platform, our speeches, our conventions, or anywhere? If not, withdraw the charge.

A rhetorical question, then prolepsis:

Sheil, speech in the House of Commons (1834)

You have got so much, then, of the revenue of Ireland, which you ought never to have received. Has no injustice been done to Ireland in this respect? But you will tell me that you have cured all this by the consolidation of the exchequers of the two countries. You have not; because, at the time of the Union, you agreed that the surplus revenue of Ireland should be spent in Ireland. . . .

Prolepsis, then perhaps hypophora, then a rhetorical question (and a dash of isocolon as well):

> "But," says an honorable gentleman near me, "the impost will be a partial tax; the Southern States will pay but little in comparison with the Northern." I ask, What reason is there for this assertion? Why, says he, we live in a cold climate, and want warming. Do not they live in a hot climate, and want quenching?

Ellsworth, speech at Connecticut Ratifying Convention (1788)

Hypophora, then a rhetorical question – and then the same pattern again, along with a dash of epimone to finish the book where we began:

> How was the franchise in the English counties fixed? By the act of Henry the Sixth, which disfranchised tens of thousands of electors who had not forty shilling freeholds. Was that robbery? How was the franchise in the Irish counties fixed? By the act of George the Fourth, which disfranchised tens of thousands of electors who had not ten pound freeholds. Was that robbery?

Macaulay, speech in the House of Commons (1831)

BIBLIOGRAPHICAL NOTE

THE GENERAL LITERATURE on rhetoric is extensive, but the books dealing with our branch of it – rhetorical figures – are fewer in number. Here is a brief review of them.

First are the classical sources. The most substantial ancient discussions of rhetorical figures to survive are Quintilian's *Institutio Oratoria* (Institutes on Oratory – c. 95 AD) and the *Rhetorica ad Herennium* (Rhetoric for Herennius – c. 90 BC), once attributed to Cicero but now agreed to be of unknown authorship. These books, so far as their treatment of figures is concerned, have been influential and remain interesting to the connoisseur, but they are likely to be a little disappointing to the typical modern reader; they contain only brief discussions and few examples of each device. Various other ancient handbooks on rhetoric mention the devices examined here and contain interesting remarks on some of them – for example, Cicero's *De Oratore*, and works by Demetrius (*de Elocutione*, c. 270 BC) and Longinus (*de Sublimitate* – the date and author of which are both somewhat uncertain). George Kennedy's *A New History of Classical Rhetoric* (1994), and R. Dean Anderson's *Ancient Rhetorical Theory and Paul* (1998) contain helpful surveys of the development of rhetoric and rhetorical theory in ancient times, with discussions of the sources just mentioned and many others.

Much the same can be said of discussions from the Renaissance, when figures of speech were studied and classified with much ardor but again without results that are likely to be of great interest to the modern student of the subject. The most prominent are Sherry's *Treatise of Schemes and Tropes* (1550), Wilson's *The Arte of Rhetorique* (1553), Peacham's *The Garden of Eloquence* (1577), Puttenham's *Arte of English Poesie* (1589), and *Directions for Speech and Style* by John Hoskins (ca. 1599). Later came Hugh Blair's *Lectures on Rhetoric and Belles Lettres* (1785), an attractive new edition of which was released in 2004 by the Southern Illinois University Press. Blair's book was quite influential during the nineteenth century and contains some discussions of figures and of style generally that are still helpful now.

Next are compilations of rhetorical figures from particular sources. Shakespeare's uses of rhetorical figures – not metaphors, but the sorts of fig-

◈ 251

ures examined in this book – have been the subject of two prominent studies. First is Sister Miriam Joseph's fine and scholarly *Shakespeare's Use of the Arts of Language* (1947); more recent and also excellent is *Shakespeare's Wordcraft* by Scott Kaiser (2007), which offers an impressively wide-ranging collection of verbal patterns and illustrations of them (with scrupulous avoidance of terms from Greek, for better or worse). The King James Bible has been the subject of similar inquiry: Bullinger's *Figures of Speech in the Bible* (1898), which contains little discussion but is formidable in the sheer number of figures that it organizes and illustrates. More modern authors have occasionally been treated to studies of this kind as well; a distinguished recent example is Zimmerman, *Edgar Allan Poe: Rhetoric and Style* (2005). Mardy Grothe's *Never Let a Fool Kiss You or a Kiss Fool You* (2002) provides many examples of chiasmus for those who cannot get enough of the device.

The aficionado of rhetoric needs a convenient place to look up the Greek and Latin words – sometimes seemingly endless – that have been used to name the various figures and categorize them. The best resource for the purpose is Richard Lanham's *Handlist of Rhetorical Terms* (2d ed. 1991); it has concise and lucid explanations of all the classical terms that one is ever likely to meet, with short discussions of many of them and edifying longer essays included here and there. It also has a table in the back that allows the reader to look up general families of rhetorical figures by type and then see all the terms that fit under each heading, along with one-line descriptions of each of them – a most welcome resource when one sees a technique used and wants to find the word for it. Gideon Burton's convenient and extensive website, *Silva Rhetoricæ*, is another highly useful work for this purpose, containing an enormous number of definitions and cross-references as well as links to online versions of many classical texts. For the student with a surplus of bookshelf and budget, Lausberg's massive *Handbook of Literary Rhetoric* (1963), originally in German but available in English translation, is something to consider. It has elaborate technical discussions of an immense number of rhetorical figures, often with examples in Ancient Greek or Latin. If the reader is more modestly interested in the ancient origins of modern rhetorical vocabulary, and just wants to see how the modern terms were spelled in Ancient Greek and where they were mentioned in classical writings, R. Dean Anderson's *Glossary of Greek Rhetorical Terms* (2000) is a great help.

Many books on style and rhetoric contain lists of rhetorical figures that look roughly like this book's table of contents, with perhaps a paragraph and a couple of examples for each entry. Those treatments are too numerous to cite individually here, but Bryan Garner's *The Elements of Legal Style* (2d ed. 2002) is a good specimen of the type. There also have been a few other attempts to give the subject something like the general treatment this book aims to provide, the chief instances of which are Arthur Quinn, *Figures of Speech* (1982); Sylvia Mager et al., *Power Writing, Power Speaking* (1978); and Robert A. Harris, *Writing with Clarity and Style* (2003). Those books differ from this one in various ways that I consider disadvantages (else I would not have written another), but that some readers might prefer. They mention more devices, but with fewer examples and less organization and discussion of them; and the examples they use tend to be more modern than the ones found here.

A NOTE ON THE TYPE

FARNSWORTH'S CLASSICAL ENGLISH RHETORIC has been set in Sabon Next, a type with a distinguished and complex history. Originally commissioned in the 1960s from the master tyopographer, designer, and calligrapher Jan Tschichold, Sabon is a contemporary interpretation of a roman type attributed to Claude Garamond and an italic attributed to Robert Granjon. It was named in honor of Jacques Sabon, a punchcutter who worked for the printer who created the specimen on which Tschichold based his design. Because the types were initially intended for machine composition on both Linotype and Monotype as well as for cold-metal composition, the design was carefully drawn and modified to accommodate the limitations imposed by the various methods of composition. This process resulted in a widely popular type that was somewhat compromised by its lack of kerns, a feature that limited the appeal of the italic in particular. Sabon Next was drawn in 2002 by Jean François Porchez, who set out to harmonize Tschichold's type and the types that inspired it with the possibilities that the OpenType platform offered to the contemporary type designer. The result is an elegant, highly readable type with a complete range of characters (including a generous selection of ligatures, swash characters, and ornaments) that is beautifully suited to book work.

DESIGN & COMPOSITION BY CARL W. SCARBROUGH